Book-keeping

Andrew Piper
and
Andrew Lymer

Book-keeping

Andrew Piper
and
Andrew Lymer

TEACH YOURSELF BOOKS

2 0 0 0 4 4 2 6

MORAY COUNCIL
LIBRARIES &
INFORMATION SERVICES

657 · 2

Orders: please contact Bookpoint Ltd, 39 Milton Park, Abingdon, Oxon OX14 4TD.
Telephone: (44) 01235 400414, Fax: (44) 01235 400454. Lines are open from 9.00–6.00,
Monday to Saturday, with a 24 hour message answering service.
Email address: orders@bookpoint.co.uk

Long renowned as the authoritative source for self-guided learning – with more than 30
million copies sold worldwide – the *Teach Yourself* series includes over 200 titles in the
fields of languages, craft, hobbies, business and education.

A catalogue entry for this title is available from The British Library

First published in UK 1984 by Hodder Headline Plc, 338 Euston Road, London NW1 3BH.
Second edition 1991.

The 'Teach Yourself' name and logo are registered trade marks of Hodder & Stoughton Ltd.

Copyright © 1984 A. G. Piper
Copyright © 1991 A. G. Piper
Copyright © 1999 A. G. Piper, A. M. Lymer

All rights reserved. No part of this publication may be reproduced or transmitted in any
form or by any means, electronic or mechanical, including photocopy, recording, or any
information storage and retrieval system, without permission in writing from the publisher
or under licence from the Copyright Licensing Agency Limited. Further details of such
licences (for reprographic reproduction) may be obtained from the Copyright Licensing
Agency Limited, of 90 Tottenham Court Road, London W1P 9HE.

Cover photo © Sarah Jones

Typeset by Transet Limited, Coventry, England.
Printed in Great Britain for Hodder & Stoughton Educational, a division of Hodder
Headline Plc, 338 Euston Road, London NW1 3BH by Cox & Wyman Ltd, Reading,
Berkshire.

Impression number   10 9 8 7 6 5 4 3 2
Year   2002 2001 2000 1999

CONTENTS

ACKNOWLEDGEMENTS

The author and publishers are grateful to the Royal Society of Arts Examinations Board for permission to reproduce the complete examination papers at the end of this book.

The source of the individual questions in the text has been lost through the passage of time, but the co-operation of the following examination bodies is gratefully acknowledged:

Birmingham Commercial College
College of Preceptors
East Midland Educational Union
Institute of Bankers
Institute of Book-keepers
London Chamber of Commerce
  and Industry
National Union of Teachers

Royal Society of Arts
Union of Educational Institutions
Union of Lancashire and Cheshire
  Institutes
University of Birmingham
University of Edinburgh
University of Manchester

INTRODUCTION

The style which has proved so successful in earlier editions has been retained where appropriate, and the guidance provided by previous authors is gratefully acknowledged.

The aim of this book is to provide a concise introductory text which is both readable and interesting, and clearly relevant to the routine recording of business transactions, while at the same time covering the main syllabus requirements of elementary examinations in book-keeping. The VAT rate of 17½% has been used in some examples but the principles of recording VAT remain the same whatever its rate.

Users should remember that there is a difference between book-keeping and accountancy. Book-keeping is concerned with the initial recording of financial transactions. The second chapter introduces some common business documents. These often provide the basic raw material from which the subsequent book-keeping entries and financial statements are prepared. The use of computers and direct recording of this data through a keyboard may lead to the elimination of some of them, but the accurate recording of the transaction as soon as possible remains essential. These records provide an important part, but not all, of the material which is used and interpreted by the accountant and the manager.

This edition includes an introductory chapter on the use of computers in support of the book-keeping activity. Information Technology (IT) is playing and increasing role in the collection, recording and processing of accounting data and therefore some appreciation of its impact is necessary. However, the basic principles of book-keeping remain unchanged and it continues to be important that book-keepers understand these principles.

This edition also includes 'Objectives' at the beginning and 'Key Points' at the end of each chapter. The 'Objectives' provide an overview of each chapter and after completion you should review the 'Key Points' before going on to the next chapter.

Book-keeping is neither dull nor mysterious: indeed its 'rules' are logical and straightforward, and readily mastered by practice. Thus the text includes many worked examples, carefully graded questions and three complete examination papers with fully worked solutions. You should always prepare your own solutions to each question as it is encountered and then compare it with the one provided in the text.

A Piper

A Lymer   January 1998

1 | WHAT IS BOOK-KEEPING?

OBJECTIVE

This chapter introduces you to the basics of book-keeping in the form of a conversation between two people, one of whom is familiar with the process of Double Entry Book-keeping.

Question What is book-keeping?

Answer The process of correctly recording in Books of Account cash, credit and other transactions.

Question What are Books of Account?

Answer The primary Book of Account is called the **Ledger**, so called because all transactions, after first being recorded in subsidiary books, are afterwards grouped or summarised in Accounts in the Ledger.

Question Why should goods or services be bought or sold on 'credit'?

Answer Almost all business dealings are conducted on a credit basis to avoid the inconvenience and danger of carrying large amounts of cash. The supplier of goods or services is usually content to accept payment at some future date. The main exception is the retail trade for a private individual.

Question Why is it necessary to record these transactions?

Answer Even in the smallest business the proprietor or manager will want to have accurate and up-to-date information about how much has been bought and sold, how much money has been received for sales, how much has been paid away for purchases, etc. Private individuals often find it convenient to have the same information for their cash receipts and payments. You can imagine that with a very large business, chaos would quickly result without this information.

Question So book-keeping really involves analysing in some way or another these various transactions?

Answer You could say it involves recording these transactions so as to permit analysis in a systematic fashion, and in some way that can be applied to all businesses of whatever kind, and that is intelligible not only now but at any future time.

Question Do you mean by this 'the Double Entry System of Book-keeping'?

Answer Yes.

Question Why is it called 'Double Entry'.

Answer Every transaction involves at least two parties, so the record of the transaction should reflect its twofold aspect.

Question So it does not mean recording the same transaction twice?

Answer No, not at all. If I have bought goods worth £100 from Smith on credit, the first part of the twofold aspect is that my business has received goods for the disposal of which my storekeeper, or some other person, is accountable; the second part of the twofold aspect is that Smith, my supplier, has become my creditor, and has a claim on me for £100.

Question Would it be the same if you had bought the goods and paid for them at once, instead of getting credit?

Answer Yes, that would be a cash purchase. But instead of Smith, my banker would be my creditor, having paid money away for me. They then would have the claim on me for £100.

Question I do not quite see how your banker could be your creditor. The bank would be providing a service.

Answer What you say about the position of the bank is true, but in the first place, when you began business, you would entrust a sufficient sum of money to the bank for which you would at the outset consider the bank as accountable or indebted to you. It would be your debtor. So if later it paid money away for you, such payments reduce the indebtedness which, after all, is the same thing as saying it is your creditor to that extent, the position of the creditor being the reverse of that of debtor.

Question What is the real advantage of the Double Entry System?

Answer For the reason that every transaction can be looked at from its twofold aspect, the record made is complete instead of being only partial.

The practical advantage is that you put the whole of the facts on record. These are:

■ Your storekeeper is answerable for £100 worth of goods.
■ Somebody, Smith or your banker, has a claim on you for £100.

Obviously, to know these facts is of importance in any business.

Question Well, does this hold good with other than just buying transactions? Would the same state of affairs exist with the selling of goods?

Answer In exactly the same way. The first aspect in the selling transaction is that your storekeeper has issued £100 worth of goods as an ordinary sale. The second is that the person who has received them has become your debtor, i.e. they are indebted to you, on the assumption that you, in this case, are giving credit, because *you* are the supplier.

Question Does the Double Entry System stop at this?

Answer No. It goes much further. Because of this twofold aspect I have been talking about, it enables you to compare the proceeds of the sales you have made with the cost to you of the goods you have bought, and so obtain your profit or loss on trading.

Similarly, as it shows the claims other people have on you (your creditors), and the claims you have on other people (your debtors) you can tell very quickly what is the position of affairs of your business at any particular date so far as these people are concerned.

Question Is this important?

Answer Yes. If the creditors of the business exceed in amount its debtors, any stock in its warehouse which it hopes to sell, and the 'ready' money it has available, it may be insolvent, that is to say, it cannot pay its debts as they become due.

Question When we began talking, you said the Ledger was the Book of Account, and that all transactions were first recorded in what you called 'Subsidiary Books'. What are these Subsidiary Books, and why are they kept in addition to the Ledger?

Answer The Subsidiary Books are termed *Journals* or *Day Books* because, very much like a journal or diary, they are completed daily (or should be).

They are designed to relieve the various accounts in the Ledger of a great amount of detail which, while indispensable to the business, can better be given in a subsidiary book than in the Ledger itself.

If you take, for example, the purchasing side of a business, a very great amount of detail may have to be recorded as to the supplier, the quantity, quality and price per unit of the goods, total amount payable and so on.

But, so far as the double entry or twofold aspect of all the buying transactions is concerned, they are all in the first place purchases or goods for which the storekeeper is responsible. In the second place, credit must be given to all the various suppliers from whom the purchases have been made. Thus there will be one account in the Ledger for incoming goods, or purchases, and other accounts, also in the Ledger, for the individual suppliers.

Question So the Journals or Day Books do not form part of the Double Entry System at all?

Answer That is true. These Subsidiary Books are outside the Double Entry System. Their function is to provide the information from which the Ledger Accounts are written up (or entered up) subsequently.

That is why they are often referred to as books of **prime** or **first entry**. With very few exceptions it is a well-recognised rule in book-keeping that no transaction should be recorded in a Ledger Account unless it has first been recorded in a subsidiary book, or a book of first entry or a computer based substitute.

KEY POINTS

You should now appreciate some of the basic facts about Double Entry Book-keeping as a process.

1 All transactions are fully recorded in a book of prime entry.

2 Two entries in the Ledger, one debit and one credit, are needed in respect of each transaction.

3 Detailed records are essential to enable you to manage a business.

Questions

1 Explain briefly the theory of 'Double Entry', and of 'debit and credit'.
2 What do you understand by the term Double Entry, as applied to a system of account keeping? Give examples to illustrate.
3 'Book-keeping by Double Entry means recording the same transaction twice.' Criticise this assertion briefly.
4 State the advantages to be derived from keeping a set of books on the Double Entry System and contrast this method with any other system you know of.

2 | BUSINESS DOCUMENTS

OBJECTIVE

This chapter describes several business documents. It is from these documents that you obtain most of the information you need to write up the books of prime entry. It is important that you can recognise these documents and the data they contain.

Financial documents

An **invoice** is the primary document which records details of a sale to a customer or the purchase from a supplier. An example follows, and in many systems the advice and delivery notes are produced at the same time. The data on them is very similar and provision is made for appropriate signatures to verify the details shown on each particular document.

	WHITHAMS FLOOR COVERINGS		
	HIGH GREEN	VAT REGD. NO.	
	YORKSHIRE	931–8251–80	
	INVOICE		
		Date _____	
		Invoice No 645/AB	
Quantity	Details	£	£

Example 2.1

E Whitham sells floor covering at discount prices. On 1 May xxx1, M Lowbridge was supplied with one piece of brown kitchen floor covering measuring 6 metres long by 2 metres wide, with a recommended retail price of £10 per square metre.

E Whitham gives M Lowbridge a discount of 25%, and makes a standard delivery charge of £5. Delivery to 69 Markbrook Drive, Marktown, Yorkshire. All transactions are subject to Value Added Tax of 10%.

A completed invoice would look something like this.

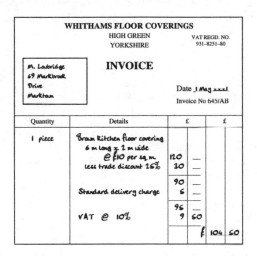

A statement in the accounting context refers to the summary of the purchase or creditor ledger account that is sent to a customer, or by a supplier to your business, at regular intervals, usually monthly, requesting payment of the amount due. Some businesses produce it at the same time as the ledger account is updated. In a very simple book-keeping system it may have to be copied from the personal ledger.

When a statement is received it should be compared with the records kept by the recipient. Sometimes the amount requested by the statement will agree with your own records, sometimes there will be a difference. This can arise for a number of reasons, for example, clerical errors, goods invoiced but not yet received, cheques paid, items in dispute, goods returned and credit notes not yet issued, and discount or other allowances not recorded. After the necessary adjustments have been made the two balances should reconcile, i.e. show the same amount. The statement can then be signed by the person who has been authorised to certify the amount that can be paid.

The statement sent by the bank is known as a Bank Statement and the reconciliation process is described in Chapter 6.

A **cheque** is the usual way in which payment is made to a supplier. The cheques used by small businesses are like personal ones and are illustrated below.

The counterfoil or 'stub' (not shown here) and the cheque are pre-numbered, e.g. 397. The other numbers are used by the bank. Generally, pre-printed cheques will also show the number of the bank account and the name of the business or person who will be writing the cheque.

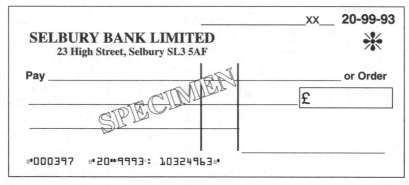

Example 2.2

Mary Smith has received goods to the total net value of £346 for her flower shop from Growmore Nurseries Ltd. Complete the cheque for full settlement of this amount on 31 July xxx1.

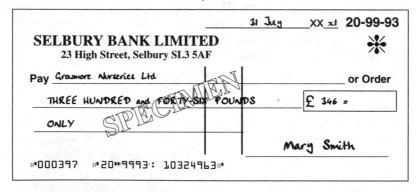

The size of the counterfoil or stub restricts the amount of information that can be recorded. Therefore, when paying a personal account in the purchase ledger, the account reference could be included and will be adequate. When paying sundry items it would be appropriate to include a reference to the invoice or other document supporting the payment.

Cash discount allowed by the supplier should also be recorded here so that a record is available to ensure that the double entry record is written up correctly.

Many organisations now use a computer to print cheques and a copy can be used as the cheque payments record, called a cheque list or sheet. This list, or the counterfoil if cheques are written by hand, is then used to write up the Cash Book.

An alternative form of payment is the Bank-giro system which allows payment to be made at any branch of the bank to any branch of any bank in the country. Service utilities such as gas, electricity, etc, send a prepared form with the invoice for this purpose. When regular payments of the same amount will be due the **standing order** (STO or S/O) can be used. This is an instruction by the debtor to their bank to make a transfer to the creditor. It is also possible for the debtor, or potential debtor, to authorise the creditor to initiate the transfer; this is known as a **direct debit** (DD or D/D).

A **'banker's draft'** is similar to a cheque but is issued by the bank at the request of the debtor and as it is guaranteed by the bank it is accepted immediately as cash.

The **Paying-in Book** is provided by the bank, in which the details of items paid into the bank are recorded. The form used for personal accounts and small business transactions is shown below and space for recording details of the separate cheques is on the reverse.

The form is perforated and the bank will retain the larger right-hand portion and leave the left-hand portion in the book after stamping it to acknowledge receipt of the amount paid in.

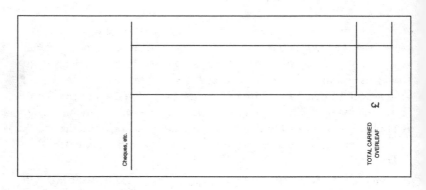

Example 2.3

You are employed by Benyon and Walkley Ltd as a cashier. Your employers keep a current account (16271763) at Selbury Bank. On 1 April xxx1, you pay the following items into the bank on behalf of your employer:

19	£20 notes
33	£5 notes
128	£1 coins
1	50p coin
3	20p coins
17	bags of £5 in each bag

plus cheques payable to Benyon and Walkley Ltd from:

C Tootill	£189.56
S Fowler	£165.45

You are required to complete all parts of the paying-in slip shown above. (Make your own entries before comparing with the solution.)

This example asks you to enter several items which in practice might be pre-printed on the paying-in slip, and if they are there will be no need to enter them by hand.

The counterfoil may be used as a prime document to write up the cash received sheet, and used to check the receipts shown on the bank statement.

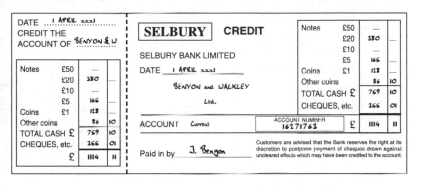

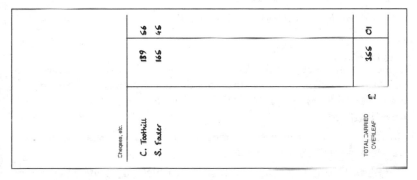

The **Receipt Book** is a memorandum book, usually duplicate or triplicate, which is used to provide a record of money (cash or cheques) received. They are usually pre-printed and pre-numbered and will show the date, amount received, person/company it is received from, nature of payments, i.e. cash or cheque, any discount allowed and the signature of the person who made out the receipt.

Example 2.4

Micklethwaite Electrics keep a cash receipt book and retain two copies of each receipt issued. Prepare the document that you would issue to Keith Miller acknowledging receipt of his cheque payment.

On 23 February xxx1 you received a cheque on behalf of Micklethwaite Electrics, 85 Leeds Road, Ripon from Keith Miller, 10 Halstead Road, Pannal Ash in full settlement of Sales Invoice No B 973 dated 6 February xxx1. The amount of the invoice was £230. Keith Miller is entitled to a cash discount of 5% if settlement is made during February.

RECEIVED WITH THANKS	Date **23-2-x1**
From KEITH MILLER	
Cash	
Cheque	**218.50**
Discount	**11.50**
Total	**£230.00**
Signed **G N Other**	
For MICKLETHWAITE ELECTRICS	
	1436

Some systems might require the full description of the debtor and if Keith Miller is not sufficient to ensure correct identification then his address could be included, as could the invoice number and description of the items involved.

Nowadays it is not usual to issue receipts for payments made by cheque or transfers through the banking system.

The **Bank Cash Book** is a book or sheet in which payments into the bank and withdrawals from the bank are recorded.

BANK CASH BOOK

	RECEIPTS						PAYMENTS		
		£	£	£			£	£	£
Date	Particulars	Discount Allowed	Details	Bank	Date	Particulars	Discount Received	Details	Bank

Example 2.5

Pauline Weldon operated a small mail-order company. All her receipts were paid immediately into the bank and all her payments were made by cheque. Her Cash Book showed a balance in hand of £748.24 on 1 October xxx1.

You are provided with the above pro-forma and are required to enter the following transactions and balance.

During October she made the following deposits into the bank:

Paying-in Book counterfoils:

Dated	In respect of cheque from	Cheque £	Discount £
Oct 7	A Abram	74.82	5.18
Oct 7	B Barrett	137.80	12.20
Oct 18	C Cook	58.75	–
Oct 18	D Dennison	24.30	–
Oct 28	B Barrett	37.18	2.82
Oct 28	C Cook	42.43	–

Her cheque book counterfoils for October showed the following details:

Date	Payable to	Cheque No	Cheque £	Discount £
Oct 5	D Dunn	342	82.00	–
7	Autos Ltd	343	189.25	10.75
9	Wages/salaries	344	237.87	–
14	E Evans	345	17.22	–
22	Brown & Co	346	98.79	–
29	Francis & Co	347	132.80	2.20

Prepare your own Bank Cash Book and enter the transactions, then check with the following solution. **Note:** Receipts are entered on the left-hand side and payments on the right.

BANK CASH BOOK

	RECEIPTS					PAYMENTS			
		£	£	£			£	£	£
Date	Particulars	Discount Allowed	Details	Bank	Date	Particulars	Discount Received	Details	Bank
xxxx					xxxx				
Oct 1	Balance			748.14	Oct 6	D. Dunn	–	342	82.00
7	A. Abram	6.18	74.82		7	Autos Ltd	10.76	343	189.26
7	B. Barrett	12.10	137.80	212.62	9	Wages/ Salaries	–	344	237.87
18	C. Cook	–	68.76		14	E. Evans	–	346	17.22
18	D. Dennison	–	14.30	83.06					
18	B. Barrett	1.82	37.18		22	Brown & Co.	–	346	98.79
18	C. Cook	–	42.43	79.61	29	Francis & Co.	2.10	347	132.80
		10.10		1123.61	31	Balance			366.69
Nov 1	Balance			366.69			12.96		1123.61

There may also be a 'folio', or reference, column for the cheque numbers.

The **Cash Book** will usually record both bank and cash transactions as described in Chapter 5, but there may be separate cash sheets and/or a Petty Cash Book as described in Chapter 7.

Wages documents

A **clock card** is the original document on which employees record the date and the time at which they arrive and leave work or when they start and finish particular jobs. A typical example of a clock card is given below.

Name ....

Department ....

	MON.	TUE.	WED.	THU.	FRI.	SAT.	SUN.
H O U R S							
NORMAL	1.1	1.2	1.5	2.0		SPLIT SH.	

A **piece work card** is the original document on which the employee records the amount or the number of units produced. It is used when payment is 'per unit'.

The time at work, and the work produced, multiplied by the appropriate rates will enable the gross wages to be calculated.

There are usually deductions to be made from this gross amount, for example, tax, national insurance and other compulsory items. There may also be voluntary deductions, such as trade union subscriptions, Save as you earn, etc, to complete the calculation of the net amount which will be paid to the employee.

Example 2.6

Jenny Stone works in the goods inwards department of Fenwold Electrical. Her clock card number is 100. She is paid £3.20 per hour for a 37-hour week. She is paid time and a quarter for any weekday overtime and time and a half for overtime worked on a Saturday.

Hours worked week ending 27 February:

Monday 8 hours	Tuesday 9 hours	Wednesday 9 hours
Thursday 8 hours	Friday 6 hours	Saturday 3 hours

Deductions for the week:

National Insurance contributions   10% of gross wage
Income Tax   25% of all earnings over £54.80 per week

Save As You Earn Scheme   £5.00 per week
Trade Union Subscriptions   £1.00 per week

Note: Employers' National insurance contribution is the same amount as the employee's contribution in this example.

You are required to calculate Jenny Stone's net pay for the week ending 27 February xxx1.

Name: Jenny Stone   **Clock Card No:**   100
Department: Goods inwards   **Week beginning:**   27 February xxx1

GROSS PAY

Hours worked: 40 hours 0 minutes during normal working hours

Basic	37	@ £3.20	£118.40
Overtime	3	3.20 x 1.25	12.00
		3 hours on Saturday	
Overtime	3	3.20 x 1.50	14.40
Total gross pay			£144.80

DEDUCTIONS

National Insurance (10% of gross)	£14.48	
Income Tax	22.50	
SAYE	5.00	
TU subscription	1.00	
Total deductions		£42.98
NET PAY		£101.82

These calculations for all employees should be entered into a **Wages Book**, or more likely onto a **Payroll Sheet,** for the week. In a computer system the details for each employee could automatically be added to their records and be used to provide the equivalent of the Payroll Sheet. A typical Wages Book (Payroll Sheet) is shown below.

PAYROLL

Department ....   Week Ending ....

CLOCK NO	NAME	HOURS		RATE	GROSS PAY	DEDUCTIONS					NET PAY	EMPLOYERS' NI
		Basic	OT			Tax	NI	Pensn	Vol	Total		

This data for Jenny Stone, calculated above, would be entered as shown below.

PAYROLL

Department ...... *Goods inwards* ....   Week Ending ...... **27 Feb xxxx** ......

CLOCK NO	NAME	HOURS		RATE	GROSS PAY	DEDUCTIONS					NET PAY	EMPLOYERS' NI
		Basic	OT			Tax	NI	Pensn	Vol	Total		
100	Jenny Stone	43	2.25	2.20	144.80	22.50	14.48	-	6.00	42.98	101.82	14.48

This particular payroll requires the total hours paid at basic rate (43) and the premium overtime hours 3 at time and a quarter (0.75) plus 3 at time and a half (1.5), a total of 2.25 hours, to be shown. Note the column for Employers' National Insurance. There are rules and regulations governing the calculation of this amount in practice but at this stage of your studies a simple rule was provided.

Note and coin analysis

When employees are paid in cash it is essential that the exact amount of their net pay can be put into individual pay packets to ensure rapid payment at the appropriate time. This requires the analysis of each net amount into the notes and coins required. It is usual to use the minimum number but sometimes it has been agreed that there will always be, say, at least four one pound coins in a packet. In this situation the usual analysis, shown below, would have to be modified to reflect the particular constraint.

Net wages	£20	£10	£5	£1		20p	10p	5p	2p	1p
using the 'maximum' rule £20 divides into the wage six times, so 6; etc.										
127.57	6		1	2		2	1	1	1	–
143.68	7	–	–	3		3	–	1	1	1
etc.										
271.25	13	–	1	5		5	1	2	2	1

When obtaining the money for the	Check	£20	@	13	260.00
pay it will be provided by the bank		10		0	0.00
(or sometimes by the cashier) in		5		1	5.00
accordance with this analysis.		1		5	5.00
		20p		5	1.00
		10p		1	.10
		5p		2	.10
		2p		2	.04
		1p		1	.01
					271.25

Naturally, computer programs are available to provide this analysis as a by-product from the payroll work. Sometimes the net wage or salary will be rounded up to the nearest pound each week and the difference carried forward to be adjusted the next week or month. There has also been some pressure from employers for employees to have a bank account into which direct payments could be made. One obvious reason for this is the avoidance of large cash amounts in transit or being held at the point of payment; also less likelihood of paying the wrong person.

Stock records

Stock is often a significant asset of an enterprise and records should be kept showing receipts, issues and the amount of stock. Some book-keeping systems will also record orders and although some records will show the quantity others may show the value as well. The procedures may be integrated into an overall system that provides the justification for paying purchase invoices, issuing sales invoices and means of controlling the amount of stock being held.

An **advice note** from a supplier is notification that goods will be delivered in response to an order. It may be used by the stores as confirmation that their request for supplies has been processed.

The **delivery note** (sometimes the advice note) comes with the goods when they are delivered to the stores. It may be used for subsequent processing, e.g. recording the receipt of the goods, or to support a goods received note made out by the stores personnel to record the receipt.

A **stores requisition note** is, as its name suggests, a request to issue goods from stock, authorised by an agreed procedure. It is used to record the issue of stock on the bin card or stores record and for crediting the stock account and debiting the recipient if the system has been designed for that purpose, usually in manufacturing enterprises.

Stock cards are records of a particular item in stock. If held in bins/racks/trays they may be called **bin/rack/tray cards**. In principle it is a record kept with the physical stock and updated at the time of any physical movement. Usually only quantity is recorded. Stock ledger records are kept in a stores office and/or the accounts department and may record quantity and value.

This record uses the 'running balance' format rather than a 'two-sided' one, and has the advantage of always showing the up-to-date balance. From time to time the physical stock should be counted and the amount compared with the bin card and the stock ledger card. There may be some differences due to transactions not yet recorded but any differences remaining should be investigated, if material, and all records amended to show the actual quantity. Other causes of a difference may be clerical error, unrecorded issue to cover scrap, theft, items stored somewhere else.

Using the form below, write up a stock record card for Jigsaws, ref no 1610:

Balance in hand on 1 February xxx1		50
2 February	issues req. no. 220	25
7 February	issues req. no. 231	10
15 February	receipts order no. 126	100
18 February	issues req. no. 261	50

STOCK RECORD				
DATE	REF	IN	OUT	BALANCE

Solution

STOCK RECORD				
JIGSAWS				Part No. 1610
DATE	REF	IN	OUT	BALANCE
xxx1 Feb 1	Balance			50
2	Req. 220		25	25
7	Req. 231		10	15
15	Order 126	100		115
18	Req. 261		50	65

This illustration only uses quantities. Some systems also record the value of receipts, issues and the balance. Purchases are usually valued at actual cost, issues at the average cost of the balance immediately before the issue. There are other bases of valuation which are acceptable.

KEY POINTS

Having completed this chapter you should:

1 be familiar with many of the common documents you will use when writing up the books of most businesses

2 now recognise what each document is for and what information it should contain

3 be able to complete the common business documents – an invoice; a cheque; a paying-in slip (Giro); wages documents; stock records.

Questions

1 Knox Sawmills have a current bank account (no 16760272) at Selbury Bank Ltd. On 2 March xxx1 the business pays in the following items into the local branch:

     3   £20 notes
     7   £10 notes
     12   £5 notes

74	£1 coins
35	50p coins
16	20p coins
200	2p coins

and cheques made payable to Knox Sawmills from

F Rigton	£108.25
AC Killinghall	£365.12
Duck and Drake	£49.96

You are required to:

■ complete all parts of the paying-in slip given below.

■ describe two possible uses of the counterfoil slip retained in the bank paying-in book.

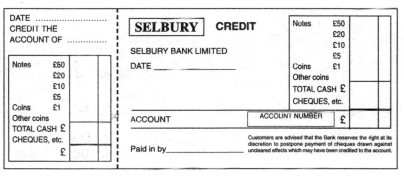

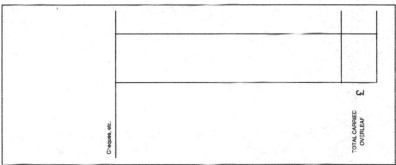

2 Josephine Swift makes all payments over £15 by cheque and pays all receipts into the bank at the end of each day. On Monday 27 February her Bank Cash Book showed a balance of £4960 Dr.

The following information is available for the next week:

Cheques drawn

27 Feb	R Loftus (creditor) £300	Cheque No 1610
27 Feb	Stock £600	Cheque No 1611
28 Feb	Advertising £150	Cheque No 1612
1 March	Electricity Board £125	Cheque No 1613
2 March	Petrol account £65	Cheque No 1614
3 March	Rover and Waters Garages (deposit on car) £1000	Cheque No 1615

Bank Lodgements:

28 Feb	Cash takings			£250
28 Feb	Cheques:	B Blue	£25.25	
		T Roe	£70.00	
		R Lamb	£82.91	
1 March	Cash takings			
	Cheques:	T Williams	£600	
		R Potter	£350 (in settlement of account of £375.00)	
3 March	Cheques:	R Lowther	£275 (debtor)	
		XY Equipment Ltd	£100 (sale of old typewriter)	

On 5 March she received her bank statement which revealed the following information:

Date	Details	Debit	Credit	Balance
27 Feb	Brought forward			4960.00
28 Feb	Bank charges	40.00		4920.00
1 March	Cash and cheques		428.16	5348.16
1 March	1611	600.00		4748.16
2 March	1610	300.00		4448.16
2 March	1612	150.00		4298.16
2 March	Sundry		1275.00	5573.16
2 March	Standing Order (XY Insurance Company)	100.00		5473.16
3 March	1613	125.00		5348.16

You are required to:

■ write up and balance the Bank Cash Book for the week beginning 27 February xxx1 (after receipt of the Bank Statement), using the format given below

■ prepare a Bank Reconciliation Statement on 5 March xxx1 after completing Chapter 6.

BANK CASH BOOK

		£	£	£			£	£	£
Date	Particulars	Discount Allowed	Details	Bank	Date	Particulars	Discount Received	Details	Bank

3 C Ponsford manages a small firm employing four workers. During the week ending 31 December xxx1 each worker earned a take home pay as follows:

L Jennett	£160.56
J Smith	£90.75
J Grala	£100.20
G Thomas	£136.40

C Ponsford pays wages at the end of each week in cash using notes and coins of £10, £5, £1, 50p, 10p, 20, 5p, 2p and 1p. C Ponsford insists that each worker receives at least one £1 coin.

You are required to:

- rule up and complete a note and coin analysis in table form using the least number of notes and coins permissible
- reconcile the value of the total notes and coins with the total pay bill.

4 D Swift maintains manually prepared stock record cards for the recording of the receipts and issues of various items of stock held in the stores.

You are required to:

- draw up a stock record card showing the following rulings and headings:

Item   STOCK CARD

Date	Details	Receipts		Issues		Balance	
		Units	£	Units	£	Units	£
Sep 1	Balance					12	144

■ record the following movements of the item of stock reference number DW/04 for the month of September xxx1. The cost price of each item is £12 and there were 12 items in stock at 1 September xxx1.

Receipts

September	8	Invoice No 784	20 units
September	15	Invoice No 847	48 units
September	22	Invoice No 984	20 units

Issues

September	6	Issue Note No A237	8 units
September	17	Issue Note No D534	18 units
September	24	Issue Note No B631	64 units

■ On making a physical stockcheck on 30 September xxx1, Swift discovered that there were eight units in stock. Adjust the stock record card for this difference and give some possible explanation.

3 THE BUSINESS TRANSACTION, PURCHASES AND SALES

> **OBJECTIVE**
> This chapter describes the process for recording the purchases and sales of a business.

The business transaction

We are familiar in our daily life with buying articles we want and paying cash for them. But unless we are in business the idea of selling goods is not so familiar, nor is the process of receiving payment for what we have sold. And yet every business is concerned with buying and selling goods or services, usually on a credit basis, so that at some later date it pays for what it has bought and is in turn paid for what it has sold.

These are recurrent transactions in particular goods which the business buys, sells or manufactures.

Merchanted goods are those which it resells in the same condition as when purchased. *Manufactured goods* are the finished article which, with the assistance of employees, are worked up from the raw materials.

Thus, from the purely trading standpoint, a kind of trade cycle can be recognised. Goods are bought first of all in sufficient quantity to meet customers' requirements, either as the finished article or a raw material. They are what is called the **Stock** or Stock in Trade of the business.

When the goods are sold in the finished state to customers at selling price, and on credit terms, these customers become the **debtors** of the business; that is, they are indebted to it, and when they in turn make payment the **Cash in Hand** or **Cash at Bank** of the business is replenished. From these increased cash resources, the business can buy more goods, and so the cycle repeats itself.

Cash and goods cycle

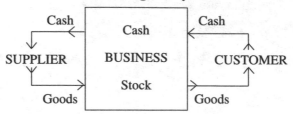

At any given time a business will possess:

- Stock in Trade
- claims on customers, which may be described as Debtors, or Book Debts
- Cash in Hand and/or Cash at Bank

These forms of property represent the trading resources of the business, and in total form part of its **Capital**.

It is very important to understand correctly the meaning of Capital in the book-keeping sense.

Supposing we bought goods from Jones, value £100, for payment a month after they had been delivered. Jones would be our creditor, and during that month we might sell the goods at a profit and so obtain the cash to pay him when the time came.

That would be an ideal case, because then the business apparently need have no cash resources *of its own*; it could rely on Jones, and other suppliers, to finance its operations. The capital invested in the business, represented by the stock of goods value £100 supplied by Jones, would be in effect *Jones's* Capital, and not the proprietor's Capital at all.

In practice, however, we find that such an ideal state of affairs can seldom, if ever, arise.

First of all, we may not be able to sell all the goods we purchased from Jones in the credit period he gives us of one month. Secondly, we shall in all probability be obliged to extend credit to our customers, just as Jones did to us. Thirdly, we shall be obliged to possess cash resources to pay our staff week by week, and fourthly, if ours is a new business, Jones or any other supplier may be unwilling to supply us with goods on credit until they have experience of what may be called our 'creditworthiness'.

It must also be remembered that an important part of every business's resources is a factory, warehouse or office (or the right to occupy these, for which a rent is paid) from which to operate. Such property does not form part of the trading resources, because it would be unusual to sell our business premises in which all the work was carried on.

For these reasons a certain minimum amount of property, or of Capital, must be possessed by the business from the time it was started. It is also clear how varied are the forms which this Capital may take.

Our task will always be easier if we think of Capital as the resources or the property of a business. Indeed, the term *Capital* has no meaning to a business person unless it is represented by property of some kind or another, property which is called the business **Assets**.

While we are going to examine Capital more fully at a later stage, remember that there are a number of types of property: **Fixed Assets**, such as the factory or warehouse mentioned above, and **Current Assets**, which correspond to our trading assets, such as stock in trade, claims on customers and money in the bank.

The distinction between these two kinds of property is important because our Fixed Assets have been bought to be retained, while our Current Assets, as we have seen, are an essential result of the business's everyday transactions. Indeed, they enter into and form part of these transactions.

Two more points must be made. The first is the business definition of Capital as representing not merely the Assets, but

The excess of the assets over the liabilities of a business.

An example will help to make this clear:

Example 3.1

Brown begins business on 1 January xxx1, with £10 000 in cash. He leases for five years factory premises at a cost of £6000, and obtains goods on credit from Smith costing £2000. The total assets of his business are:

Factory lease, cost	£6000
Stock of goods, cost	2000
Cash in bank	4000
	£12 000

but this is not the amount of Brown's Capital invested in the business because £2000 of these assets have been supplied on credit by Smith, for which the business is liable to him. What is owing to Smith is, therefore, a liability of the business and does not represent property of Brown. We therefore define Capital as corresponding to 'the excess of the Assets over the Liabilities of a business': Brown's Capital = Total Assets £12 000, *less* Liabilities £2000 = £10 000, or put in another way, Brown's capital of £10 000 is represented by:

Fixed assets		£6000
Current assets	£6000	
Less Liabilities	2000	
		4000
		£10 000

We are justified in deducting the liability to Smith from the total of the *Current* Assets, since it is out of them that we intend to pay him.

The other point which we ought now to be in a position to appreciate is that

Capital is a liability of the business to its proprietor.

At first sight this appears to be rather different from what we should expect.

We have seen that from its start the business must be provided with a certain minimum amount of property, or Capital, and initially we defined Capital as the equivalent of property or assets, and subsequently more fully as representing 'the excess of the Assets over the Liabilities of a business'.

Let us now see if we can reconcile what appears to be a contradiction in terms.

If the proprietor, instead of investing Capital in setting up the business, had lent £10 000 to a friend in consideration of a payment of interest at 12% per annum, the loan would clearly be an investment yielding an annual income of £1200, and the amount of the loan, looked at from the standpoint of the borrower, would as clearly be a liability.

The borrower's financial position could be stated thus:

Liability £10 000 represented by **Cash** £10 000

In exactly the same way, when the proprietor invests Capital in a business, it is clearly an investment, answerable to him for interest, or in this case

Profit, period by period.

From the standpoint of the business, looked at as distinct from its proprietorship, there is a **Liability** to account for the amount of the proprietor's Capital put at its disposal for the purpose of profit earning.

At any time, therefore, the business should be able to prepare a statement of its position, and of how it has dealt with such Capital, that is to say, by what kinds of property that Capital is represented.

The financial position of the business would similarly be:

> **Liability to proprietor** £10 000, represented by, in the first instance, **Cash** £10 000.

The only difference between the examples is that, in the first case, the borrower would sooner or later have to repay the loan, while in the second the repayment of the proprietor's Capital would involve shutting down the business.

For this reason, in the latter case, the Capital invested is usually regarded as a *permanent* or *fixed liability*, or indeed, as it is in law, a postponed or deferred liability.

The Purchase and Sales Journals in the book-keeping system

Most of us are familiar with the idea of using a diary to make daily notes of things that happen to us. We enter into it brief but sufficient details of what has taken place. They very often form a useful reference for the future.

In the early stages of business development it is not difficult for us to imagine the proprietor of the business making a similar record of transactions with people who had become suppliers and customers, narrating what they had bought, and from whom; what they had sold, and to whom. Just as a diary is a daily record, so also is a **Journal**. It is written up as soon as possible after the transaction has taken place. It is essentially a *primary* record, and hence we derive the meaning of the term 'Journal' in book-keeping as a book of **first entry**. No matter what subsequent use we make of the particulars recorded in it, the desirability of a primary record is obvious.

To the extent that the transactions of the business are recurrent, even in the smallest undertaking we should expect to see a record of:

- purchases
- sales
- payments to suppliers
- receipts from customers.

As soon as the transactions entered into became more numerous, some kind of analysis of the Journal would be imperative if the proprietor at any time wished to know:

- how much they had purchased
- how much they had sold
- what was the total of the cash payments
- the total of the cash receipts.

With numerous daily transactions, putting on record the fact that £100 worth of goods had been purchased on credit from Jones, and £100 worth of goods had been sold on credit to Smith, the Journal entries might take the following form:

- Warehouseman chargeable with incoming goods **at cost** £100. Jones to be credited with £100.
- Smith chargeable with goods £100. Warehouseman to be credited with issue of goods at selling price £100.

If, however, we took matters a step further, and used the symbols **Dr** (debtor) instead of 'chargeable with' and **Cr** (creditor) instead of 'to be credited', the entries could easily be stated in the following way:

- Warehouseman   Dr £100.00
  Jones   Cr   100.00

and

- Smith   Dr £100.00
  Warehouseman   Cr   100.00

This would be a much simpler and more concise way of putting the transaction on record, but the repetition of the recurrent entries over a period of time would make detailed analysis always essential to arrive at, for example:

- our total purchases, and
- our total sales for that period

as well as the need for similar analysis for cash paid and cash received.

For that reason, the first form of Journal was modified to comply with these requirements of the proprietor; in one section of it were recorded **purchases**, in another **sales** and in yet another **cash**, either in total, or as in many cases today:

- ■ **Cash received**, and
- ■ **Cash paid**.

To the first of these subsections of the Journal was given the title **Purchase Journal** (or Purchase Day Book); to the second **Sales Journal** (or Sales Day Book); and to the third **Cash Book** or **Cash Journal**, with the result that in them we now find:

- ■ our total purchases
- ■ our total sales and
- ■ our purely cash transactions in as great a detail as we desire, or the requirements of the business demand.

Certain transactions take place which it would not be appropriate to record in the three subdivisions of the Journal described above. These comparatively infrequent transactions are considered in Chapter 8.

Note that some small organisations with very few transactions will not use these journals. They will attach a slip to a batch of invoices and other documents, summarise the slips as appropriate and use the summaries to produce accounts. This is known as a **slip system**.

Supposing we begin with the **Purchase Journal** or **Day Book**:

Example 3.2

Enter the following purchases in the Purchase Day Book of H Yates, a cycle dealer, total the Day Book, but do not post the entries to the Ledger.

xxx1

Feb 2   Received invoice from the Speedy Cycle Co Ltd for:
2 Gents' Roadsters, model A625 at £125, less 20% trade discount.
2 Ladies' Roadsters, model A725 at £110, less 20% trade discount.
2 Crates at £5.00 each.

15   The Drake Cycle Co Ltd, invoiced:
3 Gents' Special Club models B21 at £140, less 15% trade discount.
3 Ladies' Special Club models B20 at £120, less 15% trade discount.
2 Crates at £6.00 each.

27   Received invoice from the Victoria Manufacturing Co Ltd:
2 Racing models A16 at £170, less 15% trade discount.
1 Crate at £5.00.

Purchase Day Book

February xxx1

Date	Supplier	Description	Details	Goods Total	Gents' Models	Ladies' Models	Crates and Packing
			£	£	£	£	£
xxx1							
Feb 2	Speedy Cycle Co Ltd	2 Gents' Roadsters, Model A625, at £125.00	250.00				
		2 Ladies' Roadsters, Model A725, at £110.00	220.00				
			470.00				
		Less 20% Trade discount	94.00				
			376.00		200.00	176.00	
		2 Crates at £5.00	10.00	386.00			10.00
15	Drake Cycle Co Ltd	3 Gents' Special Club models, B21, at £140.00	420.00				
		3 Ladies' Special Club models, B20, at £120.00	360.00				
			780.00				
		Less 15% Trade discount	117.00				
			663.00		357.00	306.00	
		2 Crates at £6.00	12.00	675.00			12.00
27	Victoria Manufacturing Co Ltd	2 Racing models, A16, at £170.00	340.00				
		Less 15% Trade discount	51.00				
			289.00		289.00	–	
		1 Crate at £5.00	5.00	294.00			5.00
				£1355.00	£846.00	£482.00	£27.00

In these three purchase transactions, we notice:

- that the goods purchased are exclusively for resale, i.e. they are goods in which Yates is dealing
- that a deduction is made on account of **trade discount**. This is a common allowance made by a supplier to a retailer with whom there are regular dealings and may represent:
  - a margin of profit for the retailer, who sells the goods at the advertised list price
  - an inducement to the retailer to continue to trade with the supplier.

  Prior to entry in the last four columns of the Day Book, it is seen that the trade discount has been deducted in the 'details' column, and we must always be careful to follow this procedure.

  All that concerns Yates is the **net cost** of the cycles which have been bought.

- that the suppliers have in each case included in their invoice price the cost of crates. These clearly do not refer to the cost of the goods dealt in, and are therefore entered in a separate column. Moreover, it is usual for the suppliers to issue **credit notes** as and when the crates are later returned to them in good condition. There may in consequence be a recovery of all or the greater part of the total purchase cost under this heading.

The solution to the example, as shown, enables Yates to see at a glance:

- from whom goods have been purchased
- what has been purchased
- the total cost of the purchases, suitably analysed, including
- the cost of crates, packing, etc.

If, as in the first transaction, trade discount of 20% is allowed by the supplier then a very simple trading account to reflect the sale of one Gents' Roadster would show Sales £125, Cost of sales £100. The difference is called *Gross profit* and is £25, or 20% of the sales, which is the amount of the trade discount. If the cycle is sold for less than the expected price then the gross profit will be less than expected, and vice versa.

The gross profit expressed as a percentage of the selling price, or sales, was 20%. It may also be expressed as a percentage of the cost of sales. In this case £25 as a percentage of £100, or 25%. Always be very careful to remember whether you are referring to sales or cost of sales. When based on cost of sales it is sometimes called the mark-up, i.e. the percentage added to cost to give estimated selling price.

What about Value Added Tax (VAT)? More about VAT is provided at the end of Chapter 4 and at this stage it is only necessary to say that an extra column would be required in the Purchase and Sales Day Books. This is illustrated in the next example, where VAT at the rate of 17½% is assumed in respect of all sales and purchases.

Example 3.3

From the following particulars compile the Purchase Day Book, Sales Day Book and Returns Book of D Morris.

Full details must be shown in the Day Books. No posting to the Ledger is required.

March 10   Sold to W Humphrey, Lincoln, 200 metres floral cotton cloth at £2 per metre; 100 metres of best blue cotton cloth at £2.40 per metre. Whole invoice less 10% trade discount.

12   Received invoice from R Ridgwell, Bolton, for 50 sheets at £3.50 each; 40 tee-shirts £2.80 each.

15   Sent a debit note to W Hunt for £12, being an overcharge on cotton supplied to D Morris on February 5.

18   Sent an invoice to S Boham, Coventry, for 100 metres of linen at £5.00 per metre, less 5% trade discount; 300 metres of floral cotton at £2 per metre; trimmings £15.

20   Bought goods from B Davis, Ely, 500 metres of floral cotton at £1.00 per metre; 400 tee-shirts at £2 each; sundry remnants £15.

22   W Humphrey, Lincoln, returned 50 metres of the floral cotton supplied on March 10, as being of inferior quality.

23   Received a debit note from A Jenkinson, Wolverhampton, for 20 metres of linen returned to D Morris at £7 per metre less 20% trade discount.

24   Sent an invoice to T Butterworth, Norwich, for 300 metres of linen at £7.00 per metre less 5% trade discount; 150 metres of best blue cotton at £2.40 per metre less 10% trade discount; assorted buttons £10.

27   Received a credit note from V Luxton, for 30 metres of white cotton returned by D Morris at £1.00 per metre.

29   Bought from General Supplies Ltd, London, showcases and fittings £1000 net.

You are required to calculate the appropriate trade discount and VAT. The actual invoice from your supplier and your own sales invoices would include these amounts.

Note: Great care must be exercised in setting out the Day Books. It may be a useful exercise for students to prepare their own day books, and then compare them with the entries which follow rather than merely reading the entries. You may be wondering why time is spent recording data from an invoice into a journal; why not file the invoice or summarise several invoices together, or enter details into a computer? Any of these methods, or other similar ones, may be used according to the wishes and objectives of the owner or manager depending upon the availability of data processing equipment and staff.

What is essential is that the basic data is accurately recorded, in a **permanent** form, to which **access** can be obtained **rapidly** whenever required. The latter two objectives have already been illustrated by the use of separate Purchase and Sales Journals. These can easily become separate files of Purchase invoices received and copies of our own Sales invoices. However, to encourage you to appreciate the system of the recording cycle a Journal approach is used.

Computer software is readily available for use with PCs or other computers that will provide an integrated system of Journals; but the basic principles of Journals as described in this chapter and the Ledger as described in Chapter 4 will continue to be observed.

Before beginning to record these transactions in the Purchase and Sales Journals, it is essential for us to realise that they are being stated from the point of view of the business of which D Morris is the proprietor.

The first process is to classify each of them as being:

■ a purchase transaction
■ a sales transaction
■ the return of goods to a **supplier**, or the obtaining of an allowance *from* them
■ the return of goods by a **customer**, or the granting of an allowance *to* them.

They can then be recorded in the appropriate Journal. In the latter two cases the result will be that the amount of the original purchases and sales will be reduced accordingly, but *instead of altering* the entries in the Purchase and Sales Journals, we shall make use of **Purchase Returns Journals** and **Sales Returns Journals** (see pages 39–40).

Let us now summarise the points arising in this and Example 3.2 on pages 31–32.

In the first place, the *analysis columns* which follow the total column enable us to analyse as fully as we may wish the details of our purchases and sales.

Secondly, we see that an *Invoice No* column is provided. In this is entered the reference number *given by the business* to its suppliers' invoices, as well as to its own invoices to customers. If for any reason the original purchase invoice or copy sales invoice has to be consulted, it can quickly be referred to in the purchase or sales invoice files.

Thirdly, Returns and Allowances Books, whether for purchases or sales, are ruled in almost exactly the same way as the Purchase and Sales Journal themselves, the difference being that the heading 'Invoice No' is replaced by 'Debit Note No' and 'Credit Note No' respectively, thus facilitating reference to these documents.

Fourthly, it is apparent that a check can be placed on the arithmetical accuracy of the book-keeping work by agreeing periodically, often at the end of each month, the 'cross' cast or 'cross addition' of the Analysis Columns with the cast or addition of the Total Column in each of the subsidiary books.

Finally, we have an example of the purchase by the business of capital goods or Fixed Assets, the showcases and fittings.

As these have been bought for retention and not for resale, it is essential to provide an additional analysis column, in this case headed 'Special Items'. Alternative headings might be 'Capital Items' or 'Capital Additions'.

The provision of this column enables us to see at a glance the total value of such special or capital purchases during the period.

As VAT (Value Added Tax) was applicable to these transactions we required an additional analysis column in which to record the VAT. On the purchase from R Ridgwell, which totalled £287.00, there would be VAT; at 17½% this is £50.22 and would be added to the invoice to give a total of £337.22. Similarly with the invoice from B Davis, VAT of £230.12 is added, giving a total of £1545.12, and with that from General Supplies VAT

D MORRIS

Purchase Day Book

Date	Supplier	Description	Invoice No	Details £	Total £	VAT £	Cotton £	Linen £	Sheets £	Tee-shirts £	Sundries £	Special Items £
xxx1 March 12	R Ridgwell, Bolton	50 sheets at £3.50 each		175.00					175.00			
		40 tee-shirts at £2.80		112.00						112.00		
				287.00								
		VAT 17½%		50.22		50.22						
			1		337.22							
20	B Davis, Ely	500 metres floral cotton at £1.00 per metre		500.00			500.00					
		400 tee-shirts at £2.00 each		800.00						800.00		
		Remnants		15.00							15.00	
				1315.00								
		VAT 17½%		230.12		230.12						
			2		1545.12							
29	General Supplies Ltd, London	Showcases and fittings		1000.00								1000.00
		VAT 17½%		175.00		175.00						
			3		1175.00							
					£3057.34	£455.34	£500.00		£175.00	£912.00	£15.00	£1000.00

D MORRIS

Sales Day Book

Date	Customer	Description	Invoice No	Details	Total	VAT	Cotton	Linen	Sheets	Tee-shirts	Sundries
				£	£	£	£	£	£	£	£
xxx1 March 10	W Humphrey, Lincoln	200m Floral cotton @ £2 per m		400.00							
		100m best Blue Cotton @ £2.40 per m		240.00							
				640.00							
		Less 10% Trade discount		64.00							
				576.00							
		Add VAT 17½%		100.80		100.80	576.00				
			4		676.80						
18	S Bonham, Coventry	100m Linen @ £5 per m		500.00							
		Less 5% Trade discount		25.00							
				475.00				475.00			
		300m Floral cotton @ £2 per m		600.00			600.00				
		Trimmings		15.00							15.00
				1090.00							
		Add VAT 17½%		190.75		190.75					
			5		1280.75						
23	T Butterworth, Norwich	300m Linen @ £7 per m		2100.00							
		Less 5% Trade discount		105.00							
				1995.00				1995.00			
		150m best Blue cotton @ £2.40 per m		1995.00							
		Less 10% Trade discount		360.00							
				36.00							
				324.00			324.00				
		Assorted buttons		324.00							10.00
				10.00							
		Add VAT 17½%		2329.00		407.57					
				407.57							
			6		2736.57						
					£4694.12	£699.12	£1500.00	£2470.00			£25.00

Purchases Returns and Allowances Book

D MORRIS

Fo 1

March xxx1

Date	Supplier	Description	Debit Note No	Details	Total	VAT	Cotton	Linen	Sheets	Tee-shirts	Special Items
				£	£	£	£	£	£	£	£
xxx1											
March 15	W Hunt	Overcharge goods supplied Feb 5		12.00			12.00				
		Add VAT 17.5%		2.10		2.10					
			7		14.10						
27	V Luxton	30 metres White cotton returned at £1.00 per metre		30.00			30.00				
		(Their credit note)									
		Add VAT 17½%		5.25		5.25					
			8		35.25						
					£49.35	£7.35	£42.00				

D MORRIS

Fo 2

March xxx1

Sales Returns and Allowances Book

Date	Supplier	Credit Note No	Description	Details	Total	VAT	Cotton	Linen	Sheets	Tee-shirts	Special Items
				£	£	£	£	£	£	£	£
xxx1											
March 22	W Humphrey		50 metres floral cotton, invoice Mar 10, inferior at £2.00 per metre	100.00							
			Less 10% Trade discount	10.00							
				90.00			90.00				
			Add VAT 17½%	15.75		15.75					
		9			105.75						
23	A Jenkinson, Wolverhampton		20 metres Linen at £7.00 per metre	140.00							
			Less 20% Trade discount	28.00							
			(Their debit note)	112.00				112.00			
			Add VAT 17½%	19.60		19.60					
		10			131.60						
					£237.35	£35.35	£90.00	£112.00			

is £175, making a total of £1175. These will be recorded in the Purchase Day Book and the VAT analysed into the extra column that has been added.

Exactly the same procedure takes place with the Sales. The VAT must be added to each invoice. This will increase each one by 17½%, e.g. invoice number 4 to W Humphrey for goods costing £576.00 will have VAT of £100.80 added and the invoice total will be £676.80; and similarly for the other sales, and purchases and sales returns.

KEY POINTS

On completion of this chapter you should be:

1 familiar with the Purchase and Sales Journals, their structure, purpose and how invoices should be recorded in them

2 able to recognise that purchase and sale returns follow a similar pattern

3 aware that complete accuracy is essential at this initial stage. Any error made will be processed throughout the book-keeping system.

Questions

1 In the context of an accounting system for a manufacturing company, list your recommendations for dealing with purchase invoices and give the ruling of the book in which you suggest they should be entered.

2 Explain the functions of the Purchase Analysis Journal. Give a specimen ruling and make six entries in it. Total all columns and check the cross cast.

3 Goods purchased by a business may comprise either goods for resale at a profit, or goods for retention and use. Give two examples of each, and explain how such purchases are recorded in the books of account.

4 'The books of prime entry are developments from the ordinary Journal.' Comment on this statement, and give draft rulings for a Purchase Day Book and a Sales Day Book in a business having three main departments.

5 PQ & Co, Merchants, have three departments, A, B and C. It is desired to keep separate trading accounts for each. With this end in view, give the ruling of the Sales Day Book, making four specimen entries, and explain how the book would function.

6 A trader wishes to ascertain separately the gross profit earned by each of the two departments which comprise his business.

Show how the columnar system of book-keeping would allow him to do this without opening any additional books or accounts. Give any necessary rulings and explain how the system works.

7 What are the Returns Inwards and Outwards? Where should these items be entered in the books of a trader? What effect has each upon the profits of a business?

8 On 1 February, B Grey owed A White £16 for goods supplied.

On 13 February he bought from White on credit three shirts at £8 each, six pairs of socks for £7 and a pair of jeans for £17.

Set out in full the invoice made out by White relating to the purchases on 13 February. Include VAT at 17½%.

9 XY is a manufacturer of electrical appliances. Give the ruling for a Purchase Book which you would recommend he should keep. Enter the following invoices received. Ignore VAT.

Feb 2   AB, £250 for goods.
     4   PQ, £120 for repairs to machinery.
     5   CD, £70 for advertising.
     6   AB, £575 for goods.
     8   X City Council, £1240 for general rates. PO telephones, £84.
     12   GH, £100 for goods.
     14   Overnite, £30 for carriage.
     15   AB, £2250 for new plant.

10 On 1 February xxx1, you supplied to T Thomas, 200 grey pullovers at £7 each, less a trade discount of 7½%. Thomas returned 50 pullovers as not up to sample and you agreed to credit him with their value.

Enter the items in the Returns Book concerned and draw up the credit note to Thomas, including VAT at 17½%.

11 G Bath, a retailer, purchased two items for resale in his shop, one of Product A and one of Product B. The following figures relate to these two items.

	Product A	Product B
Manufacturer's Recommended Retail Price	£1500	£4000
Trade Discount allowed to retailers	20%	25%

It is G Bath's intention to sell these two products at the recommended retail price. You are required to:

■ calculate the price which G Bath will pay for each product;
■ calculate the gross profit as a percentage of selling price on each product, if the products are sold at the recommended retail price;
■ calculate the gross profit as a percentage of cost price for each product.

Ignore VAT.

12 Enter the following transactions of Milner & Co Ltd in the appropriate books of prime entry; rule off at 28 February xxx1, and post as necessary to the Impersonal and Private Ledgers.

Note: Special care should be taken in drafting the form of the books of prime entry. **Read Chapter 4 before posting to the ledgers.**

Feb 4   Bought of T Lloyd, Lincoln, 500 metres of baize at £2.35 per metre, 2000 metres of satin at £5.60 per metre, less 10% trade discount in each case.

      10   Sold to T Williams, York, 400 metres curtain material at £6.50 per metre, and sundry fittings £8. Box charged £10.

      11   Bought showcase and counter for showroom from Universal Supplies Ltd, London, £750.00.

      12   Returned to T Lloyd, Lincoln, 200 metres of satin as invoiced on 4 February.

Feb 18   Bought of J Grey, Taunton, 300 metres linen at £7.25 per metre, less 5% trade discount and 250 metres baize at £2.35 per metre net.

      20   Received debit note from T Williams, York, for box invoiced on 10 February.

      24   Sold to D Wilson, Coventry, 300 metres baize at £4.00 per metre net, and 600 metres satin at £7.00 per metre less 10% trade discount.

Ignore VAT.

4 PURCHASE AND SALES TRANSACTIONS AND THE LEDGER ACCOUNTS

OBJECTIVE

In this chapter you are introduced to the Ledger and the relationship between the books of prime entry and the Ledger are explained.

This chapter includes details of how the Ledger is made up and how information is entered into it. The important distinction is also drawn between Personal and Impersonal Ledgers and some details of their interactions are given. The section concludes with a brief comment on VAT.

Question As I see it, the Purchase and Sales Day Books are written up from the original purchase invoices, and the copies of the sales invoices to customers?

Answer Yes, that is right, but it is of the utmost importance that every purchase invoice, whether for goods or services, should be certified by the responsible officials of the business that it is correct before being entered in the Purchase Journal.

Question The final column in the first example's Purchase Journal was headed 'Crates and Packing', but there was no similar column in the second one. Why is this?

Answer Suppliers may or may not charge for crates and packing material. If they do so, a record must clearly be made of the expense. It is a cost which we should record separately because it may be recoverable if and when such items as crates are returned to the suppliers; otherwise the cost must be borne by the business.

Question With both the Purchase and the Sales Journals there is then no one particular form of ruling?

Answer No. There cannot be. The system of book-keeping must be such as will give the information in each particular case in the form in which it is required, or can be of the greatest use. For this reason care must be exercised in the choice of the analysis columns. These may represent the principal materials dealt in, or the departments responsible for their production and sale, and so on.

Question If goods are bought and sold on credit, I should have thought it was also very important to know:

- how much the business has purchased *from any one supplier*, and
- how much it has sold *to any one customer*.

But as there are numerous transactions with different suppliers and customers, how could this be done from the Journals alone?

Answer By means of the Ledger, or principal book of account, we are able to discover very quickly not only what has been purchased from or sold to any particular person, but *how that person stands in relation to the business at any particular time*, that is, whether they are its creditor or debtor. Put in another way, we want to know how much we have sold to each customer period by period because if possible we hope to increase our sales to them, and we also want to know how much that customer owes us for goods delivered, since their payments to us provide the monies out of which we have to pay our suppliers.

Question So the Ledger Account records not only the trading aspect of our transactions, but also the *cash aspect*?

Answer Yes. Both aspects must be recorded as affecting suppliers and customers, but at the moment we are only concerned with the *trading aspect*.

The Ledger

Personal Accounts

We have spoken of Ledger Accounts as playing an essential part in summarising the transactions of the business so far as they concern those with whom it deals.

It is now necessary to describe the Ledger Account rather more precisely, and to consider its other functions.

Its usual format is as follows:

JONES

Dr   Cr

Date	Details	Amount	Date	Details	Amount
		£			£

In the format we notice:

- ■ Name of Account. This may be the name of the person, in this case Jones, who is either a supplier or a customer of the business. In other cases it may also represent the impersonal subject-matter with which the account deals such as the name of a particular expense or asset of the business.
- ■ The vertical double line in the centre divides the account into two equal parts. That on the left we term the **Debit** side, denoted by the symbol **Dr**, and that on the right the **Credit** side, with the symbol **Cr**. *On both sides* of the account, it will be observed, there are three columns headed respectively: Date, Details and Amount.

In the ordinary way, a separate page, or folio of the Ledger, is used for each account opened, and the Ledger itself may be a bound book; a loose-leaf book; in the form of cards, with a separate card for each account; or a series of files in a computer-based system.

If we assume that Jones is a supplier of goods to the business, the structure of the account enables us to put to his credit, i.e. on the right-hand, or *credit* side, the value of the goods supplied by him. The right-hand side may also be regarded generally as that on which we enter benefits received *by the business*. The supply of goods on credit is clearly such a benefit and Jones may be said to have performed, to this extent, a 'credit-worthy' action.

Furthermore, his account is said to be 'in credit', in that he is a *creditor* of the business. Let us suppose Jones has supplied goods to the value of £10. This being an ordinary purchase transaction, the first record will be made in the Purchase Journal, as we have seen. It will ultimately be put (or 'posted' as this action is usually called) to the credit of Jones's account, as follows:

JONES

Dr								Cr
Date	Details	PRJ Fo	Amount	Date	Details	PJ Fo	Amount	
				xxx1 Jan 1	Goods	2	£ 10.00	

At this point we must remember:

■ it is not necessary, but in appropriate circumstances it might be helpful, to repeat here the full description of the goods. By inserting a column for the Purchase Journal folio (PJ Fo) we can readily turn back to the initial entry in the Purchase Journal and, if we wish, to the original document, on which it was based, i.e. in this case the supplier's invoice

■ the purpose of our Ledger Account with Jones is to summarise or assemble within it *all our transactions* with him; otherwise it would be impossible to determine the position of the business in relation to him.

Because we are now thinking of Jones as a *supplier*, it is logical to assume, in the first instance, that any items on the left-hand or *debit* side will be in respect of payments made to him; off-setting the amounts standing to his credit.

If, however, the business has had occasion to return goods to him because of unsatisfactory quality, or error in price, and a *credit note* is received signifying his acceptance of them, this also is a matter which must be recorded on the *debit* side. The effect of the return of the goods is *to reduce the liability of the business* to Jones as its creditor. In this case, the initial entry will have been made in the **Purchase Returns** or **Allowances Book**, and from that we shall post to the *debit* of Jones's Ledger Account, as under:

JONES

Dr								Cr
Date	Details	PRJ Fo	Amount	Date	Details	PJ Fo	Amount	
xxx1 Jan 6	Returns or allowances	3	£ 1.50	xxx1 Jan 1	Goods	2	£ 10.00	

Should Jones, on the other hand, be a *customer* of the business a Ledger Account will be opened in identical form, but if goods to the value of £10 are *sold* to him, his account will be debited, that is the entry will be made on the *left-hand* side:

JONES

Dr								Cr
Date	Details	SJ Fo	Amount	Date	Details	SRJ Fo	Amount	
xxx1 Jan 1	Goods	2	£ 10.00					

He now appears as a *debtor* to the business, as indeed he is, the details of the original sale being found on Folio 2 of the **Sales Ledger**.

The business in this case has performed the 'creditworthy' action, and as such is entitled to regard Jones as *chargeable* with it. He is *indebted* to the business, and therefore the entry appears on the debit side.

Finally, should goods be returned by him, or the business make him any kind of allowance, the amount, as posted from the **Sales Returns and Allowances Book**, will be put to his credit.

The result will be, as we should expect:

- to offset by that amount his original indebtedness of £10
- to indicate that the business, having delivered defective goods, or made an overcharge, now proceeds to give Jones the necessary *credit*.

The Ledger Account would then appear:

JONES

Dr								Cr
Date	Details	SJ Fo	Amount	Date	Details	SRJ Fo	Amount	
xxx1 Jan 1	Goods	2	£ 10.00	xxx1 Jan 16	Returns or allowances	3	£ 1.50	

When the *cash* as well as the *trading aspect* of these transactions has been dealt with, we shall be in a position to determine, at any time and irrespective of the number of items, the *balance of indebtedness* due either *to* or *by* the business.

So far as we have been dealing with persons *external* to the business, the *personal* aspect of the sales and purchase transactions has now been recorded.

By that we mean *the effect upon the people* with whom the transactions have been entered into, resulting in their becoming the creditors or debtors of the business.

If we have carefully followed the construction of the Ledger Account as shown, it is apparent that the entries are postings from the various books of first entry – from the Journals. That is to say, the Journals provide the basis for the writing up of all Ledger Accounts.

We may even lay it down as a rule with very few exceptions that: *No entry shall be made in a Ledger Account, unless it has first appeared in the Journal.*

We should remember that the Journal will not necessarily be a bound book. It may consist of tabulation prepared by a computer or a file of invoices.

Impersonal Accounts

It was stated at the beginning of the previous section that the name of the account might be that of the person with whom the business dealt, or of the impersonal subject-matter referred to in it.

The former we have now called a **Personal Account**, and the latter is called an **Impersonal** or **Nominal** Account.

Jones's account, whether he be a supplier or a customer, is a *Personal Account*. His position, as someone external to the business, has been looked at from the *personal* aspect.

There is, however, another aspect to be considered, and that is *the effect upon the business* as an impersonal unit, of the transactions with Jones and any other suppliers and customers.

When in the first place we regarded Jones as a *supplier* his account was credited with £10, but at the same time we must remember that the business then came into possession of £10 worth of *goods*. It is therefore natural to regard the stores or warehouse as *chargeable* with this amount. As a department of the business it may be regarded *impersonally*, and the necessary charge made to it in an *impersonal account*, headed 'Warehouse' or 'Goods purchased' or, more usually, **Purchases**.

Thus the heading refers to the *subject-matter* of the account and not to the name of the warehouseman or storekeeper, which is immaterial because he represents the *business*. If this seems strange we must remember:

■ the essence of the Double Entry System is to record the dual aspect of each transaction *within the Ledger*, or book of account. In the event of no 'Warehouse' or 'Purchases' Account being opened we should have recorded in the Ledger *one aspect of the transaction only* – the personal aspect.

■ the business, or its proprietor, desires to know, period by period, how much has been *purchased* of the various kinds of goods dealt in.

The opening of the Ledger Account for 'purchases' permits the periodic totals of the Purchase Journal to be posted to it on the chargeable, or *debit*, side.

Sometimes it is contended, and truthfully, that the total cost of purchases, suitably analysed, can be seen at a glance in the Purchase Journal.

This, however, is no reason for eliminating the Ledger Account for 'purchases', because, as stated above, we desire to complete the *double entry within the Ledger*, and also obtain, *in the summarised form which the Ledger account gives*, the total charge to the warehouse for goods received by it month by month during the trading year.

As, in practice, the various subdivisions of the Journal are ruled off at monthly intervals, a note of the monthly totals in summarised form is clearly very helpful and this role is performed by the **Purchases** Account in the Ledger.

The following illustrates in another way what has been described above:

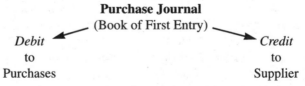

Purchase Journal
(Book of First Entry)

Debit   *Credit*
to   to
Purchases   Supplier

or, in account form, assuming the total purchases for the month were £1410:

Nominal Ledger Account
PURCHASES

Dr							Cr
Date	Details	PJ Fo	Amount	Date	Details	Fo	Amount
xxx1 Jan 31	Total purchases for month	2	£ 1410.00				

We may also add that, from the point of view of the business, the charge or *debit* to the 'Purchases' Account may be made by taking the *total* only of the appropriate column in the Purchase Journal.

This is in striking contrast to the necessity for giving *credit* to each separate supplier in *his own personal account.* We cannot avoid this latter step because we must know at any time *how the business stands in relation to each supplier.*

Purchase returns and allowances

It was seen on page 46 that Jones, as a supplier, was charged or *debited* with the goods returned to him, or the allowance claimed from him. As the result in either case is to *reduce the initial debit to* 'Purchases' Account, the double entry will be completed by *crediting* that account, as follows:

Purchase Returns and Allowances Book

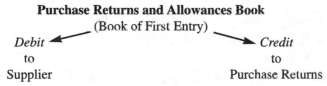

(Book of First Entry)

Debit	*Credit*
to	to
Supplier	Purchase Returns

or, in account form, assuming total purchase returns for the month were £71.50:

Nominal Ledger Account

PURCHASE RETURNS AND ALLOWANCES

Dr								Cr
Date	*Details*	*P.J Fo*	*Amount*	*Date*	*Details*	*PRJ Fo*	*Amount*	
			£				£	
xxx1 Jan 31	Total purchases for month	2	1410.00	xxx1 Jan 31	Total returns and allowances for month	3	71.50	

Purchases of a capital nature

In Example 3.3 we saw that the purchase by D Morris of showcases and fittings was recorded, together with his other purchases, in the Purchase Journal kept by him.

The personal aspect of this transaction is a credit to the suppliers in the Ledger Account opened in their name, i.e. a *personal account.*

But, as with the receipt of goods by the warehouse on behalf of the business, we have similarly to put on record somewhere the purchase of these capital goods, or as they are usually called, *fixed assets*.

There can be no question of charging them to the purchases since they are not goods in which the business is dealing.

But, nevertheless, an account must be opened for them in the Ledger, in order to complete the double entry *in the Ledger*, and so we may decide to open an account under the general heading of 'Fixtures and Fittings'.

In this case the business has acquired property, the use or value of which it is liable to account to its proprietor, even though such property is not intended for resale, and it is right that it should be charged or, as we say, *debited* with the purchase cost of £1000.

The question now arises: in which *section* of the Ledger shall the account be opened?

What we have already done is to describe:

   ■ **Personal Accounts**, as with Jones
   ■ **Impersonal Accounts**, e.g. Purchases,

the latter being the counterpart, in summarised form, of the former, so far as the effect upon the business is concerned.

Because of the existence of these two types of account, it is customary, in practice, to use *two entirely separate Ledgers*, known respectively as the **Personal Ledger** and the **Impersonal** or **Nominal Ledger**.

It is also usual to keep *separate personal ledgers*, one for customers, usually called the **Sales Ledger**, the other for suppliers, the **Purchase Ledger**.

If it would be useful to divide either of these ledgers there is no reason why not. The usual basis is by alphabet – to spread the work amongst different operators; by area so that different salesmen can be provided with relevant information; and sometimes but not very often, by particular categories of sales.

By contrast, the accounts in the Impersonal Ledger are unlikely to be very numerous, and in the main they relate to those matters which affect the business in its *ordinary trading activities*, such as purchases, sales, wages, etc.

We could, of course, from the standpoint of the effect upon the business, open the 'Fixtures and Fittings' Account in the Impersonal Ledger, and in that account record all dealings in that particular type of property. But, because the fixtures and fittings have no direct relation to the day-to-day trading activities, *a further section of the Ledger* is provided for the accounts of this and similar types of fixed asset.

This further section is termed the **Private Ledger**, and represents the third and final division of the Ledger as a book of account. It was called the **Private Ledger** from the days when only the owner or a director would have access to these '**private accounts**'. It is merely another illustration of the division of the Ledger into whatever sections the owners or managers think will be useful.

One again, we post the *total* of the 'special items' or 'capital items' column in the Purchase Journal, so that the Fixtures and Fittings Account appears as follows:

FIXTURES AND FITTINGS

Dr							Cr
Date	Details	PJ Fo	Amount	Date	Details	Fo	Amount
xxx1 March 31	Showcases and fittings	1	£ 1000.00				

or in diagram form:

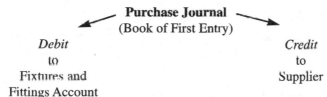

Purchase Journal
(Book of First Entry)

Debit to Fixtures and Fittings Account

Credit to Supplier

Sales

Much of what we have said in regard to the completion of the double entry under the heading of purchases will apply in the case of sales, although in the reverse direction.

We are still dealing with the *impersonal aspect* or *the effect upon the business* of the delivery of goods from the warehouse to the customer.

What we must realise is that if goods are sold to Brown, for example, in his capacity as a *customer*, the warehouse having delivered the goods is entitled to take credit to itself, as representing the business, for the goods that have passed out of its possession.

From the *personal aspect*, the customer Brown must, of course, be charged or *debited* with what he has received at *selling price*.

Impersonally the business is thus entitled to credit in an impersonal account, which may be headed 'Warehouse', or 'Goods sold', or more usually, **Sales**.

Our reasons for so doing are:

■ as in the case of purchases, the double entry must be completed *within the Ledgers*.

■ the business, or its proprietor, desires to know, period by period, how much has been sold of the various kinds of goods dealt in.

Therefore, we will open an account in the Impersonal Ledger, headed 'Sales', the periodic totals of the Sales Journal will be posted to it on the *credit* side, and, as with purchases, the Sales Journal will usually be ruled off and posted at monthly intervals.

At any time, therefore, we may obtain a comparison of the *cost of purchases*, with the *proceeds of sales*, by examining these two accounts in the Impersonal Ledger.

Stated in another way, we have:

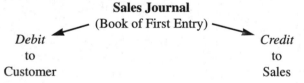

Sales Journal
(Book of First Entry)

Debit	*Credit*
to	to
Customer	Sales

or, in account form, assuming the sales value for the month to be £2000.00:

SALES

Dr								Cr
Date	Details	Fo	Amount	Date	Details	SJ Fo	Amount
				xxx1 Jan 31	Total sales for month	2	£ 2000.00

At this stage we record the total sales as shown in the Sales Journal, but see page 63 for a more detailed analysis.

This is because, irrespective of the *kind* of goods sold, they may all be regarded as *sales*, and dealt with in the Ledger as one item.

In recording the *personal aspect*, however, a separate debit to each customer in their own *personal account* is essential if we are to know precisely:

- how much has been sold to them
- the amount of their indebtedness to the business at any particular time.

Sales returns and allowances

Should Brown, to whom £20 worth of goods have been sold, return any part of the goods, or make a claim on the business for an allowance in respect of the invoice price to him, the effect upon the business will be to reduce the initial *credit* to the 'Sales' Account. In other words, the latter account will be *debited*:

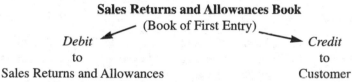

Sales Returns and Allowances Book

(Book of First Entry)

Debit	*Credit*
to	to
Sales Returns and Allowances	Customer

or, in account form, assuming the total amount of the sales returns and allowances for the month to be £50:

Nominal Ledger Account

SALES RETURNS AND ALLOWANCES

Dr								Cr
Date	*Details*	SRJ Fo	*Amount*	*Date*	*Details*	SJ Fo	*Amount*	
xxx1 Jan 31	Total returns and allowances for month	5	£ 50.00	xxx1			£	

Sales of a capital nature

These are far less frequently encountered than purchases of this class of goods. However, the need for a systematic approach to data processing means that all transactions will be processed in accordance with pre-planned procedures.

It is possible to record such sales by inserting a 'Special Items' column in the Sales Journal, but in practice use is almost always made of the earliest form of Journal, or the ordinary Journal (without analysis columns) as illustrated in Chapter 8.

Examples that may be cited of this type of 'sale' are the disposal of a lorry, salesperson's motor car or machinery.

The Journal entry in such a case provides the basic narrative of the transaction for entry in the Ledgers, these being the personal (Sales) Ledger so far as the person to whom they are sold is concerned, and the account of the particular asset in the Private Ledger so far as concerns the effect on the business. For example,

Journal

Date	Narrative	Dr	Cr
xxx	Person to whom sold	XX	
	Capital asset account		XX
	being sale of lorry, car, etc, to AN Other		

Consider the following example.

Example 4.1

On 1 January xxx1, D Morris had in his factory machinery with a book value of £5000 (i.e. cost in the accounts at the time). On 15 January a stitching machine was sold to a dealer, realising £150.

Private Ledger Account
MACHINERY

Dr							Cr
Date	Details	Fo	Amount	Date	Details	Fo	Amount
xxx1			£	xxx1			£
Jan 1	Balance		5000.00	Jan 15	A Dealer, Stitching machine		150.00

An important point in connection with this transaction would be the loss or profit on sale, i.e. the proceeds of sale of £150 would have to be compared with that proportion of the opening balance of £5000 which represented the actual machine sold. The principles describing how this comparison will be made are described in Chapter 15. The important fact to note with 'sales' of a capital asset is that they are not recorded in the 'Sales Account' in the Ledger but simply credited to the Asset's Impersonal account or to a Disposal account to record the effect on the business.

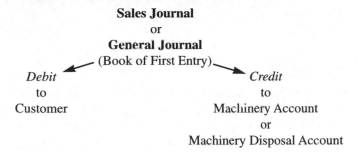

Impersonal, or Nominal, and Private Ledgers

While the Personal Ledger is restricted to the accounts of suppliers and customers in its purchase and sales sections respectively, the following examples are typical of the accounts appearing in the Impersonal Ledger and the Private Ledger:

Impersonal Ledger (Also called the **Nominal Ledger**)	**Private Ledger**
Purchases	Capital (of Proprietor)
Sales	Factory, warehouse or office
Purchase returns	premises
Sales returns	Machinery
Wages	Tools
Carriage	Fixtures and fittings
Salaries	Motor vehicles
Cash discounts allowed	Patents
Cash discounts received	Trade marks
Bad debts	Stock
Travelling expenses	Investments
Packing expenses	Loans
Repairs	
Interest paid	

Interest received

Rent

Rates

Commission

It might be added that in a general way, of the items appearing above, those under the heading 'Impersonal Ledger' relate to accounts in which we find details of the *profit and loss*, or *revenue position* of the business.

Those, on the other hand, under the heading of 'Private Ledger' relate to the *assets and liabilities* of the business.

Several of the accounts in the Private Ledger are sometimes called **Real** accounts, in particular factory premises, plant and machinery, etc., as they refer to assets that are 'real' in the physical sense. Clearly the Private Ledger, particularly in the case of a sole trade or partnership, relates to matters of a more private nature and may be more closely controlled by the proprietor rather than being part of the routine book-keeping.

Ledger Accounts

Now that we have become acquainted with the general application of Double Entry principles to the recording of Purchases and Sales transactions *within the Ledgers*, let us carry Example 3.3 (p. 34) a stage further and *post to the Ledger Accounts* from the various books of Prime Entry which we have already written up.

1 Purchases

In the Purchase Day Book of D Morris we see it is necessary to give **credit** to each one of the three suppliers who have supplied goods. Such credit will clearly be given in the Personal (Purchase) Ledger, and the three accounts required will be opened as follows:

D MORRIS

Purchase Ledger

R RIDGWELL, BOLTON

Dr							Cr
						PJ	
Date	Details	Fo	Amount	Date	Details	Fo	Amount
				xxx1			£
				March 12	Goods & VAT	1	337.22

B DAVIS, ELY

Dr								Cr
Date	Details	Fo	Amount	Date	Details	PJ Fo	Amount	
				xxx1 March 20	Goods & VAT	1	£ 1545.12	

GENERAL SUPPLIES LTD, LONDON

Dr								Cr
Date	Details	Fo	Amount	Date	Details	PJ Fo	Amount	
				xxx1 March 29	Goods & VAT	1	£ 11175.00	

In each case the entries appear on the *credit side* since, until payment is made to them, the suppliers are creditors of the business.

The use of the words 'Goods and VAT' in the 'Details' column is all that is necessary, as full particulars of the goods can quickly be found on Folio 1 of the Purchase Journal itself.

We must now consider the *impersonal aspect*, which is the charge to the warehouse for 'Goods Purchased' or 'Purchases'. It is necessary, too, for us to remember that by this is meant 'goods purchased for resale', so that we must in any event exclude the item of Showcases and Fittings.

Our Impersonal Ledger Account for Purchases will then be:

PURCHASES

Dr		PJ						Cr
Date	Details	Fo	Amount	Date	Details	Fo	Amount	
xxx1 March 31	Total for month:		£					
	Cotton		500.00					
	Sheets		175.00					
	Tee-shirts		912.00					
	Sundries		15.00					
		1	1602.00					

It is unlikely that we will be content with the *form* of this account, because month by month new totals will appear in it, and the subsequent addition of the 'Amount' column will be somewhat complicated.

For this reason, it may be preferred to open a separate Purchases Account *for each class of goods*, or to enter them in one account, but in *columnar* form.

If the first method is chosen we will have four separate purchases accounts:

Nominal Ledger

PURCHASES – COTTON

Dr							Cr
Date	Details	PJ Fo	Amount	Date	Details	Fo	Amount
xxx1 March 31	Total for month	1	£ 500.00				

PURCHASES – SHEETS

Dr							Cr
Date	Details	PJ Fo	Amount	Date	Details	Fo	Amount
xxx1 March 31	Total for month	1	£ 175.00				

PURCHASES – TEE-SHIRTS

Dr							Cr
Date	Details	PJ Fo	Amount	Date	Details	Fo	Amount
xxx1 March 31	Total for month	1	£ 912.00				

PURCHASES – SUNDRIES

Dr							Cr
Date	Details	PJ Fo	Amount	Date	Details	Fo	Amount
xxx1 March 31	Total for month	1	£ 15.00				

For the showcases and fittings purchased, an account in the Private Ledger will be opened, as below:

FIXTURES AND FITTINGS

Dr							Cr
Date	Details	PJ Fo	Amount	Date	Details	Fo	Amount
xxx1 March 31	Total for month	1	£ 1000.00				

It must be noted that the charge to the business for *purchases* and *fixtures and fittings* is made on the *debit* side, the amount in each case being the *total* of the appropriate analysis column in the Purchase Journal.

We now see that:

- the Purchase Journal as a Book of Prime Entry provides a basis for the Double Entry
- the dual aspect of the transactions has been recorded *within the Ledgers*
- arithmetical agreement has been obtained, in that the sum of the *credit* entries or postings in the Purchase Ledger is equal to the sum of the *debit* postings in the Impersonal and Private Ledgers
- while the postings to the Impersonal and Private Ledger Accounts are made on 31 March and in *total* only, those to the Personal Ledger are made as soon as possible after the initial record in the Journal and use the dates of the original transactions. It is essential to have our Ledger Account with each supplier 'up to date'.

2 Purchase Returns and Allowances

In the Purchase Returns Book we see there are two entries relating, in the first case, to an overcharge, and in the second, to the return of goods by the business to one of its suppliers.

In recording the *personal aspect* we must therefore remember that the suppliers' accounts in the Purchase Ledger will be *debited*, resulting in a reduction of any amounts previously standing to their *credit*.

This is a logical step to take because, had the overcharge not been detected, we should have *debited* Hunt with a payment *greater* than was actually due to him. The issue of a Debit Note now clearly reduces the amount of any subsequent payment to him by the business.

Further, the *receipt of a Credit Note* from Luxton enables the business to debit him with the cost of the goods returned for which, when purchased, it had originally given him credit.

The Purchase Ledger Accounts for the two suppliers will then appear as follows:

Purchase Ledger
W HUNT

Date	Details	PRJ Fo	Amount	Date	Details	PJ Fo	Amount
Dr							Cr
xxx1			£				
March 15	Overcharge	1	14.10				

V LUXTON

Dr								Cr
Date	Details	PRJ Fo	Amount	Date	Details	PJ Fo	Amount	
xxx1 March 27	Returns	1	£ 35.25					

As to the *impersonal* aspect, the warehouse will need to be *credited*. The reason for giving it credit now, is that it was originally charged or *debited* with the goods purchased at the invoice or cost price to the business. The credit thus given to it puts on record the fact that its responsibility is lessened by the amount of goods returned and adjustments, in total, of £42.00.

The **Purchase Returns** or **Returns Outwards Accounts**, will then be credited on 31 March with the **total of** the appropriate analysis columns in the Purchase Returns Journal as below:

PURCHASE RETURNS – COTTON

Dr								Cr
Date	Details	Fo	Amount	Date	Details	PRJ Fo	Amount	
				xxx1 March 31	Total for month	1	£ 42.00	

You will have noticed that the suppliers of goods were credited with the total of 'Goods and VAT' and the purchases accounts debited with the cost of goods only from the analysis columns. To complete the double entry and record the position of the business in respect of VAT the appropriate entries must be made in the VAT account in the Nominal (Impersonal) Ledger, using the monthly totals from the analysis columns in the books of prime entry.

When the Impersonal/Nominal Ledger account is written up, the balance will be the amount that is due to be paid to the Customs and Excise. Occasionally more may have been paid with purchases than has been charged on sales and a claim can be made for repayment.

Nominal Ledger Account

VAT

Dr								Cr
Date	Details	Fo	Amount	Date	Details	Fo	Amount	
xxx1			£	xxx1			£	
March 31	Total for purchases during month	1	455.34	March 31	Total for sales during month	2	699.12	
	Total for sales returns and allowances for month	2	35.35		Total for purchase returns and allowances for month	1	7.35	

These figures show that VAT of £699.12 has been charged to customers and will be collected from them, less £35.35 in respect of returns and allowances, i.e. 663.77

We have been charged, and will pay to
the suppliers £455.34 less £7.35 i.e. 447.99

so the remaining balance of 215.78

is due to the Customs and Excise. VAT is not a charge on the business: the business charges the customer and accounts for the total charge to the Customs and Excise after the appropriate allowance is made for the VAT that has been paid to suppliers.

Once more, it is seen that:

■ the double entry is completed within the Ledgers, Personal and Nominal

■ arithmetical agreement is maintained, the sum of the *debit* items being equal to the sum of the *credits*, and

■ while the postings to the accounts of Hunt and Luxton are made on the dates of the transactions with them, those to the Purchase Returns Accounts are made in total on 31 March.

3 Sales

The Sales Journal gives us full particulars of the sales to the three customers for whom we shall open separate accounts in the Sales Ledger.

To record the personal aspect, we must show that they are debtors to the business, and therefore their accounts will be in *debit*, taking the following form:

W HUMPHREY, LINCOLN

Dr   Cr

Date	Details	SJ Fo	Amount	Date	Details	Fo	Amount
xxx1 March 10	Goods and VAT	2	£ 676.80				

S BONHAM, COVENTRY

Dr   Cr

Date	Details	SJ Fo	Amount	Date	Details	Fo	Amount
xxx1 March 18	Goods and VAT	2	£ 1280.75				

T BUTTERWORTH, NORWICH

Dr   Cr

Date	Details	SJ Fo	Amount	Date	Details	Fo	Amount
xxx1 March 24	Goods and VAT	2	£ 2736.57				

We should now be able to understand the meaning of what has been done in our book-keeping work. If in the case of *personal* accounts, like those set out above, the entries appear on the debit side, or there is an excess in value of debit entries over credit entries, the person whose name appears at the head of the account is always a debtor to the business. They are chargeable to the extent of paying the business for the goods it has sold to them.

If a similar state of affairs is found to exist in an *impersonal* account, such as 'Purchases', it indicates that the official of the business under whose control the goods have come is chargeable to account for them until the time of their ultimate sale.

When dealing with *sales*, it is necessary to give *credit* to the warehouse which has parted with goods on the instructions of the Sales Department, and has therefore reduced its responsibility to account in the proper way.

Thus, an account will be opened in the Impersonal Ledger for Sales, as follows:

SALES

Dr								Cr
						SJ		
Date	Details	Fo	Amount	Date	Details	Fo	Amount	
				xxx1			£	
				March 31	Total for			
					month			
					Cotton	2	1500.00	
					Linen		2470.00	
					Sundries		25.00	
							3995.00	

As explained on page 59, in connection with the analysis of purchases, we shall, however, almost certainly prefer to open separate Sales Accounts for the various kinds of goods to correspond with the columns in the Sales Journal.

The result will then be:

SALES – COTTON

Dr								Cr
						SJ		
Date	Details	Fo	Amount	Date	Details	Fo	Amount	
				xxx1			£	
				March 31	Total for			
					month	2	1500.00	

SALES LINEN

Dr								Cr
						SJ		
Date	Details	Fo	Amount	Date	Details	Fo	Amount	
				xxx1			£	
				March31	Total for			
					month	2	2470.00	

SALES – SUNDRIES

Dr								Cr
						SJ		
Date	Details	Fo	Amount	Date	Details	Fo	Amount	
				xxx1			£	
				March31	Total for			
					month	2	25.00	

By means of these analysed Impersonal Accounts it is now possible for the proprietor of the business to compare, month by month, the **purchase cost** with the **proceeds of sale** of the various articles in which they are dealing.

Obviously, in the long run sales should exceed purchases but from month to month there will be changes in the level of stocks owned by the business and the direct comparison of purchases and sales may be inappropriate.

4 Sales Returns and Allowances

As with Purchases, we find in this book two entries which must be posted to the Ledger, involving the completion of the *personal aspect* at once and as a separate posting to the account of each customer, and of the *impersonal aspect* at the end of the month, and in total only.

We find, however, this difference from Purchases: the goods returned by Humphrey are part of those sold to him during the month under review; while both items come under the head of 'Returns', there being no question of an overcharge.

Let us try to visualise what these two entries mean. It may be simpler to deal first with the Impersonal aspect.

The warehouse has received the goods, increasing its stock, for which it is accountable. It is, therefore, logical that we should charge or *debit* it with the *total* value of the returned goods.

At the same time, the customers have performed a 'creditworthy' action, to this extent offsetting the original charge or debit made to them individually. It is equally reasonable, therefore, to *credit* them with the returned goods. This credit, in the case of Humphreys, will cause his account to appear as follows:

W HUMPHREY, LINCOLN

Dr								Cr
Date	Details	SJ Fo	Amount	Date	Details	SRJ Fo	Amount	
xxx1 March 10	Goods and VAT	2	£ 676.80	xxx1 March 22	Returns	2	£ 105.75	

and from it we can see that his original indebtedness is now reduced, *which is in line with the facts*.

As for Jenkinson, he too will receive *credit*, as follows:

A JENKINSON, WOLVERHAMPTON

Dr								Cr
Date	Details	Fo	Amount	Date	Details	SRJ Fo	Amount	
				xxx1 March 23	Returns	2	£ 131.60	

However, since we know nothing of his original indebtedness to the business, the position is that he appears as a creditor for the amount shown above. Payment may either be made to him in settlement, or more probably, the credit will be taken into account by him when he next pays for any further goods supplied.

Finally, to complete the double entry, we shall post the totals of the appropriate columns in the Sales Returns Journals to the Debit of the Impersonal Ledger Accounts for 'Sales Returns – Cotton' and 'Sales Returns – Linen', just as we did with Purchases.

In both cases, the warehouse has received goods, either from a supplier, or from a customer.

SALES RETURNS – COTTON

Dr							Cr
Date	Details	Fo	Amount	Date	Details	Fo	Amount
xxx1 March 31	Total for month	2	£ 90.00				

SALES RETURNS – LINEN

Dr							Cr
Date	Details	Fo	Amount	Date	Details	Fo	Amount
xxx1 March 31	Total for month	2	£ 112.00				

Summary

With each of the Journals we have been careful to regard them as providing the basis for the completion of the double entry *within the Ledgers*. They have, therefore, served their purpose in enabling us to look at each one of the *purchasing* and *selling transactions* from their *dual aspect*, or the Personal and Impersonal aspect.

Irrespective of the *number* of these transactions during any particular period, we are now in a position to tabulate the information contained in the Ledger Accounts in the form of *balances* that now exist. These balances will be obtained by a scrutiny of each account, so that the amount of one item or of the total items on the debit side will be termed a *debit balance*, and one on the credit side a *credit balance*. Where entries appear on both debit and credit sides, the excess of the one side over the other will also be termed the balance, but this we shall appreciate more readily after dealing with Cash Receipts and Cash Payments.

In this example there are only two accounts with both debit and credit entries: VAT, which has been summarised on page 63 and W Humphrey, shown below. Inspection shows us that the debits are greater than the credits so the net balance will be a debit. At the end of each month, or whenever a balance is needed, two entries are made. A balancing amount which ensures that the total credits equals the total debits is entered on the credit side, the two columns total and the balancing amount brought down as the new debit, completing the double entry.

W HUMPHREY, LINCOLN

Dr								Cr
Date	Details	SJ Fo	Amount	Date	Details	SRJ Fo	Amount	
xxx1			£	xxx1			£	
March 10	Goods and VAT	2	676.80	March 22	Returns	2	105.75	
				31	Balance	c/d	571.05	
			676.80				676.80	
31	Balance	b/d	571.05					

We can extract and list the balances as they now appear in the various Ledger Accounts:

Page	Ledger	Name of Account	Dr	Cr
			£	£
58	Purchase	R Ridgwell		337.22
59		B Davis		1545.12
59		General Supplies Ltd		1175.00
61		W Hunt	14.10	
62		V Luxton	35.25	
64	Sales	*W Humphrey	571.05	
64		S Boham	1280.75	
64		T Butterworth	2736.57	
66		A Jenkinson		131.60
60	Impersonal	Purchases – Cotton	500.00	
60		Sheets	175.00	
60		Tee-shirts	912.00	
60		Sundries	15.00	
62		Purchase returns – Cotton		42.00
65		Sales – Cotton		1500.00
65		Linen		2470.00
65		Sundries		25.00
67		Sales returns – Cotton	90.00	
67		Linen	112.00	
63		VAT		215.78
60	Private	Fixtures and fittings	1000.00	
			£7441.72	£7441.72

* Note that the Ledger account on page 64 with only the sale recorded has been subsequently updated to reflect the 'returns and allowances' as above.

It should be mentioned that in the average business by far the greater number of accounts will be found in the Personal Ledgers, and especially in that section of those Ledgers containing the accounts of customers, or Sales Ledger. So large may this become as a result of the business enlarging its sales that its division on an alphabetical or territorial basis may be essential if the Accounting Department is to do its work with speed and efficiency.

Control accounts

Reference was made earlier (page 4) to 'one account in the ledger for incoming goods or purchases and other accounts for the individual suppliers'. If these suppliers become numerous it may be simpler to have one account, called a **Creditors Control Account**, for recording the totals of the transactions, and subsequently analysing these totals to the individual suppliers. Similarly there would be an account for the customers, for which the control account would be called the **Debtors Control Account**.

The illustration on pages 59–60 showed first an account for total purchases which was subsequently replaced by separate accounts for different types of purchases. Use of the total purchases account provides one illustration of a control account – in this case a control account for purchases. The more usual control account is for the personal accounts, and it is preferable to have at least two, one for debtors (as listed in the Sales Ledger) and the other for creditors (as listed in the Purchases Ledger).

If a Creditors Control Account had been used, the entries made in it for the transactions in the recent example would have been

Creditors Control Account

Dr							Cr
Date	Details	PJ Fo	Amount	Date	Details	PRJ Fo	Amount
xxx1			£	xxx1			£
March 31	Purchases returns and allowances for the month	1	49.35	March 31	Goods supplied for the month, and VAT thereon	1	3057.34

and separate *subsidiary* records would be kept to show the position of each individual supplier. The net balance on the creditors control account (£3057.34 minus £49.35, i.e. £3007.99) should equal the sum of the balances on the individual suppliers accounts.

		£
R Ridgwell	Cr	337.22
B Davis	Cr	1545.12
General Supplies Ltd	Cr	1175.00
		3057.34

minus	W Hunt	Dr	14.10	
	V Luxton	Dr	35.25	
				49.35
				£3007.99

With opening balances and more entries, as is usual in practice, the benefits from the use of the control account become more apparent. Control Accounts may be used wherever it is considered useful to a particular situation; maybe merely to divide the Personal Ledger (sales) into alphabetical sections, or areas of the country, or the responsibility of particular sales staff.

Value Added Tax

Question What is VAT?

Answer Many countries have introduced a tax calculated as a percentage of the sales of the business. In Britain this is known as the Value Added Tax (VAT) (and in other countries it may be called a Sales Tax) and the appropriate percentage (currently 17½% for most goods and services) on the value of sales has to be accounted for to the Customs and Excise. As allowance is given for VAT paid on purchases, a business in effect pays over the VAT on the value added by the business and recovers it from the customer. The balance of VAT charged to customers over the VAT suffered on purchases must be handed over to the Commissioners of Customs and Excise. On the other hand, if the tax suffered by it exceeds that which has been charged, repayment is due. Only registered businesses are affected by this tax. Any business may register, however it is not obliged to register unless turnover exceeds £48,000 per annum for 1997/98. A business not registered cannot charge VAT nor can it recover VAT suffered on its purchases.

Question What extra records does the business have to keep?

Answer The business with proper records will require very little extra; another column in the Purchase and Sales Day Books and an additional nominal ledger account is all that is necessary. The example in this chapter illustrated the book-keeping requirements.

Similarly, an extra column would be required in the cash book for the VAT on cash transactions when purchases and sales are not made with credit.

Question This seems to be a simple procedure. Why do some people complain about the complexity of VAT?

Answer The book-keeping is straightforward. The difficulties arise because certain goods and services are exempt from VAT (i.e. have VAT charged at 0%), others are zero rated.

Question Where should a trader go for advice?

Answer The local officer of the Customs and Excise or the accounting advisor should be consulted for the precise details applicable to a particular enterprise.

Exemption

Exemption for a transaction means that no liability to account for tax to the tax authorities arises when the transaction is performed. Equally, the trader undertaking the exempt transaction is given no credit by the tax authorities for any tax invoiced by suppliers for the goods and services used for the exempt business. The operation of the credit mechanism throughout a chain of transactions is therefore interrupted by an exempt business transaction.

Zero rating

Zero rating a transaction means that it is brought within the scope of the tax, but the rate applied to output is zero. If the person carrying out the transaction is a taxable person they are accountable in the usual way; but the result is that their outputs carry no tax because a zero rate is applied to them, while they are allowed credit for or repayment of tax on their inputs. Exports are relieved from tax by means of this technique.

KEY POINTS

On completion of this chapter you should be familiar with:

1 the basic principles of Debiting and Crediting accounts and the nature, use and inter-relation of the following:

■ Day Books/Journals   Personal Accounts
    Purchases   Purchase Ledger
    Sales   Sales ledger
    Purchase returns   Control Accounts
    Sales returns
■ The Ledger   Impersonal Accounts
                             (or Nominal)
                             Real Accounts
                             Private Accounts

2 the principles of VAT and the recording of the VAT aspects of purchases and sales

3 the principle and use of Debtors and Creditors Control Accounts.

Questions

1 Name the different Ledgers employed in the ordinary trading concern, and mention the classes of account you would expect to find in each.

2 Explain:

    a Nominal Accounts

    b Real Accounts

    c Personal Accounts.

3 On which side of the following Ledger Accounts would you expect to find the balance? Give reasons for your answer in each case:

    a Bad Debts Account

    b Plant and Machinery Account

    c Sales Account

    d VAT Account

    e Returns Outwards Account.

4 W Green has the following transactions with J Black:

xxx1			£
July	10	Goods sold to W Green	422.00
	15	Goods returned by W Green	20.00
Oct	10	Goods sold to W Green	392.00
	10	Goods returned by Green	10.00
	11	W Green charged extra due to pricing error	45.00

You are required to show how each of the above items would be recorded in the books of J Black.

5 During the month of October xxx9, Ian Webster's transactions on credit were as follows:

Oct			£	
	1	Purchases from D Hudson	180.00	subject to 20% trade discount
	4	Sales to M Whitehead	85.00	
	7	Sales to A Woods	115.00	
	10	M Whitehead returns goods	20.00	
	15	Purchases from M Douglas	420.00	subject to 25% trade discount
	23	Returned goods to M Douglas (part of stock purchased on October 15)	30.00	list price
	25	Sales to M Whitehead	170.00	
	28	Purchases from D Hudson	86.00	
	30	Received credit note from Hudson in respect of goods (which had been purchased on October 28) with a list price excluding VAT of	16.00	
	31	Whitehead returns goods	36.00	

(**Note:** All purchases, sales and returns are subject to Value Added Tax at 10%)

You are required to:

    a write up Webster's sales, purchases, returns inwards and returns outwards day books for the month of October xxx9

    b write up and balance the VAT account for the month of October xxx9, showing the amount due to/from the tax authorities.

6 The following sales have been made by Sevenoaks Trading during the month of July xxx1. The values represent the value of the goods, before adding VAT at 15%.

xxx1			
July	1	to High Rise	£120
	5	to Brown & Co	£70
	10	to Carter Brothers	£240
	12	to Singh & Co	£160
	31	to Jones Ltd	£190

You are required to enter these transactions in the Sales Day Book, Sales Ledger and Nominal Ledger.

7 The credit sales and purchases for the month of October xxx1 for Teachers & Co are shown below exclusive of VAT.

xxx1

Oct	1	Bought from Kent Traders	£170
	3	Bought from Canterbury Ltd	£360
	5	Sold to Davenport & Co	£250
	10	Sold to East Ltd	£120
	12	Bought from Canterbury Ltd	£420
	31	Sold to Davenport & Co	£460

You are required to enter these transactions in the appropriate records of the company assuming that Teachers & Co are **a** not registered for VAT; **b** registered for VAT. Assume 10%.

8 The following transactions relate to November xxx1.

xxx1			£
Nov	1	Sales Ledger balances	3276
	30	Totals for the month:	4347
		Sales Day Book	
		Sales returns and allowances	265
		Cheques received from customers	1984
		Discounts allowed	29
	30	Total of individual Sales Ledger balances	5345

You are required to write up the Sales Ledger control account.

(Do not attempt this question until you have completed Chapter 5.)

5 | CASH TRANSACTIONS

OBJECTIVE
This chapter describes the process of recording cash and bank receipts and payments, and their posting to the Ledgers. Discount allowed and received is also discussed.

Question From what you have been saying about the accounts in the various Ledgers, am I correct in thinking that all they show are balances of Trading Transactions?

Answer Yes, of Purchases and Sales on Credit Terms. What we now have to do is to consider the Receipt and Payment of *Cash* by the business, usually at the end of the period of credit allowed to or by it.

Question You said earlier that some portion of the Capital with which the business was begun must be in the form of Cash. That would be in order to pay its running expenses?

Answer Not only such expenses as Wages and Salaries, but also to pay suppliers who might initially be unwilling to give credit to a new business.

Question Would it be right to describe such Cash as the **Working Capital** employed?

Answer It forms a part, but by no means the whole, of the Working Capital. A better definition for cash would be that it is a **Liquid Asset**, part of the Current Assets. Its subsequent use by the business may result in its remaining a **Current Asset**, as when goods are bought for stock, or becoming a **Fixed Asset**, when Plant, Fittings, etc., are purchased.

Question In the case of goods in which the business dealt, you said these were entrusted to the warehouse manager, who was responsible for their receipt and issue. Is the cashier similarly responsible for the Cash assets?

Answer No, only for what is termed **Cash in Hand**; this, however, is negligible in amount as compared with the money in the bank account of the business, or **Cash at Bank**. Between the two, there is this difference; the *Cashier*, as a servant of the business, will always be, on balance, accountable to it for cash held by them. The *Bank*, on the other hand, may sometimes be the creditor of the business, for instance where money is advanced on loan or by way of overdraft.

Some business transactions take place by the use of cash in the form of coin and notes. Others, including most large transactions, use cheques or electronic transfers. There are clearly differences between cash and cheques but there are similarities in the book-keeping entries when purchases or sales are settled. Instead of using separate cash received and cheques received books and ledger accounts, one is used for all receipts (and payments) except when a cash fund is used for small payments under the control of a particular person.

A small business may use one cash book to record all receipts and payments whether cash, cheques or transfers. As it grows it will become more convenient to use separate books; one for small cash payments (petty cash see Chapter 7), another for larger payments and a third for receipts. The principles and procedures are similar in either case.

Office procedure on receipt of cash

When each day's incoming mail is opened, all remittances from customers will be passed on to the cashier. They will usually be accompanied by the statements of accounts which the business has issued at monthly intervals to its customers. These statements are copies of the Personal Account in the Ledger and show the customer what should be paid. If it is up to date and the customer agrees that it records all the transactions accurately, the requested amount will be paid. Sometimes there are differences; perhaps cash or goods in transit, queries over price or quality that have not yet been agreed. In this case a smaller amount will be paid and every effort must be made to identify and settle the disputed items.

The cashier will:

■ compare the amount remitted with the total of the statement and, at the same time, check the *Cash Discount* which the customer may have deducted. **Cash Discount** is the inducement offered by the business to its customers to pay within the recognised period of credit. As such it is an expense to the business, which must always be taken into account with the accompanying remittance. If the terms upon which business is done are '2½% monthly account', and Mr Green's debt is £100, then *if he pays on or before the end of the month following delivery of the goods to him, he need pay* £97.50 (i.e. £100 – 2½%) only. On the other hand, if he pays after the expiry of the credit period, the discount will not ordinarily be allowed.

Where Cash Discount refers to the customers of the business, it is termed **Discount Allowed**. It differs from *Trade Discount*, which we discussed on page 33, in that it always relates to the cash or financial aspect of each transaction. Looked at in another way, it assists the business in collecting what is due from its customers by encouraging timely payments of money owing.

The cashier will also:

■ enter the remittances in detail in either a rough cash diary or Journal, as a preliminary to entry in the Cash Book proper, or enter them at once in the Cash Book. Whichever alternative is adopted, such initial entry is a **Prime** or **First** entry, and therefore corresponds to the record of Purchases or Sales in the Purchase and Sales Journals/Day Books

■ list the remittances on the counterfoil of the bank paying-in book, so that the total agrees with the total of the entries for the particular business day appearing in the Cash Book of the business. Thus, the amount actually banked will agree with the business records

■ make out formal receipts in the name of each customer, which may be attached to the statements of account and then issued to the customers for retention by them. (In most businesses it is no longer usual to issue receipts for cheque payments.)

The Cash Book or Cash Journal will then be available for the ledger clerks, whose duty it will be to post the amount of each remittance *to the credit of the Ledger Account of the customer from whom it was received.*

The procedures described above are those that a very small business might use to ensure that there is a record of every stage in the process. In practice, many businesses would combine some of these activities. All the cheques may be listed by hand or computer and the total entered in the bank account, and the same list used to support the paying-in slip.

Also, there may be notifications from customers that they have paid the account by credit transfer to your bank.

Book-keeping entries: Cash receipts

We can best approach these by considering the cashier as being very much in the same position as the warehouseman, with the difference that they are responsible for **cash** instead of **goods**.

If, therefore, we apply the same reasoning to their responsibility as a servant of the business we shall charge them with *all incoming cash*. It is logical to do this, so that they may at any time be accountable for its safe custody and disposal.

Using a term with which we have now become familiar, the cashier will be *debited* with all money received and, as was indicated above, each of the customers will be *credited*, the latter having performed a 'creditworthy' action in paying to the business what is due by them.

We commence our records by opening a **Cash Received Journal** or **Cash Received Book**, in which all money received from customers, whether in the form of cheques, notes, coin, etc., will be entered. Bearing in mind the fact that in many cases Cash Discount has been allowed to the customers, it will be helpful to show the amount of the discount *by the side of* the item to which it relates. The entry for the payment of cash received from G Green would therefore be recorded as follows:

Cash Received Journal

Date	Customer	Total	Discount	Cash
		£	£	£
xxx1 Feb 20	G Green	100.00	2.50	97.50

From this it is apparent that G Green has now settled the debt of £100, and in collecting what was due, the business has incurred an expense of £2.50 which, clearly, must reduce the figure of profit it expects to make.

Like the Purchase and Sales Journals, the Cash Book will probably be ruled off and totalled at the end of each month, with the result that, as with our Purchase and Sales transactions, we shall find it desirable:

■ to give *credit* to *each customer* immediately on receipt of the separate remittance

■ to *debit* or charge the *cashier* in total with the cash receipts, irrespective of the individual details making up the total.

The Cash Received Journal enables us to do this, and at the same time to comply with *double entry principles*, as the following diagram shows:

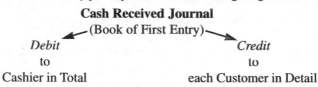

Cash Received Journal
(Book of First Entry)

Debit	*Credit*
to	to
Cashier in Total	each Customer in Detail

or in account form which also records £50 received from D Brown (with no discount allowed):

Cash Received Journal

Date	Customer	Total	Discount	Cash
xxx1		£	£	£
Feb 20	G Green	100.00	2.50	97.50
22	B Brown	50.00	–	50.00
		£150.00	£2.50	£147.50

Sales Ledger
G GREEN

Dr								Cr
Date	Details	Fo	Amount	Date	Details	CRJ Fo	Amount	
xxx1			£	xxx1			£	
Feb 1	Sales		100.00	Feb 20	Cash	1	97.50	
					Discount	1	2.50	
			£100.00				£100.00	

P BROWN

Dr								Cr
Date	Details	Fo	Amount	Date	Details	CRJ Fo	Amount	
xxx1			£	xxx1			£	
Feb 1	Sales		50.00	Feb 22	Cash	1	50.00	

Private Ledger

CASH

| Dr | | CRJ | | | | | | Cr |
Date	Details	Fo	Amount	Date	Details	Fo	Amount
xxx1 Feb 28	Total cash received	1	£ 147.50				

In the above, we note firstly that the *Cash Account* appears in the *Private Ledger*. This is as we should expect because the Private Ledger is concerned with Assets and Liabilities, and Cash Received is clearly an Asset.

Secondly, we note that, while our aim is to complete the double entry *within the Ledgers*, the sum of the two credit balances on the accounts of Green and Brown is £150, whereas we have a debit balance on Cash Account of £147.50 only.

That is to say, so far as *discount allowed* is concerned, we have given credit to G Green personally *in the Ledger* for that amount, but we have not impersonally noted its effect upon the business. The business must be charged with that amount as an expense or loss resulting from its dealings with Green, and it is therefore necessary to open in the Nominal Ledger an account for discount allowed.

DISCOUNT ALLOWED

| Dr | | CPJ | | | | | | Cr |
Date	Details	Fo	Amount	Date	Details	Fo	Amount
xxx1 Feb 28	Total discount	1	£ 2.50				

Arising from this we see that:

- the double entry is completed within the Ledgers
- a Debit Balance in an Impersonal Ledger Account, e.g. Discount, is a business *expense*, and a debit balance on a Private Ledger Account is for our present purpose an *asset* of the business.
- the Debit Balances formerly appearing on the accounts of Green (£100) and Brown (£50) in the Sales Ledger will have been settled by the posting to their credit of the cash received.

Office procedure on payment of cash

Periodically, say at monthly intervals, the business will pay its *suppliers* for what has been purchased from them. At the end of each month a statement of account may have been received from them setting out the balance in their favour. This will be compared with the total standing to their credit in the various Purchase Ledger Accounts. Care will be taken to deduct the value of any goods returned to them by the business, if omitted in the statement, and similarly a deduction will be made for Cash Discount which, from our point of view, is called **discount received** or **receivable**.

Thus on or before the end of the month following delivery of the goods a list will be prepared for all *accounts payable*, setting out:

- the folio of the supplier's account in the Purchase Ledger
- the name of the supplier
- the total amount due
- the amount of the discount, and
- the sum now payable.

This list, together with the Statement of Account received from the suppliers, will be submitted to the proprietor or to a responsible official of the business, who will sign the cheques issued in settlement.

Many businesses pay in accordance with their own records rather than using a statement from the supplier. This is a simpler process but eventually the two records must be reconciled (see page 105).

Book-keeping entries: Cash payments

When the warehouseman issued goods to customers he would be given credit for their value at *selling price*, the credit being given in 'Goods Sold' or *Sales* Account.

With the *payment* of cash, we have likewise to give *credit* to the cashier, which is only logical, having charged or *debited* them with cash *received*.

At the same time, we shall *debit* the cash payment to each of the suppliers, thus offsetting the amounts for which they appear as *creditors*, and indicating that the liability of the business to them is now discharged.

For this purpose, a *Cash Paid Journal*, or *Cash Paid Book*, may be opened, as a Book of First Entry, ruled with columns for discount and the actual cash paid.

Cash Paid Journal

Date	Supplier	Total	Discount	Cash
		£	£	£
xxx1 Feb 23	L Lindsay	30.00	0.75	29.25

The record shown above indicates that a liability to L Lindsay of £30 has been satisfied by a cash payment of £29.25 and that a **profit** in the form of £0.75 has been earned.

The Cash Paid Journal enables us to:

■ charge or *debit each supplier* immediately on payments of money

■ *credit the cashier* in total with the total cash payments irrespective of the individual details.

This may be put in another way:

Cash Paid Journal
(Book of First Entry)

Debit   *Credit*

to each Supplier in Detail   to Cashier in Total

or in account form which also records £58.50 paid to M Morris and £1.50 discount received.

Cash Paid Journal

Date	Customer	Total	Discount	Cash
		£	£	£
xxx1 Feb 23	L Lindsay	30.00	0.75	29.25
26	M Morris	60.00	1.50	58.50
		£90.00	£2.25	£87.75

Purchase Ledger

L LINDSAY

Date	Details	CRJ Fo	Amount	Date	Details	Fo	Amount
			£				£
xxx1 Feb 23	Cash	2	29.25	xxx1 Feb 1	Purchase		30.00
	Discount	2	0.75				
			£30.00				£30.00

Dr   Cr

M MORRIS

Dr								Cr
Date	Details	CRJ Fo	Amount	Date	Details	Fo	Amount	
xxx1 Feb 26	Cash	2	£ 58.50	xxx1 Feb 1	Purchase		£ 60.00	
	Discount	2	1.50					
			£60.00				£60.00	

Private Ledger

CASH

Dr								Cr
Date	Details	Fo	Amount	Date	Details	CPJ Fo	Amount	
				xxx1 Feb 28	Total cash paid	2	£ 87.75	

As the counterpart of cash received, but in the reverse direction, the Cash Account in the Private Leger has a credit balance, which here denotes a *liability*. This will be clearer to us if we think of the banker of the business instead of its cashier. If they have paid money away on behalf of the business to its suppliers, the banker will have a claim upon it to that extent, and this claim is, of course, a liability of the business.

So far as the balances on the Ledger Accounts are concerned, the sum of the *debits* in the Purchase Ledger is seen to be £90, while the *credit* on Cash Account is £87.75.

The impersonal aspect of discount received or discount earned is that a profit of £2.25 has been made for which credit may be taken. We may therefore open the following account in the Impersonal Ledger:

DISCOUNT RECEIVED

Dr								Cr
Date	Details	Fo	Amount	Date	Details	CPJ Fo	Amount	
				xxx1 Feb 28	Total discount	2	£ 2.25	

Once more, the double entry is completed *within the Ledgers*, and we see that a credit balance on an Impersonal Ledger Account is a business *profit*, while a similar balance on a Private Ledger Account is a *liability* of the business.

Goods and cash compared

1 When *goods* are bought, the Purchases Account is debited and the individual suppliers credited; when goods are sold, the individual customers are debited, and Sales Account is credited.

In the Impersonal Ledger there are therefore two accounts used for the trading transactions; purchases and sales.

But in our *cash* dealings, recorded in total in the Private Ledger, we have *only one cash account*, debited as regards cash received and credited with cash paid.

2 Goods purchased will be valued at *cost price* per unit, but goods sold at *selling price*. Moreover, in a manufacturing business at least, goods purchased may largely consist of raw materials, while goods sold will be the finished product – an essentially different article. With cash, however, whether it is cash received or cash paid, the value per unit is the same.

For these reasons, we are able to **merge** our cash received and our cash paid **in one account** only, or by using the figures given above:

Dr   CASH   Cr

Date	Details	CRJ Fo	Amount	Date	Details	CPJ Fo	Amount
xxx1 Feb 28	Total cash received	2	£ 147.50	xxx1 Feb 28	Total cash paid	2	£ 87.25

It is clear that the excess of the debit side, or £60.25, represents an *asset* of the business, while if the larger amount appeared on the credit side, it would be a *liability*.

From this we may draw three conclusions:

■ That instead of having two Books of First Entry – a Cash Received Journal and a Cash Paid Journal – *one book* will suffice, and we may call it the Cash Journal or, as is more usual, the **Cash Book.**

■ Because it contains all our cash receipts and payments, *the Cash Book is not only a Book of Prime Entry, but is also a Ledger Account*, in that,

■ Whether the cashier or the banker is entrusted with the cash resources, *the position of the business in relation to either* can quickly be seen from the Cash Book.

Proceeding on the basis that incoming cash remittances are banked intact on the day of receipt, and all payments are made by cheque, writing up the Cash Book daily as Book of First Entry is equivalent to writing up the Ledger Account with the bank.

If, however, a minimum amount of cash must be retained by the business in order to pay petty expenses, and if, also, wages and salaries have to be paid in cash and not by cheque, it is necessary to provide *additional columns* in the Cash Book to record purely cash, as distinct from banking transactions or to use a separate petty cash book (see Chapter 7).

We will now work through an example to make this clear:

Example 5.1

From the following particulars, draw up the three-column Cash Book of V Treat. No posting to the Ledger is required and no money is to be paid into the bank unless and until instructions are given.

xxx1

Jan   1   Commenced business with cash in hand £60 and a balance at the bank of £325.

      3   Cash sales £336.

      4   Drew cheque £70 for private use; paid wages by cash £260.

      5   Paid rent by cheque £220.

      6   Paid into bank additional capital £1000.

      8   Received a cheque from Light Bros £240 in settlement of their account of £250 allowing cash discount of £10.

      9   Paid Brown & Sons cheque for £480, receiving discount £20.

Jan   10   Received a cheque from Bilton Ltd, value £140, in settlement of their account £145 after cash discount of £5.

    11   Drew cheque £120 for cash for office use.

    12   Paid into bank the two cheques received from Light Bros and Bilton Ltd, respectively.

    13   Paid Jennens Ltd cheque £190, having deducted discount 5% from their account.

    16   Light Bros' cheque was returned by the bank marked R/D. This means 'Refer to drawer', in this case the person – Light Bros – who signed the cheque.

    18   Paid wages by cash £230.

    31   Bank charges for the month £15.

Balance off the Cash Book and bring down the balances as on 31 January xxx1.

Note: The three columns of a three-column Cash Book refer to Discount, Cash and Bank, and there are also three columns for receipts and three for payments. There is also space to record the reference for the posting of the personal aspect of the transactions to the appropriate supplier or customer account.

If we look more closely at this example, we will see that provision is made in the columns headed 'Cash' and 'Bank' respectively for a statement at any time of the position of the business as regards:

■ its cashier, and
■ its banker.

At the beginning of the month the proprietor introduced as Cash Capital £385, divided as shown, and the description of the item 'Capital A/c' indicates that that is the Account in the Ledger which is to be credited.

During the month cheques are drawn on the bank account in order to replenish the money in the hands of the cashier. The bank pays out money, and thereby reduces its accountability to the proprietor of the business. For this it must be **credited**, but, simultaneously, the accountability of the **cashier** is increased, and so, on the left hand, or debit side of the Cash Book, we enter the amount of £120 in the **cash** column.

In our wording of the items in the Cash Book, we must be careful to choose words which will indicate at once *where the corresponding (debit or credit) entry is to be found.*

When a cheque received from a customer is returned by the bank marked R/D (refer to drawer, or Light Bros) we must bring the Cash Book into line with the bank's own view of the position, and having *charged* the bank with £240 on 12 January we must now give them credit on 16 January. We therefore cancel the original charge to the bank and, *to complete the double entry within the Ledgers*, post the amount to the *debit* of Light Bros' account, reviving the original debt due from them. Their position is now the same as it was before the worthless cheque was received.

We see that columns are provided in which to record cash discount *allowed* and *received*. When the cheque from Light Bros was first received on 8 January, £10 was allowed to them as discount, the *total* due by them being £250. But as their cheque is returned on 16 January it is not enough merely to credit the bank with the amount of the *cheque*; we must in addition write back to Light Bros's account the discount which was, of

Cash Book
V TREAT

Dr

Date		Fo	Discount	Cash	Bank
xxx1					
Jan 1	Capital A/c			60.00	325.00
3	Cash Sales			336.00	1000.00
6	Capital A/c				
8	Light Bros		10.00	240.00	
10	Biltor Ltd		5.00	140.00	
11	Bank			120.00	
12	Cash, cheques per contra				380.00
16	Light Bros				
	discount charged		(10.00)*		
			£ 5.00	£896.00	£1705.00
xxx1					
Feb 1	Balances b/d			26.00	370.00

Cr

Date		Fo	Discount	Cash	Bank
xxx1					
Jan 4	Drawings				70.00
4	Wages			250.00	
5	Rent				220.00
9	Brown and Sons		20.00		480.00
11	Cash				120.00
12	Bank, cheques from Light Bros and Bilton Ltd			380.00	
13	Jennens Ltd		10.00		190.00
16	Light Bros cheque returned				240.00
18	Wages			240.00	
31	Interest and bank charges				15.00
31	Balances c/d			26.00	370.00
			£30.00	£896.00	£1705.00

*When Light Bros' cheque is returned the discount previously allowed to him must be *deducted* from discounts allowed and *debited* to his account. Note that the original entry is not cancelled; the new transaction is recorded with an appropriate new entry.

course, only allowed by the business in the belief that the cheque was good. It is this third column for discount which led to the use of the phrase 'three-column cash book'.

Credit is given to the bank for charges made by them for the month. They will, *in their own books*, have debited the business with this sum, and in order that the two sets of records shall agree, this entry must be made.

On 31 January balances can be inserted on the *credit side* of the Cash Book (representing the amount by which the debit side exceeds the credit side) and *brought down* on 1 February, as the *opening balances* for the new period. The balances, it will be noted, are in both cases *debit balances*, indicating the existence of an asset in the form of:

- cash in hand £26.00, and
- cash (or balance) at bank £370.00.

Before we pass from this example let us look at the Discount Allowed and Discount Received Accounts in the Nominal Ledger.

DISCOUNT ALLOWED

Dr							Cr
Date	Details	Fo	Amount	Date	Details	Fo	Amount
xxx1 Jan 31	Total for month		£ 5.00				

DISCOUNT RECEIVED

Dr							Cr
Date	Details	Fo	Amount	Date	Details	Fo	Amount
				xxx1 Jan 31	Total for month		£ 30.00

Considering Discount Allowed we notice that while both the cheques received from *and* the discount allowed to Light Bros and Bilton Ltd appear on the *debit* side of the Cash Book, these customers will each receive *credit* for the **total** in their respective Ledger Accounts. But only the amount of the *actual money* they pay is debited in the cash and bank columns. Accordingly, to complete the double entry, we must have in the Nominal Ledger an account for *discounts allowed*, in which the further debit required will be shown, *and correspondingly for discounts received*.

The control account described and illustrated on page 69 will also include the total payments made to creditors, month by month, and any discount received.

Running balance account

So far ledger accounts have used the two-sided, Dr and Cr, format. An alternative is the three-column running balance.

Example 5.2

John Smith, a merchant, does not pay all cash received into his bank. He wants to record all cash received and paid and all his bank transactions in one Cash Book. His transaction during the first few days of January xxx1 were as below:

xxx1			£
Jan	1	Cash in hand	150
		Bank overdraft	72
		Received cash from AB (after allowing him discount £10)	150
	2	Paid into bank	245
	3	Drew cheque for CD (after deducting discount £3)	27
	4	Received cheque from EF (after allowing him discount £30) and paid it into bank	270
	5	Drew from bank in cash	20
		Paid wages (on presentation of an open cheque at bank)	80
	7	EF's cheque returned by bank, dishonored	
	8	Received cash from GH (after allowing discount £2)	48
	9	Paid into bank	25
	10	Paid cash to JK (after deducting discount £4)	36

You are required **a** to record these transactions in a three-column Cash Book; **b** to rule off and balance the book; **c** to state clearly how the discounts are dealt with in the Ledger. (Prepare your own record and then compare it with the printed solution.)

A bank overdraft occurs when arrangements have been made for more to be withdrawn from the bank than has been paid into it. It is like a loan for a fixed amount and there is usually an upper limit placed on the 'loan' by the bank. Unlike a normal loan, interest is only paid to the bank if the account becomes overdrawn. If the business doesn't need an overdraft then no interest is paid. In effect it is a flexible loan.

An overdraft is **not** an asset, it is a liability and when there is an overdraft at the beginning or end of an accounting period it will appear as a **credit** balance in the Cash Book.

a The three-column cash book is shown on page 91.

b To calculate the cash and bank balance it is useful to total the columns. For the cash Dr £368, Cr £306, so the net balance to be carried down (or forward) is £62. Similarly for the Bank Dr £540, Cr £469, £71 net. Record these balances so that the totals agree and complete the double entry by carrying them down to the opposite side. They will appear as debits, i.e. assets.

c Discounts allowed. Individual items, e.g. £10.00 for AB, will be posted to Cr of AB in Sales Ledger and the total £12.00 to the Debit of Discount Allowed/Discounts Received. Individual items, e.g. £3.00 from CD, will be posted to Debit of CD in Purchases Ledger and the total of £7.00 to the Credit of Discounts Received.

Example 5.3

The nominal ledger account for VAT on page 63 could be recorded:

Date	Detail	Fo	Dr	Cr	Balance
			£	£	£
xxx1					
March 31	On purchases	PJ1	455.34		455.34 Dr
	On sales	SJ2		699.12	243.78 Cr
	On purchase returns	PRJ1		7.35	251.13 Cr
	On sales returns	SRJ2	35.35		215.78 Cr

The balance is calculated automatically after each posting and is indicated as Dr or Cr. Some systems use + and − instead of Dr and Cr as do other accounts, e.g. the bank statement, etc.

Cash Book postings to Ledger Accounts

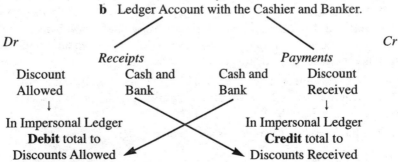

Cash Book being
a Book of First Entry, and
b Ledger Account with the Cashier and Banker.

Dr   Cr

Receipts   Payments

Discount   Cash and   Cash and   Discount
Allowed   Bank   Bank   Received
↓   ↓
In Impersonal Ledger   In Impersonal Ledger
Debit total to   **Credit** total to
Discounts Allowed   Discounts Received

Cash Book

JOHN SMITH

Dr   January xxx1 Cr

Date	Receipts	Discount	Cash	Bank
xxx1				
Jan 1	Balance b/d		150.00	
1	AB	10.00	150.00	
2	Cash			245.00
4	EF	30.00		270.00
5	Bank		20.00	
7	EF discount not allowed	(30.00)*		
8	GH	2.00	48.00	
9	Cash			25.00
		£12.00	£368.00	£540.00
xxx1				
Jan 12	Balances b/d		62.00	71.00

Discount column: Debited to 'Discount Allowed' Account

Date	Payments	Discount	Cash	Bank
xxx1				
Jan 1	Balance b/d			72.00
2	Bank		245.00	
3	CD	3.00		27.00
5	Cash			20.00
5	Wages			80.00
7	EF cheque returned			270.00
9	Bank		25.00	
10	JK	4.00	36.00	
11	Balances c/d		62.00	71.00
		£7.00	£368.00	£540.00

Discount column: Credited to 'Discount Received' Account

*When EF's cheque is returned, the discount previously allowed to him, £30, must be recharged to him. It is therefore *deducted* in the discounts allowed column and *debited* to EF's account.

a In Purchase Ledger **debit** to individual suppliers total of cash and discount.

b In Nominal Ledger **debit** to wages, cash purchases or other expense accounts.

c In Private Ledger **debit** to Asset Accounts (if purchased) or Liability Accounts if paid off or reduced.

a In Sales Ledger **credit** to individual customers total of cash and discount.

b In Nominal Ledger **credit** to bank interest received, cash sales or other income accounts.

c In Private Ledger **credit** to Asset Accounts (if sold) or Liability Accounts if, for example money borrowed or new capital introduced.

Other bank accounts

So far we have only considered one bank account, the Current Account. A business may have several accounts, e.g. a Deposit Account on which higher rates of interest may be earned, or a Loan Account where the bank has lent money to the business on agreed terms of interest and repayment.

When the business has more money than it needs for day-to-day activities it could transfer the surplus from the Current Account to the Deposit Account. This is similar to a payment; the Current Account (which up to now we have called the bank account) will be credited and a new account, the Deposit Account, will be debited. This is just like the entries made when Cash is paid into the bank, Debit bank and Credit Cash. We have already explained that the Cash and Bank Book is sometimes the Ledger Account as well, but the Deposit Account will usually have its own Ledger Account.

KEY POINTS

On completion of this chapter you should:

1 be aware of the purpose of cash received and cash paid books, whether they are separate books, one book or computer-generated lists

2 be able to use a three-column cash book and make the appropriate entries in the Discount, Cash and Bank columns

3 appreciate the possible role of the cash book as a book of prime entry and a ledger

4 post the cash book entries to the appropriate Ledger Account.

Questions

At this stage ignore VAT.

1 Define trade discount and cash discount. State clearly how these are treated in books of account.

2 A trader receives an account from XY, the landlord, for £250 in respect of one month's rent, which is paid on the date of receipt.

Explain the different ways which might be adopted to record this item in books kept on the Double Entry System.

3 On 1 January xxx1, R Rich sold G Jones goods to the amount of £50.25; on 13 February Jones paid Rich £25 on account; on 27 February Rich sold Jones £48.50 of goods; on 3 March Jones returned to Rich £7.75 goods (not being up to sample); on 13 March Jones paid Rich £24 and was allowed £1.25 discount to clear the January account. On 31 March Rich sent a quarterly statement to Jones. Set out the statement in proper form.

4 From the following particulars write up A Bondman's Cash Book for the week commencing 5 July xxx1 and balance the Cash Book as at 10 July xxx1.

July 5 Cash in hand £15.50, and in bank £176.
      5 Paid by cheque to F Abbott his account of £47, less 5% cash discount.
      6 Paid in cash, postage stamps £2.75.
      7 Purchased goods by cheque £10.50.
         Received cheque from R Beal in payment of his account of £40, less 2½% cash discount, and paid the cheque into bank.
      8 Purchased by cheque office desk £30.
     10 Paid wages in cash £120.
         Cash sales for week £150.75.
         Withdrew from bank for office purposes £20.
         Withdrew from bank for self £15.

Post the items in your Cash Book to the Ledger.

5 Leslie Morris commences business on 1 January xxx1. Record in a suitable ruled Cash Book the following transactions for the first week of January xxx1 and bring down the balances on 7 January:

xxx1			£
Jan	1	L Morris paid into bank on account of Capital.	700.00
	2	Received and paid into bank direct the following:	
		Jones (after allowing discount £5)	45.00
		Wilson (after allowing discount £0.50)	12.50
		Graham (after allowing discount £0.75).	15.00
	2	Drew cheque for office cash.	40.00
	4	Wilson's cheque returned by bank unpaid.	

5	Drew cheque for		330.00
	Paying wages	£200.00	
	salaries.	130.00	
5	Bought goods for cash.		25.00
6	Received the following (in cash):		
	Peters, payment for goods	£250.00	
	Rent receivable	10.00	
	Sanders (after allowing discount £1).	60.00	
			320.00
6	Paid cash into bank.		300.00
7	Paid by cheque:		
	Lister (after deducting discount £0.50)		19.50
	White (after deducting discount £1.50).		58.50

How would you deal with the totals of the columns Discounts Allowed and Discounts Received, when the Cash Book is ruled off on 7 January xxx1?

6 On 20 June xxx1, H Rivers received from S Wells an invoice for £514. Of this amount £510 represented the cost of goods purchased and £4 the carriage on them.

On 30 June xxx1, H Rivers returned to S Wells goods to the value of £60.

After the invoice had been entered in the books, it was discovered that a trade discount of 20% had not been deducted from the cost or from the item relating to goods returned and an adjusting entry was made to correct these mistakes.

The account was paid by cheque on 31 July xxx1, less 2½% discount.

You are required to show the entries in the respective books of account of H Rivers to record the above transactions.

7 From the following particulars write up the Cash Book of Thomas Mixture for the month of January xxx2, and bring down the balances at the end of the month. It is not Mr Mixture's rule to bank all cash and make all payments by cheque.

xxx2			£
Jan	1	Cash in hand.	18.00
	1	Balance overdrawn at bank.	36.75
	2	Received cash sales.	242.50
	4	Banked cash.	115.00
	4	Paid Jackson & Co by cheque.	14.25
	5	Received Jones' cheque (direct to bank).	14.50
	6	Paid salaries in cash.	134.75
	7	Bought goods for cash (paid from office cash).	11.00
	8	Drew office cash from bank.	16.00
	9	Received cash sales.	225.00
	13	Paid salaries in cash.	133.50
	16	Received Smith's cheque (direct to bank).	56.75
	20	Paid Brown by cheque.	16.00

20	Received from Jones in coins and notes.	55.50
20	Paid salaries in cash.	134.75
23	Drew office cash from bank.	135.00
26	Received Jones' cheque (direct to bank).	17.50
27	Paid salaries in cash.	134.75
27	Paid office cash into bank.	20.00
28	Jones' cheque returned by bank unpaid.	17.50

8 The Cash Book of Thomas Jones for the first week of January xxx1 is as follows:

xxx1		Discount £	Bank £	xxx1		Discount £	Bank £
Jan 1	Balance		752.00	Jan 3	Wages		159.00
2	Sundry customers:			5	Sundry suppliers:		
	L Smith	1.00	39.00		G Green	3.00	57.00
	V Latham	4.00	76.00		T Robson	2.00	78.00
4	Rents receivable		117.00	5	V Latham cheque		
6	Plant A/c (machine				returned		76.00
	tool sold)		26.00	6	Cash purchases		18.00
		£5.00	£1010.00			£5.00	£388.00

You are required:

a to indicate to which Ledger each entry in the Cash Book would be posted.

b to make the cash postings in such Ledger Accounts, including the Discount Account.

9 From the following particulars you are required to write up the three-column Cash Book of K Walker. No posting to the Ledger is required:

xxx1

March	1	Cash in hand £246.50.
	1	Overdrawn at bank £93.60.
	2	Paid into bank £30.00.
	3	Paid wages by cash £141.50.
	4	Received cheque from R Francis value £35.75 in settlement of an amount owing £37.00.
	4	Cash sales £153.60.
	4	Received a cheque from M Scott £23.75, and allowed him discount £0.75.
	5	Paid S Marsh cheque the balance of his account £34.00, less 5% discount.
	5	Cash purchases £33.00.
	6	Paid cheques from R Francis and M Scott into the bank.
	8	K Walker paid into the bank addition capital £240.00.
	9	Drew cheque £36.00 for office use.
	10	Paid L Hopecraft cheque £18.80, being allowed discount £0.80.
	10	Paid wages by cash £90.60.
	10	M Scott's cheque was returned by the bank marked R/D.
	11	Drew cheque £15.00 for private use.
	11	Bought plant and machinery £370.00 and paid the amount by cheque.
	12	Paid sundry small expenses by cash £16.40.
	31	Bank charges £7.20.

Balance the Cash Book as on 31 March and bring down the balances.

10 Apart from in the cash book, in what Ledger or other accounts, and upon which side of these accounts, would you expect to find the following?

a £500 paid for new machinery.

b £170 received from J Robinson in full settlement of his account of £172.60.

c £600 received from an insurance company in settlement of a claim for damages to premises by fire.

d £750 received for the sale of old motor van.

e £250 paid to Jane Fitter in full settlement of an account due to her three months hence of £260.75.

6 | THE BANK RECONCILIATION

OBJECTIVE

This chapter describes the importance of ensuring that the balance at the bank shown by the books of the business is the same as the balance shown by the records of the bank. The reconciliation should be carried out on a regular basis, and the chapter explains the procedure for achieving this.

Banks usually send to their customers, whether they are businesses or private individuals, a statement of their position in relation to the bank at regular intervals. This statement is a copy of the customer's account in the bank's Ledger, and usually will be shown from the bank's standpoint. That is to say, money paid in or *lodgements* by the customer will be shown as credits, and money withdrawn by cheque will be debited. At any time, there will be a balance either in favour of or against the customer.

Before the use of book-keeping machines and computers became common, *Bank Pass Books* were issued to all new customers, which were written up by the bank for the customer to compare with the bank columns in their own Cash Book. The customer could therefore be satisfied that the bank had given credit for all money which had been debited to it in the Cash Book. Similarly, when the bank *debited* the paid cheques, it could be seen that the name of the payee and the amount for which the cheque had been drawn were also in agreement with the *credit* side of the Cash Book.

At intervals it was, of course, necessary for the Pass Book to be returned to the bank in order to be written up to date.

In many cases today, however, the bank's statement is given in the form of *loose sheets*, so that there is a continuous record of the bank's version of the position between them and the customer.

We have seen elsewhere that it is the custom for suppliers of goods to the business to send statements of account which are valuable evidence of the accuracy of the Purchase Ledger Accounts.

The importance of a similar statement from the bank can readily be appreciated, more particularly if the bank is the *creditor* of the business, as with a loan or overdraft account to which a limit has been set.

It is rare for a bank to make a mistake in writing up the Pass Book or loose sheets, but we do find that at times mistakes are made by the cashier in the Cash Book, and also in *omitting to record* some particular receipt or payment.

Many banks, to prevent lack of agreement between their own records and the Cash Books of their customers, print at the bottom of each statement sheet:

> 'The items and balance shown on this statement should be verified and the bank notified promptly of any discrepancy.'

In ordinary business practice, it is the custom to rule off and balance the Cash Book at monthly intervals, bringing down the balance to the beginning of the new period. For the bank columns in the Cash Book, this balance represents either

- Cash at bank (Dr) or
- Bank overdraft (Cr)

It will, therefore, be the cashier's duty to prepare at the end of each month what is termed a **bank reconciliation** or **bank agreement**, confirming the accuracy and completeness of their Cash Book records. Some authorities suggest that the person responsible for preparing or reviewing this reconciliation should *not* be the cashier, but someone independent, who is not involved with the actual handling of cash or cheques.

A bank reconciliation requires that every item entered in the Cash Book as being paid into the bank and each cheque recorded as paid, be checked against the bank statement. This will identify cheques which have not been paid by the bank (called unpresented cheques) and receipts paid into the bank just before the balancing date but not appearing on the bank statement until afterwards (uncleared or items not yet cleared).

In the affairs of a private individual, this reconciliation may be easily and quickly prepared; it may take a few minutes only, but with a business, where lodgements are being made daily throughout the month, and the number of cheques drawn by the business is very large, the labour involved may be much greater.

We must now consider the nature of the work to be done, bearing in mind that the bank statement shows the position of the business *in the light of the information in the bank's possession.*

Supposing the reconciliation is to be prepared on 31 January; we may commence with the statement balance at that date, using a sheet of cash-ruled paper which we can later file away for future reference. Our task is then to *reconcile* or *agree* this balance with the balance appearing in the Cash Book.

If, as is usually the case, there is a difference between the two balances, it may be due to:

■ *Cheques drawn and issued by the business to its suppliers* and entered in the proper way on the credit side of the Cash Book, *but not yet presented* by the collecting banker for payment.

As the cheques so drawn have to be sent to suppliers, banked by them, and subsequently passed through the clearing system, several days may pass before they reach the paying bank. We must therefore *deduct* the amount of the unpresented cheques from the statement balance if favourable to the business, or *add* if an overdraft exists. On the other hand, if we have begun by taking the Cash Book figure, we should add the amount to a debit balance, or deduct it from a credit balance.

■ *Cheques paid in by the business* which on presentation to the paying bank are refused because of, for example:

lack of funds to meet them
– countermand of instructions to pay by the Drawer
– death of the drawer
– some irregularity on the face of the cheque, such as absence of Drawer's signature, difference between amount in words and figures, etc.

In these cases, the collecting banker, having given credit when the cheque was lodged, will now *debit the account*, returning the unpaid cheque to the business. The latter will take this up with its customer, and endeavour to resolve the difficulty.

In any event, as we saw on page 89, the cashier should credit the bank with the amount involved, i.e. enter it as though it were a payment on the credit side of the Cash Book. Should they have omitted to do this, for purposes of the reconciliation they must, if beginning with a favourable statement balance, add the amount or deduct it if unfavourable.

In beginning with the Cash Book balance, the reverse steps would of course be taken.

■ – *bank interest allowed*

– *bank interest and commission charged.*

We have already explained these items as representing, so far as the business is concerned, either a *profit* or an *expense*.

The bank will enter them in is own account with the customer at regular intervals (usually half-yearly or perhaps monthly), but does not usually give the customer a separate advice that it has done so. The customer will be unaware of these items until they receive their statement. The proper course is then to *debit* the Bank Column in the Cash Book with the interest allowed by the bank, or *credit* it with the interest and commission charged.

If this has not been done, we shall proceed as follows in preparing the Bank Reconciliation:

Interest allowed

a *Commencing with statement balance.*
   If 'in favour', deduct.
   If overdrawn, add.

b *Commencing with Cash Book balance.*
   If a debit balance, add.
   If overdrawn, deduct.

Interest charged

The reverse, of course, applies with interest and commission charged, i.e:

a *Commencing with statement balance.*
   If 'in favour', add.
   If overdrawn, deduct.

b *Commencing with Cash Book balance.*
   If a debit balance, deduct.
   If overdrawn, add.

In making these adjustments, we must always remember the aim in view, which is *to link the statement balance with the Cash Book balance*, or vice versa. Whether we begin with the statement or the Cash Book does not affect the result, but the former may give the more reliable commencing figure, as it is so much less likely to contain errors.

Example 6.1

The balance shown by the bank statement on 31 March xxx7 indicates an overdraft of £209.80, while, on the same date, the Bank Column in the Cash Book shows a credit balance of £419.00.

Comparing the two records, you find that two cheques drawn on 31 March, one for £204.00 and the other for £77.20, had not been presented for payment, while one of £72.00 paid into the bank on the same date had not yet been credited.

Prepare a Reconciliation Statement.

	£	£
Overdrawn as in bank statement		209.80
Add cheques drawn but unpresented:		
March 31	204.00	
,, 31	77.20	
	———	281.20
		491.00
Less cheque paid in but not yet credited		
by bank		72.00
Credit balance as in Cash Book		419.00

In the Example 6.2, we will begin instead with the balance according to the Cash Book.

Example 6.2

On 30 March xxx5, your Cash Book shows that you have in the bank the sum of £817.24. The bank statement shows a balance of £955.00.

On checking your Cash Book with the bank statement you find that cheques drawn by you amounting to £214.17 have not passed through the bank, that a cheque for £84.12 has not yet been credited to you, and that the bank has credited you with interest £22.07, and debited you with sundry charges £14.36. Draw up a reconciliation statement, showing adjustments between your Cash Book and Bank Pass Book.

	£
Balance in hand as in Cash Book	817.24
Add cheques drawn but unpresented	214.17
	1031.41
Less cheque paid in but not credited	84.12
	947.29
Add interest credited by bank	22.07
	969.36
Less charges made by bank	14.36
Balance as in bank statement	£955.00

Note: After completing the reconciliation remember to enter the appropriate items in the cash book.

Example 6.3 introduces some of the errors which may be made in the Cash Book and entries which may have been omitted.

Example 6.3

From the following particulars, prepare a reconciliation of the bank statement balance with the Cash Book balance.

	£
Balance as in bank statement (in customer's favour)	60.00
Balance as in Cash Book (overdrawn)	80.00
Unpresented cheques	144.00
(cheques paid by the business, sent to the suppliers but not yet paid by the bank)	
Uncleared cheques inwards	26.00
(cheques received from customers and paid into the bank, but not yet credited by the bank to the business account)	

Further,

■ a cheque for £20 paid to J Jones has been entered in error in the Cash Column of the Cash Book

■ the debit side of the Cash Book (Bank Column) has been undercast by £50

■ the cashier has omitted to record bank commission charges of £8.

If we decide to begin with the bank statement figure:

	£
Balance as in bank statement (in customer's favour)	60.00
Adjust unpresented cheques	144.00
i.e. when presented there will be an **overdraft** of	84.00
Less uncleared cheques (paid in but not credited by bank)	26.00
	58.00
Less cheque to J Jones (as this has been paid	
by the bank and will appear in the statement)	20.00
	38.00
Less Commission (charged by the bank and	
appearing in the statement)	8.00
	30.00
Add undercast in Bank Column of Cash Book	50.00
Overdrawn as in Cash Book	£80.00

If preferred, we could begin instead with the Cash Book:

	£
Overdrawn as in Cash Book	80.00
Adjust unpresented cheques (prepared and entered	
in Cash Book but not in bank statement)	144.00
Favourable balance of	64.00
Less uncleared cheques (paid in but not credited	
in statement)	26.00
	38.00
Less cheque to J Jones (paid by bank and therefore	
appearing in statement)	20.00

Less Commission charged by bank	8.00
	10.00
Add undercast in Bank Column of Cash Book	50.00
Balance as in bank statement (in favour)	£60.00

Having identified these errors, we must remember to make the appropriate entries in the books of original entry. The reconciliation confirms that the data is correct but does not correct the original error. If these adjustments are not made, the balances in the statement and Cash Book will not agree next time a reconciliation is prepared.

We have produced a reconciliation between these two balances. If during this process we discover errors in or omissions from the Cash Book then the Cash Book must be corrected.

Using the data from Example 6.3:

a Dr Bank column, Cr Cash column £20
b Increase total of Dr Bank column by £50
c Cr Bank column, Dr Bank Charges £8.

Starting with the original balances in the Cash Book

Date	Receipts	Cash	Bank	Date	Payments	Cash	Bank
30.3.x5	Balance b/d	200.00		30.3.x5	Balance b/d		80.00
	Transfer (a)	20.00			Transfer (a)		20.00
	Undercast (b)		50.00		Bank charges (c)		8.00
		220.00	50.00			0.00	108.00
	Balance c/d		58.00		Balance c/d	220.00	
		220.00	108.00				108.00
	Balance b/d	220.00			Balance b/d		58.00

Perhaps it will be worthwhile to check that these entries have been made correctly by preparing a new reconciliation:

Balance as in bank statement (in customer's favour)	60.00
Add unpresented cheques	144.00
(which produces an overdraft)	84.00
Less uncleared cheques	26.00
Balance overdrawn as in Cash Book	58.00

The bank statement and Cash Book now agree. The unpresented and uncleared cheques should clear in due course.

The cash balance should also be checked with the cash actually held by the cashier from time to time. This should also identify any errors such as the recording of a payment in the wrong column of the cash book as appeared in this example.

Customer/Supplier Statements

Where statements of account are received from customers or suppliers (debtors or creditors to the business) it is common practice to perform a similar reconciliation between the business's version of each account and the version illustrated by the statement received. Any differences not explainable by new sales/suppliers or payments made/received should be investigated.

KEY POINTS

On completion of this chapter you should

1 know how to prepare a bank reconciliation statement

2 recognise the need to record in the Cash and Bank Books any errors discovered by the reconciliation and any items correctly entered by the bank on their statement which have not been recorded by the business.

Questions

1 A cashier receives the statement from the bank and finds that the amount of the overdraft differs from that shown by the Cash Book. Give the possible explanations for this difference.

2 From the following particulars prepare a statement showing how the differences between the Cash Book balance and the bank statement balance is reconciled:

	£
Statement balance – 30 June xxx1	1401.62
Cash Book Balance – 30 June xxx1	577.52

Cheques drawn prior to 30 June xxx1, but not presented until after that date:

	£
P	29.20
Q	801.17

R	5.73
S	132.32

	£
Cheques paid into the bank on 30 June xxx1, not credited until 2 July xxx1	116.20
Bank charges and interest to 30 June xxx1, not entered in the Cash Book	8.12

3 On 30 November xxx1, the Cash Book of E Simpson disclosed a debit balance of £212, and his bank statement at the same date a balance in his favour of £361.

Prepare a bank reconciliation at 30 November, taking into account that a cheque payable to E Simpson in respect of a 3% dividend on this holding of 1000 ordinary shares of £1 each in Greystones Foundry Ltd was entered in the Cash Book on 30 November, but not credited by the Bank until 1 December, and that cheques drawn by E Simpson on 28 November, as follows, were not presented at the bank by the payees until 3 December.

	£
H Simpson, salary	108.32
Corporation electric supply	35.68
Trade Supplies Ltd (a creditor)	35.00

4 On 31 December xxx9, Jane Smith found that her bank statement showed a balance in the bank of £88.62, whereas according to her Ledger the bank account was overdrawn by £57.69. On checking over the figures she discovered that the following cheques had not been presented:

	£
Wilkins & Co	96.17
Turnbull & Snow	63.00
Samuel & Son	85.50

while a payment in of £90 on 31 December had not yet been credited by the bank, and the bank's charges for the half-year amounting to £8.36 had not been entered in the Ledger.

Prepare a reconciliation between the two balances and state which other account would be affected.

5 A Shiner's Cash Book for July xxx6 is as follows:

Dr					Cr
xxx6		£	xxx6		£
June 30	Balance	817.22	July 3	Lomas & Co	151.23
July 4	J Bell	15.75	8	Smith Ltd	32.00
9	Salt & Son	92.53	10	C Jervis	1.84
18	Williams Ltd	31.22	20	Evans & Co	10.91
29	E Harris	81.17	27	PMG	35.32
31	James & Co	14.81		Telephones	
			29	D Greene	1.80
			30	J Johnson	84.89
			31	Kenrick Ltd	25.72

His bank statement shows, for August xxx6, the following:

xxx6		£	xxx6		£
July 31	Balance	806.59	Aug 3	Kenrick Ltd	25.72
Aug 2	James & Co	14.81	6	F David	10.53
3	Saul & Co	100.78	7	D Greene	1.80
			7	J Johnson	84.89

Prepare a Bank Reconciliation as at 31 July xxx6.

6 At 31 January xxx8, the Cash Book of Sue Gibson shows a balance overdrawn of £117, while according to her bank statement at that date there was a balance in her favour of £72. A comparison of the two records revealed the following:

- ■ a cheque for £25 sent to B Murray had been entered in the cash column of the Cash Book
- ■ bank charges of £17 at 31 December xxx7 were not entered at all in the Cash Book
- ■ the bank had debited Gibson's Account with a cheque for £11 received from D Carter, which had been returned dishonoured. The fact of dishonour was not shown in the Cash Book
- ■ the Bank Column on the Receipts side of the Cash Book was found to be undercast £10
- ■ unpresented cheques amount to £232.

You are required to prepare the Bank Reconciliation at 31 January xxx8, in proper form, setting out your adjustments clearly.

7 On 1 January xxx4, a trader obtained her statement and on comparing it with her Cash Book discovered that all items agreed except the following:

- ■ cheques drawn and entered in the Cash Book, totalling £317.28, had not been presented at the bank
- ■ a cheque for £17.50, lodged the previous day, did not appear in the statement
- ■ the statement showed an item of interest on overdraft amounting to £14.09 not entered in the Cash Book.

The trader's Cash Book showed a balance, on 31 December xxx3, of £219.87 overdrawn.

State **a** what balance the statement showed on the same day, and **b** what would be the balance of the trader's Cash Book after making the necessary additional entries.

8 On 30 July xxx6, a trader's Cash Book showed his bank balance to be £71.18 overdrawn.

When he received his statement from the bank he found that a cheque for £19.50, lodged by him on 29 June, had not yet been credited by the bank, four cheques drawn on 30 June, amounting in total to £181.34, had not yet been presented for payment, and the bank on 30 June had entered a charge of £10.27 for commission and interest.

Draw up a statement showing the balance as shown by the Pass Book.

7 | PETTY CASH

OBJECTIVE

This chapter describes the procedure for the recording of small items of cash purchases or reimbursements to employees. The use of the Imprest system to provide control is explained.

We have seen that the general rule in cash transactions is to pay all cash received into the bank on the day of receipt, and to make all payments by cheque.

We have also seen that for wages and salaries payable by the business to its employees, some departure from this rule is inevitable, although in the first instance a cheque is issued to the Cashier so that they may obtain the necessary notes and coins from the bank.

However, it is necessary in all businesses, irrespective of their type or size, to make provision for the payment in notes or coins of a variety of *small amounts* which may be regarded as sundry or incidental expenses. They are usually termed **Petty Cash payments**, and must be considered because:

- they recur at regular intervals
- it is usually impracticable to issue a cheque in payment of any one of them
- the person receiving payment may be an employee of the business
- in total they may amount, period by period, to a considerable amount.

From the standpoint of the business it is most desirable to separate the records of Petty Cash payments from the main Cash Book records. It would clearly be inconvenient to include a large number of miscellaneous small payments in the Cash Book and for this reason, *as a separate book of prime entry*, it is usual to keep a Petty Cash Book. The responsibility for the entries in this, and for the *Petty Cash balance* may be entrusted to the Cashier or to someone else whose job involves monitoring and managing the Petty Cash.

Weekly or monthly, the Petty Cashier will be handed cash sufficient to meet all demands for petty cash for the period. They will then submit a list of all their payments to the Cashier and receive a sum to replenish the reduced cash balance.

It is usually a rule in most businesses that the Petty Cashier will take a receipt for each petty cash payment, and frequently specially printed forms bearing the name of the business are provided for this to be done. These receipt forms, when completed with the name of the recipient, and details of the amount and nature of the expense, are kept by the Petty Cashier as independent evidence of payment.

To permit a suitable classification of expense items, the Petty Cash Book may be ruled with *analysis columns* into which the total paid can be detailed. This facilitates the subsequent posting of the analysis columns to the Nominal and other Ledger Accounts. The best way to illustrate the operation of a Petty Cash book is by an example:

			£
March	1	Postage stamps	20.00
	3	Carriage	2.30
	4	Bus fare	0.30
	5	Shorthand note books	5.20
	6	Postage stamps	10.00
	8	Fare to London	12.55
	9	Sundry trade expenses	5.14
	11	Pencils	1.40
	14	Newspaper	0.50
	16	Envelopes	2.41
	18	Stationery	8.70
	31	Carriage	7.20

Rule a Petty Cash Book in analysis form, with five analysis columns headed Postages, Carriage, Travelling Expenses, Stationery and Sundry Trade Expenses respectively. Enter the above items and close the books as on 31 March, showing clearly the balance of Cash in Hand.

Petty Cash Book

Dr									Cr
Cash Received	Date	Details	Receipt No	Total	Postages	Carriage	Travelling Expenses	Stationery	Sundry Trade Expenses
£				£	£	£	£	£	£
100.00	xxx2 March 1	From Cashier							
	1	Brown, Stamps	1	20.00	20.00				
	3	Collins, Carriage	2	2.30		2.30			
	4	Hunt, Fares	3	0.30			0.30		
	5	White, Notebooks	4	5.20				5.20	
	6	Brown, Stamps	5	10.00	10.00				
	8	Lyle, Rail fare, London	6	12.55			12.55		
	9	Sundry expenses	7	5.14					5.14
	11	White, Pencils	8	1.40				1.40	
	14	Hunt, Newspaper	9	0.50					0.50
	16	White, Envelopes	10	2.41				2.41	
	18	White, Stationery	11	8.70				8.70	
	31	British Rail, Carriage	12	7.20		7.20			
				75.70	30.00	9.50	12.35	17.71	5.64
	31	Balance	c/d	24.30					
£100.00				£100.00					
24.30	April 1	Balance	b/d						

Note: If the business is registered for VAT then the analysis columns must include a VAT column.

It should be noted that in certain cases, for example rail fares, the nature of the payment may not provide a receipt from an outside source. For this reason, the employee receiving the money should be required to fill in a pre-numbered Petty Cash Voucher Form giving the required details and approval by an appropriate authority when necessary. Wherever possible an independent receipt should always be filed with the firm's voucher.

Further, *like the main Cash Book*, the Petty Cash Book is not only a book of First Entry; it is also a Ledger Account with the Petty Cashier. In other words, they are debited with what is received, and given credit for what is paid away on behalf of the business. The balance of £24.30 is therefore the sum for which they are accountable at the end of the month. Since credit is given to them personally for payments, we have to consider *their effect upon the business*. Impersonally, the business must be debited with the **totals** of the expenses set out in the analysis columns. For each one an account will be opened in the Nominal Ledger. For example, in the case of Postages we should have:

POSTAGES

Dr							Cr
Date	Details	PCB Fo	Amount	Date	Details	Fo	Amount
xxx1 March 31	Petty Cash total	1	£ 30.00				

Imprest System

When applied to Petty Cash, this means that a definite sum of money, say £100, is handed to the Petty Cashier when the Petty Cash system is established and at the end of each week or month the *amount expended* is reimbursed, e.g. £75.70 in the above example. The Petty Cash balance is thus restored to its original figure.

The merits of the system are that:

■ at any time actual cash or vouchers and receipts should be available for the imprest of £100

■ as the periodic reimbursements are the actual expenses paid, and not mere advances on account only, they are brought prominently to the notice of the Chief Cashier or other responsible official of the business.

Note: If the business is registered for VAT purposes, we should separate and record as VAT paid any VAT included in the payments made through the Petty Cash. An extra analysis column is required, headed VAT Paid, and any VAT identifiable from the invoices, receipts or vouchers supporting the payments should be included in this column. The total for the month will be posted to the debit of the VAT account (as for any other purchase) as shown on page 62.

Postage Book

In the last example an analysis column headed 'Postages' was provided in the Petty Cash Book. This is a typical Petty Cash payment, recurring at regular intervals. The person responsible for the stamp money may or may not be the Petty Cashier, but in any case it is usual to have a record of the outgoing mail.

For this purpose it is customary to use a **Stamp Book** or **Postage Book**, set out as suggested below.

Date	Cash Received	Name of Addressee	Town	Stamps used
	£			£

The Postage Book may be properly described as a **Memorandum Book** whose purpose is to amplify and serve as a check upon the payments appearing in the 'Stamps' column. It does not form a part of the Double Entry System.

The Petty Cashier, when making each payment, should enter the *date* and *amount* in the first two columns, and it should be expected that the difference between the 'Cash Received' column and the 'Stamps Used' column represents either the value of the stamps in hand and unused or, alternatively, the balance of cash in hand available for their purchase.

It is recommended that when further advances are made for buying stamps, the Postage Book should be shown to the Petty Cashier and initialled by them after seeing that it is written up to date and verifying the balance shown.

KEY POINTS

On completion of this chapter you should:

1 understand the need for a Petty Cash Book

2 understand the principles and advantages of the Imprest System

3 be able to enter receipts and payments into the Petty Cash Book

4 be able to balance the book and calculate the amount required to reimburse the float

5 be able to post the totals for the month to the appropriate ledger accounts.

Questions

1 What is the Imprest System of dealing with Petty Cash?

2 F Salmon keeps her Petty Cash Book on the Imprest System. The imprest figure was set at £350. On 1 November Year 8 the balance of petty cash brought forward was £155. The following transactions took place during November Year 8:

Year 8

1 Nov	Drew cash from the bank to restore the Imprest
4 Nov	Postage stamps £20
6 Nov	Train fare reimbursed £25
9 Nov	Petrol £15
10 Nov	Stationery £38
12 Nov	Bus fares £2
15 Nov	Paid £16 to P Gates – this was to refund an overpayment on his account in the Sales Ledger
16 Nov	Stamps £30
18 Nov	Motor van repairs £35
20 Nov	Stationery £47
23 Nov	Petrol £28
25 Nov	Miscellaneous expenses £17
28 Nov	Parcel post charges £19
30 Nov	Travelling expenses £38

Draw up F Salmon's Petty Cash Book, using the following analysis columns: Postage; Travelling expenses; Motor Van expenses; Stationery; Miscellaneous expenses; Ledger Accounts. Balance the account at 30 November, bring down the balance of cash in hand at that date, and show the amount of cash drawn from the bank to restore the Imprest on 1 December Year 8.

3 Alexander Field runs his own small business and he makes all payments of under £30 through his Petty Cash Book which is operated on an imprest system. At the end of each week he restores the imprest to its nominated figure of £100. All other payments are made by cheque, and all receipts are paid into the bank.

The balance at the bank was £1605.27, and the petty cash balance was £48.83 at the beginning of the final week of April, and the following receipts and payments occurred:

April 24: The petty cash imprest was restored from the bank, not having been done at the end of the previous week.

      : Paid amount owing to P Simpson of £200, less 7½% cash discount.

      : Paid taxi fare – £6.80.

      : Paid 15% salary advance on £500 to A Roe, a new employee.

      : Paid rail fare of £15.60 and parcel post of £5.20 (grouped on one voucher).

April 26: M Roe settled his credit account of £100 less 5% cash discount.

      : Purchased large envelopes £2.45, pencils £3.69 and packing tape £1.93 (grouped on one voucher).

      : J Lowbridge settled his account of £120, less 2½% discount.

      : Paid C Bell, a creditor, £10.95 (his account number is 251).

April 28: Paid cleaner £12.65 for work done in the office.

      : E Gillard paid his credit account of £160, less 5% cash discount.

      : Received 28% of annual rent income of £200.

      : Purchased Postage Stamps – £7.45.

      : Restored imprest account from Bank Cash Book.

Prepare a Petty Cash Book sheet and Bank Cash Book sheet as shown below, and:

a Write up the Bank Cash Book for the week ending 30 April xxx9, and balance the book at that date. The name of the ledger account to be debited or credited in respect of each transaction should appear in the 'particulars' column.

b Write up the Petty Cash Book for the week ending 30 April xxx9, making use of the analysis columns and using petty cash voucher numbers with a separate voucher number for each transaction, except where otherwise indicated (the last voucher number issued in the previous week was 44).

Balance the Petty Cash Book at the end of the week and restore the imprest figure.

Petty Cash Book

Receipts	Date	Details	Voucher No.	Total Payments	Travelling	Cleaning	Postage & Stationery	Ledger

Bank Cash Book

Date	Particulars	Discount Allowed	Details	Bank	Date	Particulars	Discount Received	Details	Bank

8 | THE (GENERAL) JOURNAL

OBJECTIVES

In this chapter you will be introduced to the General Journal as a Book of Prime Entry for items not appropriate for the Books met so far. A number of examples are used to illustrate the practice of completing this record.

Question You said on page 31 that the Journal in its earliest form was still used for certain purposes, and that it would be referred to at a later stage?

Answer Yes. While the majority of the transactions carried out in a business relate to purchasing, selling and the receipt and payment of cash, there are nevertheless others which do not fall under these headings.

Question If there are transactions that do not relate to any of these items do we not use a Book of Prime Entry?

Answer As was stated earlier, *no entry shall be made in a Ledger Account unless it has been recorded in a Book of Prime Entry*. Therefore in certain cases the use of the Journal, or General Journal as it is sometimes termed, is essential. While the information that can be given in the ordinary Ledger Accounts is limited, as much information as is required, including reference to documents, correspondence, etc., may be shown in the Journal. This we describe as the **Narration**.

Question Can you give me examples of such entries?

Answer It will help you to consider them as representing business transactions which are not capable of entry in the ordinary Purchase, Sales and Cash Books of Prime Entry. For example, if Brown, a customer, owes the business £20 which he cannot pay, a Bad Debt of £20 has arisen. Brown will be *credited* with £20 in his Personal Account in the Sales

Ledger, and *Bad Debts* Account (an expense to the business) will be *debited* with that amount in the Nominal Ledger. Supposing also that Smith both buys goods from and sells goods to the business; in the Purchase Ledger there will be an account with him as a supplier, and in the Sales Ledger as a customer. If on balance he is indebted to the business he will only remit the difference in full settlement, therefore the balance on his Purchase Ledger Account must be transferred or posted to the credit on his Sales Ledger Account.

Question   In effect for these and other similar transactions the Journal is the only book in which the prime or first entry can be made?

Answer   Yes, but it is also appropriate, as we shall see shortly, for recording what are termed **opening** and **closing** entries. The former relate to the introduction into the business of Capital in one form or another; the latter refer either to the construction of the periodic *Profit and Loss Account* or to changes in the ownership of business property, and so on.

Question   And in all these cases it is important to give adequate *narration*?

Answer   Yes, if this were not done, it might be difficult to explain the exact meaning of each Journal entry at some later date. Also, the entry enables us conveniently to summarise the position for subsequent posting to the Ledger Accounts. A few examples will help to make the process clear.

Example 8.1

Give the necessary Journal entries to record the following:

    a Having deducted 5% cash discount when paying the account of Lakeside Ltd, a letter is received from them notifying us that only 2½% can be allowed. The difference (£2.77) is being carried forward in their books.

    b Goods to the value of £50 have been purchased from C Ridley and goods value £30 sold to him. Both accounts are subject to a cash discount of 5%, and a cheque for the net balance is forwarded to him.

Fo 1

			Dr	Cr
a			£	£
xxx8				
Feb 1	Discounts received	Dr	2.77	
	To Lakeside Ltd			2.77
	Being discount not allowed as per their letter 29 January			
	xxx8			
b				
Feb 4		Dr		
	C Ridley (PL A/c)		30.00	
	To C Ridley (SL A/c)			30.00
	Being transfer of Sales Ledger Balance to			
	Bought Ledger on settlement			

Should it happen that *either* the *debit* or *credit* aspect affects more than one Ledger Account, it is usual to prefix the word 'Sundries' to the entries.

C Ridley's account in the Purchase Ledger will then be as follows:

C RIDLEY

Dr							Cr
Date	Details	Fo	Amount	Date	Details	Fo	Amount
xxx8			£	xxx8			£
Feb 4	Sundries	J1	30.00	Feb 1	Balance	b/d	50.00
4	Bank	CB2	19.00				
	Discount	2	1.00				
			£50.00				£50.00

The entries in the Sales Ledger would be:

C RIDLEY

Date	Details	Fo	Amount	Date	Details	Fo	Amount
xxx8			£	xxx8		£	
Feb 1	Balance	b/d	30.00	Feb 4	Sundries	J1	30.00
			£30.00				£30.00

In posting from the General Journal to the Ledger Accounts, the word 'Sundries' appears in the 'Details' Column. It is unnecessary to repeat all of the information in the Ledger Account, when all that is required can be found on Fo 1 of the Journal.

The two entries for the cheque £19.00, and discount £1.00, will, of course, be posted from the Cash Book in the ordinary way.

The examples **a** and **b** illustrate that adequate narration is always an essential feature of Journal entries.

Example 8.2

AB purchased from CD a delivery van for cash £8980 in April xxx5, and
on 29 October he bought another for £11 210, giving the one bought in
April in part payment, and paying the balance of £4360 in cash. Show
these entries in AB's books of entry, and post to the relevant Ledger
Accounts. Ignore VAT.

Fo 6
Purchase Journal

Date	Supplier	Description	Inv No	Ledger Fo	Total	Goods	Special Items	
xxx5					£		£	
Apr	CD	Delivery Van	1	2	8 980.00	£	8 980.00	Motors a/c PL8
Fo 34								
xxx5								
Oct	CD	Delivery Van	40	2	11 210.00		11 210.00	Motors a/c PL8

Fo 10
Cash Book
Dr   Cr

Date	Details	Fo	Amount	Date	Details	Fo	Amount
				xxx5			£
				April	CD	2	8980.00
Fo 25				Oct	CD	2	4360.00
(the October							
entry)							

Fo 19
Journal

xxx5			Fo	Dr	Cr
Oct	Sundries	Dr		£	£
	Motors A/C		PL8		8980.00
	CD		BL2	6850.00	
	Loss on Sale of Assets A/c		IL9	2130.00	
	Being Sale in part exchange of Van per				
	CD's invoice No 40, 29 October xxx5				

Fo 2
Purchase Ledger
CD
Dr   Cr

Date	Details	Fo	Amount	Date	Details	Fo	Amount
xxx5			£	xxx5			£
April	Bank	CB10	8 980.00	April	Goods	PJ6	8 980.00
Oct	Sundries	J19	6 850.00	Oct	Goods	34	11 210.00
	Bank	CB25	4 350.00				
			£11 210.00				£11 210.00

Private Ledger
MOTORS

Dr							Cr
Date	Details	Fo	Amount	Date	Details	Fo	Amount
xxx5			£	xxx5			£
April	Goods	PJ6	8 980.00	Oct			
Oct	Goods	34	11 210.00		Sundries	J19	8 980.00

In looking at this example, we see that the cost of the van purchased in April is extended in the Purchase Journal into the 'Special Items' column. It would be wrong to analyse it as *goods*, because it is apparently a *Capital Asset*, i.e. an asset for use in the business not for resale. As such, it is debited to Motors A/C in the Private Ledger of AB. When the second van is bought in October, exactly the same procedure is followed. At this point, however, a record has to be made of the disposal of the first van in part payment.

Having charged the business with two vans, we must, in effect, give it credit in *Motors Account* for:

- the part exchange value of £6850. As we paid £4360 for the new van which cost £11 210 the difference of £6850 is the value allowed on the old one
- Loss on Sale of £2130. The old van cost £8980 and its part exchange value was £6850, the difference of £2130 represents a loss. This amount will be recorded in the Profit and Loss Account at the end of the period.

We may charge only the former to CD as we have done in his personal account. The latter is a special kind of expense remaining to be borne by the business and will be shown separately in the Nominal Ledger.

Nominal Ledger

LOSS ON SALE OF ASSETS

Dr							Cr
Date	Details	Fo	Amount	Date	Details	Fo	Amount
xxx5			£				
Oct	Sundries	J19	2130.00				

We will now consider the usefulness of the Folio Column in each Ledger Account. The insertion of the folio numbers prefixed by the initial letter of the book of prime entry makes immediate reference a simple matter.

Example 8.3

Give Journal entries for the following transaction in the books of L Denton.

Jan   1   L Denton commenced business with stock valued at £1493, cash at bank £2078, and fixtures value £655. £140 was owing to M Robinson.

March 10   Plant and machinery bought on credit from Langham Bros, value £523.

April   1   K Atkins, a debtor for £23, is known to be insolvent and the debt is written off as bad.

June   23   Goods valued £118.15 bought from Blake Bros entered in the Purchase Day Book and posted in error to the debit of Blake Bros' Account in the Bought Ledger.

June   28   Cheque £15.17 posted to the debit of Jones Bros instead of to the debit of Jones Ltd.

The entries on 1 January are an example of the use of the Journal for *opening* the books of a business. It is also apparent that the amount of Denton's Capital at this date is £4086, being Assets minus Liabilities.

The Cash Book balance will be debited in the bank column of the Cash Book, and the £140 owing to M Robinson credited to his personal account in the *Purchase Leger*. The other items will be posted to accounts in the *Private Ledger*.

The purchase of machinery on 10 March could be shown in the 'Special Items' column of the Purchase Journal as seen in the previous example. The following is an example of alternative treatment where the Journal is used to record the private entry of these transactions.

Journal

			Fo	Dr £	Cr £
Jan	1	Sundries	Dr		
		To Sundries			
		Cash at bank		2078.00	
		Stock		1493.00	
		Fixtures		655.00	
		M Robinson			140.00
		Capital			4086.00
		Being Assets and Liabilities introduced this day.			
March	10	Plant and machinery	Dr	523.00	
		To Langham Bros			523.00
		Being purchase on credit of drilling machinery and lathe for tool shop.			
April	1	Bad debts	Dr	23.00	
		To K Atkins			23.00
		Being amount written off per collector's report dated 1 April.			

June	23	To Blake Bros			236.30
		Being goods purchased £118.15 posted in error			
		to the debit of A/c and now adjusted.			
June	28	Jones Ltd	Dr	15.17	
		To Jones Bros			15.17
		Being cheque posted in error to debit of Jones Bros			

The entry on 23 June is interesting as its shows the correction of an error in *one Ledger Account*, that of Blake Bros.

Purchases Account in the Impersonal Ledger will have been *debited* on 30 June with the total of the Purchase Day Book for the month, which includes the item of £118.15.

At the same time, because of the error, there is also a *debit* on a personal account in the Purchase Ledger of £118.15. Clearly Blake Bros should have been credited originally with £118.15, and to adjust the position it will now be necessary to enter in the Journal a credit to them of double the amount, i.e. £236.30. In so doing, we shall cancel the debit error and record their position as creditors for £118.15. Because the original error was two debits instead of a debit and a credit, the correcting entry must be a credit; either one credit of twice the amount of the error or two credits of the same amount, one cancelling the wrong entry and the other recording the correct entry.

The 28 June entry is simpler as a debit entry had been made, but to the wrong account. The credit to this account and debit to the proper one is straightforward.

The ability to make Journal entries successfully presupposes a thorough understanding of double entry principles. Transactions of the kind dealt with in the above example, while not as common as purchasing, selling and cash transactions, will inevitably arise in all businesses at some time or another, and call for initial record in the General Journal, in the way illustrated.

KEY POINTS

On completion of this chapter you should be:

1 familiar with the purpose of the General Journal

2 experienced in making entries into the General Journal for opening a business and for making day-to-day entries relating to the appropriate activities of the business.

Questions

1 Explain the uses of the Journal in the system of Double Entry Book-keeping.

2 Explain the use of the General Journal. What entries, other than the opening entry, would you expect to find in this book?

3 The following errors are discovered in the books of a business concern:

    a £47.50 paid for new office furniture has been charged to office expenses.

    b £39.18, representing a monthly total of discounts allowed to debtors, has been posted from the debit side of the Cash Book to the *credit* of Discount Account

    c an entry of £10, representing the retail value of goods returned to X & Co, wholesalers, has been made in the Returns Outwards Book and posted. The amount should have been £7, the invoiced value of the goods in question.

Show the entries necessary to correct these errors. The original wrong entries are not to be deleted. Subject to this restriction, make the corrections in whatever form you consider most appropriate.

4 You are required to give the Journal entries necessary to correct the undermentioned errors in the books of a business:

    a Cost of advertising the Prospectus, £2200, charged to Advertising Account. (A prospectus is the document produced in connection with the sale of shares in a company.)

    b Allowance of £50 made by a supplier of machinery entered in the Returns Outward Book and included in the total posted to Purchases Account.

    c £500 received from a customer for goods yet to be delivered posted to the credit of Sales Account.

    d Imprest of £100 handed to the Petty Cashier debited to General Expenses Account.

5 Give the Journal entries necessary to record the following facts in the books of I Markham, a manufacturer:

xxx4

Jan   1 I Markham commenced business with cash in hand, £136; cash at bank, £2141; plant and machinery, £2180; and stock value £1200.

    28 Bought plant and machinery on credit from Speed & Co Ltd, value £1130.

March 3 A debt for £25 owing by B Sykes proves worthless.

    10 The plant and machinery purchased on credit from Speed & Co was returned as not being according to specification.

    31 £25 interest on capital to be allowed.

6 Record by way of Journal entry the following in the books of A, a merchant:

    a X is both a supplier and a customer. The debit on his Sales Ledger Account is £40, and the credit on his account in the Bought Ledger is £60.

    On 28 February xxx6, a cheque in full settlement is sent to him, less 2½% cash discount.

    b Purchase of office fixtures £400, and stationery, etc., £50, from Office Supplies Ltd.

    c Sale of delivery van of book value of £4300 in part exchange at the price of £2250, against a new van costing £7500.

7 Give Journal entries to record or correct the following:

Jan   6   £25 cheque received credited to John White, instead of James White, both being customers.

      14   Cuthbert agreed to accept 0.75 in £ in full settlement of the balance of £180 appearing on his account in the Bought Ledger at 21 December xxx5.

      17   Matthews, a customer, owed the business £200 on 31 December xxx5. It is agreed to allow him £50 for window display expenses, and 5% gross for special trade discount.

      19   Arnold, a customer, to be charged by agreement £40 interest on his overdue account.

      24   Wilkins, a supplier, takes over plant and tools valued at £200 as part payment of the balance due to him of £325.

8 (**Note:** Complete Chapters 9 and 10 before attempting this question.)

The book-keeper employed by John Horton handed you a Trial Balance (see Example 9.1 and page 135) which included on the debit side an item: Suspense Account, £90.90. He stated that this was the difference between the two sides of the Trial Balance which he could not trace. On investigation you find that the difference is caused by the following errors:

    a The Sales Day Book has been over-cast by £100.

    b The Returns Outwards for November, amounting to £30.58, have been posted to personal accounts only.

    c A cheque for £70.32 received from Barton Bros has been posted to their Sales Ledger account as £73.20.

    d A first and final dividend amounting to £5.88, received from the trustee in bankruptcy of Huber Wilkins, has not been posted to the Sales Ledger account. The full amount of the debt (£19) has been written off as bad during the year.

    e A cheque for £12.24, paid to J Smithson for goods supplied, has been posted to his credit in the Sales Ledger.

Show the entries (Journal *or* Ledger) which are necessary to correct the above errors.

9 | WRITING UP THE BOOKS

OBJECTIVES

The purpose of this chapter is to bring together all of the items illustrated in the chapters considered so far and prepare ourselves for producing summary financial statements.

We have now become acquainted with the various books of prime entry and the Ledgers which they serve. You should have realised in particular that *double entry is completed within the Ledger* and the books of prime entry are not directly part of the double entry process itself.

The examples that have been used up to this point have largely dealt with the ordinary purchasing, selling and cash transactions of the business, and have been selected to illustrate the meaning of double entry.

We ought now, therefore, to be in a position to look at other examples which include these transactions and aim at the preparation of the Final Accounts, as they are termed, or the **Revenue Account** (often divided into a Trading Account and a Profit and Loss Account) and **Balance Sheet**.

It is important that in working through them we try to put ourselves in the position of the book-keeper, and consider *every transaction* from the standpoint of its effect on:

■ the Profit or Loss result of the business, and

■ its Asset and Liability, or Capital position.

Example 9.1

On 1 February xxx1, R Ready had the following Assets and Liabilities: Cash in hand £100; Cash at bank £1110; Creditors: B Bright £75 and C Clowes £95; Debtors: R Wright £60 and S Tune £70; Furniture and fittings £180; Stock on hand £1340.

Open the books by Journal entry, find and credit the capital, and then enter the following transactions in the proper subsidiary books, post to the Ledger and extract a Trial Balance (a list of balances, see page 135) at 28 February xxx1. The Cash Book and Personal Accounts should be balanced, and the balances brought down. Use a VAT rate of 17½%.

xxx1				£
Feb	1	Received cash from R Wright		30.00
	2	Sold on credit to M Moses goods		50.00 + VAT £8.75
	4	Bought on credit from C Clowes goods		120.00 + VAT £21.00
	5	Paid wages, cash		112.00
	6	Drew cheque for personal use		125.00
		Cash sales for week		250.00 + VAT £43.75
	9	Paid cash to bank		140.00
	12	Received cash from S Tune	£67.00	
		Allowed him discount	3.00	
			———	
				70.00
		Paid wages, cash		115.00
	13	Paid C Clowes by cheque	£90.00	
		Discount received	5.00	
			———	
				95.00
		Cash sales for week		387.00 + VAT £67.72
	17	Sold on credit to R Wright, goods		252.00 + VAT £44.10
	19	R Wright returned goods		10.00 + VAT £1.75
		Paid wages, cash		116.00
	20	Cash sales for week		296.00 + VAT £51.80
	22	Paid cash to bank		590.00
	26	Paid wages, cash		119.00
	27	Paid rent, cash		120.00
		Cash sales for week		182.00 + VAT £31.85

Before we begin the work of opening the books for the month, it will be helpful to consider first the transactions and the business practice concerning them.

■ The amount of the proprietor's capital is not stated, but as we know it to be the excess of the Assets over the Liabilities we can easily discover it, *and record it together with the other opening balances.*

■ It is apparent that in the Cash Book there must be columns for 'Cash' as well as for 'Bank' and Cash Discounts.

■ Both Cash and Credit Sales are made. Only the Credit Sales will be recorded in the Sales Journal, in order to put on record the position of the customer as a debtor to the business, before payment is received.

■ There is no need to open columnar or analysis Purchase and Sales Journals. The one word 'goods' is the only indication we have of the purchases and sales as a whole.

■ This example includes VAT at the rate of 17.5%. If VAT was not applicable the only changes would be those connected with the VAT and the VAT account.

R READY

Journal

Fo 1

xxx1			Fo	Dr	Cr
Feb 1	Sundries	Dr		£	£
	To sundries				
	Cash in hand		CB2	100.00	
	Cash at bank		2	1110.00	
	R Wright		SL20	60.00	
	S Tune		25	70.00	
	Furniture and fittings		PL65	180.00	
	Stock to hand		70	1340.00	
	To: B Bright		BL15		75.00
	C Clowes		10		95.00
	Capital		Pl75		2690.00
	Being Assets, Liabilities and Capital at this date				
				£2860.00	£2860.00

Fo 1

Purchase Journal

Date	Supplier	Fo	Total	Goods	VAT
xxx1			£	£	£
Feb 4	C Clowes	BL10	141.00	120.00	21.00
				NLFo 30	NLFo 52

Note:

	Abbreviation
Cash Book	CB
Purchase Journal	PJ
Sales Journal	SJ
Sales Returns Journal	SRJ
Journal	J
Bought Ledger (or Suppliers, or Creditors)	BL
Sales Ledger (or Customers, or Debtors)	SL
Nominal Impersonal Ledger	NL
Private Ledger	PL

Cash Book

Dr

Date		Fo	Discount	Cash	Bank
			£	£	£
xxx1					
Feb 1	Balances	J1		100.00	1110.00
1	R Wright	SL20	3.00	30.00	
6	Cash sales	NL40		250.00	
6	VAT	NL52		43.75	
9	Cash	C			140.00
12	S Tune	SL25		67.00	
13	Cash sales	NL40		387.00	
13	VAT	NL52		67.72	
20	Cash sales	NL40		296.00	
20	VAT	NL52		51.80	
22	Cash			182.00	590.00
27	Cash sales	NL40			
27	VAT	NL52		31.85	
			3.00	1507.12	1840.00
			NL45		
March 1	Balances	b/d		195.12	1625.00

Cr

Date		Fo	Discount	Cash	Bank
			£	£	£
xxx1					
Feb 5	Wages	NL55		112.00	
6	Drawings	PL80			125.30
9	Bank	C		140.00	
12	Wages	NL55		115.00	
13	C Clowes	BL10	5.00		90.00
19	Wages	NL55		116.00	
22	Bank	C		590.00	
26	Wages	NL55		119.00	
27	Rent	NL60		120.00	
28	Balance	c/d		195.12	1625.00
			5.00	1507.12	1840.00
			NL50		

The Journal entries as set out above enable us to post to the various Ledgers the balances outstanding on 1 February.

Thus, the cash items will appear on the *debit* side of the Cash Book; accounts will be opened in the Sales Ledger for Wright and Tune, again as *debits*; and in the Purchase Ledger for Bright and Clowes, but on the *credit* side.

Similarly, *debit* balances will appear in the Private Ledger for Furniture and Stock, while R Ready's Capital Account will be *credited* with £2690.

Fo 4

Sales Journal

Date	Customer	Fo	Total	Goods	VAT
xxx1			£	£	£
Feb 2	M Moses	SL23	58.75	50.00	8.75
17	R Wright	SL20	296.10	252.00	44.10
			354.85	302.00	52.85
				NLFo 35	NLFo 52

Fo 5

Sales Return Journal
(Returns Inwards)

Date	Customer	Fo	Total	Goods	VAT
xxx1			£	£	£
Feb 19	R Wright	SL20	11.75	10.00	1.75
				NLFo 45	NLFo 52

Having first written up the Books of Prime Entry *for the transactions during the month*, and brought down the Cash and Bank Balances as instructed, we are able to post from the Journals to the appropriate Ledger Accounts.

Let us begin with the *Personal* Ledgers, dealing first with that section relating to the Accounts of Suppliers, or **Purchase Ledger**. You may find that it is useful to open up and post your own ledger accounts and then compare them with those that follow.

Fo 10

Purchase Ledger
C CLOWES

Date	Details	Fo	Amount		Date	Details	Fo	Amount
			Dr					Cr
xxx1			£		xxx1			£
Feb 13	Bank	CB2	90.00		Feb 1	Balance	JI	95.00
	Discount	CB2	5.00		4	Goods and VAT	PJ3	141.00
28	Balance	c/d	141.00					
			236.00					236.00
					March 1	Balance	b/d	141.00

Fo 15

B BRIGHT

Date	Details	Fo	Amount		Date	Details	Fo	Amount
			Dr					Cr
					xxx1			£
					Feb 1	Balance	JI	75.00

As no transactions have taken place on Bright's account, the opening balance on 1 February remains unchanged on 28 February.

Next we may turn to the **Sales Ledger**.

Fo 20

Sales Ledger
R WRIGHT

Date	Details	Fo	Amount		Date	Details	Fo	Amount
			Dr					Cr
xxx1			£		xxx1			£
Feb 1	Balance	JI	60.00		Feb 1	Cash	CB	30.00
17	Goods & VAT	SJ4	296.10		19	Returns & VAT	SRJ5	11.75
					28	Balance	c/d	314.35
			356.10					356.10
March 1	Balance	b/d	314.35					

Fo 23

M MOSES

Date	Details	Fo	Amount		Date	Details	Fo	Amount
			Dr					Cr
xxx1			£					
Feb 2	Goods & VAT	SJ4	58.75					

Fo 25

S TUNE

Dr								Cr
Date	Details	Fo	Amount	Date	Details	Fo	Amount	
xxx1 Feb 1	Balance	JI	£ 70.00	xxx1 Feb 12	Cash discount	CB2	£ 67.00 3.00	
			£70.00				£70.00	

The **Nominal Ledger**, can now be completed.

Within this, as we know, we shall expect to find the accounts dealing *with the effect upon the business* of the transactions entered into.

Nominal Ledger

Fo 30

PURCHASES

Dr								Cr
Date	Details	Fo	Amount	Date	Details	Fo	Amount	
xxx1 Feb 28	Total for month	PJ3	£ 120.00					

Fo 35

CREDIT SALES

Dr								Cr
Date	Details	Fo	Amount	Date	Details	Fo	Amount	
				xxx1 Feb 28	Total for month	SJ4	£ 302.00	

Fo 40

CASH SALES

Dr								Cr
Date	Details	Fo	Amount	Date	Details	Fo	Amount	
				xxx1 Feb 6 13 20 27	Cash Cash Cash Cash	CB2 CB2 CB2 CB2	£ 250.00 387.00 296.00 182.00	
							£1115.00	

Fo 45

SALES RETURNS

Dr							Cr
Date	Details	Fo	Amount	Date	Details	Fo	Amount
xxx1			£				
Feb 28	Total for month	SRJ5	10.00				

Fo 46

DISCOUNTS ALLOWED

Dr							Cr
Date	Details	Fo	Amount	Date	Details	Fo	Amount
xxx1			£				
Feb 28	Total for month	CB2	3.00				

Fo 50

DISCOUNTS RECEIVED

Dr							Cr
Date	Details	Fo	Amount	Date	Details	Fo	Amount
				xxx1			£
				Feb 28	Total for month	CB2	5.00

Fo 52

VAT

Date	Details	Fo	Amount	Date	Details	Fo	Amount
xxx1			£	xxx1			£
Feb 28	Total for month	PJ3	21.00	Feb 28	Total for month	SJ4	52.85
28	Total for month	SRJ5	1.75	6	Cash sales	CB2	43.75
				13	Cash sales	CB2	67.72
28	Balance	c/d	225.22	20	Cash sales	CB2	51.80
				27	Cash sales	CB2	31.85
			£247.97				£247.97
				March 1	Balance	b/d	225.22

Fo 55

WAGES

Dr							Cr
Date	Details	Fo	Amount	Date	Details	Fo	Amount
xxx1			£				
Feb 5	Cash	CB2	112.00				
12	Cash	CB2	115.00				
19	Cash	CB2	116.00				
27	Cash	CB2	119.00				
			£462.00				

RENT

Dr								Cr
Date	Details	Fo	Amount	Date	Details	Fo	Amount	
xxx1 Feb 27	Cash	CB2	£ 120.00					

Lastly, there is the **Private Ledger** to be considered.

Here we shall have first of all two Asset Accounts, for Furniture and Stock respectively, and one Liability Account, for Capital.

Private Ledger

Fo 65

FURNITURE AND FITTINGS

Dr								Cr
Date	Details	Fo	Amount	Date	Details	Fo	Amount	
xxx1 Feb 1	Balance	JI	£ 180.00					

Fo 70

STOCK

Dr								Cr
Date	Details	Fo	Amount	Date	Details	Fo	Amount	
xxx1 Feb 1	Balance	JI	£ 1340.00					

Fo 75

CAPITAL

Dr								Cr
Date	Details	Fo	Amount	Date	Details	Fo	Amount	
				xxx1 Feb 1	Balance	JI	£ 2690.00	

If, however, we look at the Cash Book, we see that on 6 February R Ready, the proprietor, drew a cheque £125 for personal use. This is withdrawing from the business a part of:

- credit on the Capital Account, or
- the profit which is being earned.

In either event, it must be debited in the Ledger in the Capital Account, or in a 'Drawings' Account opened for the purpose. Usually small withdrawals by the owner of a business will be accumulated in a Drawings Account until the year end before the total is debited to the Capital Account.

Fo 80

Dr				DRAWINGS			Cr
Date	Details	Fo	Amount	Date	Details	Fo	Amount
xxx1			£				
Feb 6	Bank	CB2	125.00				

Having now posted all the transactions to the Ledgers, and recorded *their dual aspect*, it should be the case that arithmetical agreement has been obtained, i.e. the sum of the Debit Balances should equal the sum of the Credit Balances on 28 February xxx1.

Let us therefore extract the Balances on the Accounts, that is produce a copy of the balances as a list and categorise them as Debits or Credits, according to the their nature:

Ledger	Account	Fo	Dr	Cr
Cash Book	Cash	2	195.12	
	Bank	2	1625.00	
Bought	C Clowes	10		141.00
	B Bright	15		75.00
Sales	R Wright	20	314.35	
	M Moses	23	58.75	
Nominal	Purchases	30	120.00	
	Credit sales	35		302.00
	Cash sales	45		1115.00
	Sales returns	46	10.00	
	Discounts allowed	48	3.00	
	Discounts received	50		5.00
	VAT	52		225.22
	Wages	55	462.00	
	Rent	60	120.00	
Private	Furniture and fittings	65	180.00	
	Stock, 1 February	70	1340.00	
	Capital	75		2690.00
	Drawings	80	125.00	
			£4553.22	£4553.22

In total the Double Entry is seen to be completed *within the Ledger Accounts*, regarding the Cash Book as a Ledger for this purpose.

This list, or summary of Ledger Balances, we call a **Trial Balance**. Its extraction at any time enables us:

- ■ to satisfy ourselves of the arithmetical accuracy with which the routine work of writing up the Books of Prime Entry, and posting to the Ledgers, has been carried out
- ■ to provide a basis for the preparation of the Final Accounts, or **Revenue Account** (or Profit and Loss Account) and **Balance Sheet**.

Because of its importance, we will consider this statement at greater length in the next chapter.

KEY POINTS

On completion of this chapter you should have a better understanding of the full process of recording routine transactions in the Double Entry System of a business. From this stage we will be able to consider how we present summaries of these records in the Final Accounts.

Questions

1 N Bell was in business as a wholesale merchant and on 1 January xxx1 had the following assets and liabilities: Cash in hand, £450; Bank overdraft, £4680; Stock of goods, £7100; Motor vans, £2740; Fixtures and fittings, £920; Sundry Debtors: J Betts, £640; E Evans, £600; Sundry Creditors; T Brown, £840; F Shaw, £580.

Enter the above and the following transactions into the proper subsidiary books, post to the Ledger and extract a Trial Balance. The Cash Book and, where necessary, the Ledger Accounts should be balanced and the balances brought down. Assume no VAT.

Jan 4   Received from J Betts cheque for £628 in full settlement of his account for £640. Paid cheque to bank.
      6   Sold goods on credit to E Evans, £1200.
      9   Paid wages in cash, £263.
     11   Sold goods for cash, £443.
          E Evans returned goods. Sent him credit note for £48.
     15   Sold a motor van for cash, £780.
     18   Paid cash into the bank, £800.
     23   Paid wages in cash, £263.
          Purchased on credit new motor van from the Albion Motor Co Ltd, for £8450.
     25   Received cheque from E Evans for £1740 in full settlement of the amount due from him. Paid cheque to bank.
          Purchased goods on credit from F Shaw, £800.
     27   Paid T Brown cheque for £820 in full settlement of the amount due to him on January 1.

Note: No Trading and Profit and Loss Account or Balance Sheet required until you have completed Chapter 13.

2 On 1 March xxx1, A Walker commences business with £10 000 in cash of which £9500 is paid into the bank. Enter the following transactions in the books of original entry, post to Ledger Accounts and extract a Trial Balance.

March 2 Bought premises and paid £1500 by cheque.

     4 Purchased on credit from J Raleigh:
        15 gents' cycles at £125.00 + VAT £18.75 each.
        20 ladies' cycles at £110.00 + VAT £16.50 each.
        20 children's cycles at £77.00 + VAT £11.55 each.

     5 Bought at an auction sale sundry goods for £268.00 and paid for them by cash. (No VAT.)

     6 Sold to S Taylor:
        1 gents' cycle at £160.00 + VAT £24.00
        1 ladies' cycle at £140.00 + VAT £21.00.
        1 child's cycle at £95.00 + VAT £14.25.

     8 Returned to J Raleigh:
        10 children's cycles invoiced on the 4th and received a credit note.

    10 Paid J Raleigh by cheque the amount due, less £167.00 cash discount.

    12 Bought office furniture for cash £130.75. (No VAT.)

    16 S Taylor paid by cheque the amount due.

    18 Paid by cheque rent £250.00. (No VAT.)
        Paid by cash wages £150.60.
        Paid by cheque insurance £220.75. (No VAT.)
        Cash sales for the period £597 + VAT £89.55.

    20 Paid all cash into the bank except £50.

3 R Simpson was in business as a wholesale cutler and jeweller. On 1 January xxx6, the financial position was as follows: Cash in hand, £440; Cash at bank, £2350; Stock, £2000; Fixtures and fittings, £1160. Sundry Creditors: M Marsh, £150; D Steele, £200. Sundry Debtors: H Robins, £275; J Long, £175.

Enter the above and the following transactions into the proper subsidiary books, post to the Ledger and extract a Trial Balance. The Cash Book and, where necessary, the Ledger Accounts should be balanced and the balances brought down. Assume VAT at 15%.

Jan 2 Received from H Robins on account, cheque for £200, which was paid to bank.

     3 Sold to D Dennis & Co Ltd: Goods £240 less 10% trade discount.

     4 Paid wages in cash £260.

     6 Cash sales paid to bank, £500.

     7 Bought from Silversmiths Ltd: Goods £340 subject to trade discount of 15%.

     8 Paid M Marsh by cheque £147.50 in settlement of the account of £150.

    11 Paid wages in cash £170.

    13 Cash sales paid to bank £250.

    15 Withdrew from bank for office cash £200.

    17 Sold to J Long: on credit £130.

    18 Paid wages in cash £160.
        R Simpson withdrew £80 for private purposes by cheque.

    18 Cash sales paid to bank £285.

    20 Received from J Long in full settlement of the amount due a cheque for £307. Paid cheque to bank.

Note: No Trading and Profit and Loss Account or Balance Sheet is required until you have completed Chapter 13.

4 On 1 January xxx1, the financial position of Rose Mason, owner of a children's clothes shop, is as follows: Cash in hand, £245.80; Stock, £3750.00; H Atherton (Dr), £31.75; Fixtures and fittings, £750.00; A Baker (Cr), £390.00; Bank overdraft £176.75. Assume no VAT. Find and credit her capital. During the month her transactions were as follows:

Jan	42	Bought goods from G Henry & Co, to the value of £812.80 less 12½% trade discount.
	6	Paid A Baker the amount owing, less 5% cash discount.
	7	Returned to G Henry & Co, goods to the gross value of £103.25.
	9	Sold goods to H Atherton, £68.60.
	9	Received from G Henry & Co credit note for the net amount of goods returned.
	10	H Atherton settled his account of 1 January, after deducting £1.75 cash discount.
	14	Bought new showcase £75.75 from W Dixon.
	19	Sold goods to N Dobbin £72.50.
	20	R Mason paid £300 of her own money into the business bank account.
	23	Sold shop fittings for cash £27.60.
	26	Cash sales for the period £311.80.
	28	Paid all cash into bank except £250.

Enter the transactions in the appropriate subsidiary books – post to the Ledger Accounts and extract a Trial Balance.

Note: Trading Account, Profit and Loss Account and Balance Sheet are not required until you have completed Chapter 13.

5 In the form of a three-column Cash Book, after properly heading each column, enter all the money transactions below and balance the Book. Assume no VAT.

Journalise the opening balances and remaining transactions. (**Note:** Purchases and Sales Books may be used, if preferred.)

Post the entries to the Ledger. Extract a Trial Balance. Close and balance the Ledger.

On 1 October xxx1, S Strong reopened the books with the following balances in addition to the Capital Account:

	£
Cash	47.80
K Knight & Co (Cr)	176.90
D Day (Dr)	225.75
Bank (overdraft)	217.90
Rent accrued, owing by S Strong (treat as a creditor)	120.00
Stock of goods	2741.25

The transactions during the month were:

			£
Oct	3	Received cheque from D Day to settle account	220.00
	5	Paid same into bank	220.00
	8	Sold to D Day: Goods	130.00
	10	D Day returned goods	4.20
	13	Sundry cash sales	183.70
	14	Paid into bank	100.00
	16	Bought of K Knight & Co: Goods	91.75
	19	Paid landlord by cheque	120.00
	21	Paid K Knight & Co on account	150.00
	22	Sold to D Day sundry goods and received cheque (banked)	43.75
	26	D Day's cheque returned dishonoured	43.75
	27	Cash purchases	107.30
	27	Sundry cash sales	249.40
	28	Drew cheque for self	25.00
	30	Wages and expenses for month paid by cheque and	50.40
		in cash	111.50
	31	Rent accrued (treat as an invoice)	120.00
		Bank charges	11.75
		Interest on capital at 6% per annum calculated on balance at 1 October xxx1 (treat as an invoice)	
		Stock of goods on hand valued at	2503.25

General note: The following problems may be answered assuming no VAT, or VAT at any rate that is appropriate. Obviously it makes a slight difference to the detailed answers but the general principles remain the same.

6 On 1 January xxx1, R Baxter commenced business as a fuel merchant with £10 650 in cash. On the same date he opened a current account at the bank and paid in £10 500. His transactions during the month follow:

Jan 13 Bought a second-hand lorry by cheque, £1256.00.
Bought from the Victory Colliery Co Ltd:
Coal £1970.00

4 Cash sales £277.50.

4 Sold to J Yates, Coal £184.00.

6 Paid Victory Colliery Co £1000 on account by cheque.

8 Bought from The Shell Oil Co Plc, Fuel oil £1685.00.

10 J Yates settled his account by cheque and allowed him 5% cash discount. Cheque banked.

12 Sold to W Jones, Fuel oil £473.00.

12 Paid carriage by cheque £170.50.

15 Settled the account of the Victory Colliery Co by cheque and was allowed 5% cash discount on the original account.

16 Cash sales £106.

16 Paid sundry expenses in cash £253.60.

16 Paid all cash into the bank except £100 retained for business use.

You are required to enter the above transactions in the books of original entry, to post to Ledger Accounts and to extract a Trial Balance.

No Trading and Profit and Loss Account, or Balance Sheet is required until you have completed Chapter 13.

7 On 1 November xxx1, June Maynard commenced business as a sole trader, trading under the style of The Bon Marché.

She paid £2000 into the bank account of the business on that date, and also borrowed £5000 from family sources to help finance the venture. She paid £4500 of this sum into the bank.

The following transactions were entered into during the month of November:

xxx1			£
Nov	1	Paid rent by cheque three months to 31 January xxx2	237.50
	2	Bought material on credit:	
		Forrester & Co	126.50
		Arnold & Sons	439.75
		H Meyrick Ltd	112.95
	3	Bought office fittings for cash	220.00
	3	Drew cheque for cash for own use	45.00
	4	Sold goods on credit:	
		E Walker	221.25
		J Roberts	51.00
		L Morley	147.45
		H Longden	4.85
	10	Paid wages in cash	128.25
	11	Sent cheque to Forrester & Co	125.00
		and obtained discount	1.50
	16	Received cheque from Roberts, paid into bank	50.00
		and allowed discount	1.00
	19	Received cheque from Morley, paid into bank	146.00
		and allowed discount	1.45
	24	Paid wages in cash	128.25
	27	Sent cheque to Arnold & Sons	435.00
		and obtained discount	4.75
	30	Returned defective goods to H Meyrick Ltd	9.25

Enter the above transactions in the proper books of prime entry, post to the Ledger, and extract a Trial Balance at 30 November.

10 | THE TRIAL BALANCE

OBJECTIVES

This chapter illustrates the role of the Trial Balance that was briefly introduced in Chapter 9. It also demonstrates its value to the accounting process and its limitations as a summary statement. It also discusses the idea of a four-column Trial Balance.

A number of benefits were claimed in Chapter 9 for the use of a Trial Balance as part of an accounting system. The main benefit is that it is evidence of the arithmetical accuracy of the book-keeping work, because of the dual aspect from which every transaction is regarded.

Are we therefore justified in assuming that the routine work underlying the Trial Balance requires no further examination if this statement demonstrates arithmetical accuracy? Is arithmetical accuracy alone all with which we need be concerned?

The answer is no.

Apparent proof of accuracy is not the same as conclusive proof, and it may be the case that errors exist in the underlying work which the Trial Balance will not reveal.

If, for example, a *transaction has been omitted altogether* from the books, neither its *debit* nor its *credit* aspect can have been recorded.

Goods may have been purchased from Brown, a supplier, and an invoice duly received. But if, in course of checking prior to entry in the Purchase Journal, the invoice is lost or mislaid, nothing will ultimately appear to the *credit* of the Supplier's Account. Similarly as it has never been entered in the Purchase Journal, it cannot form part of the Total Purchases for the month which are posted to the *debit* of Purchases Account.

Such an *error of omission* would be discovered only when the supplier's Statement of Account is received.

Another example would be neglect to record in the Cash Book any discount deducted by a customer.

The customer would be credited with too little in his Personal Account, causing an Asset in the form of a Book Debt to be *overstated*, and the Discounts Allowed Account would be underdebited, resulting in the *understatement* of an expense to the business.

There are also errors which we may describe as *compensating errors*. In this case, an error in one direction is counterbalanced by an error in another direction of equal amount. Hence, again the lack of agreement is not disclosed by the Trial Balance.

The following are examples of *compensating errors*:

■ The total of Sales Account on one page of the Nominal Ledger is inadvertently carried forward £10 less than it should be, i.e. there is *short credit* of £10.

At the same time, the addition of Wages Account is made £10 too little, so that there is a *short debit* of £10.

■ In extracting the balances on the Sales Ledger Accounts, an item of £110 is entered on the list of balances as £100, causing a *short debit* of £10, while a cheque for £10 from Jones, a customer, has been debited in the Cash Book but never posted to the credit of his account in the Sales Ledger. The *total book debts* are correctly shown in the List of Balances, *although the detail items are incorrect.*

We may also have to deal with *errors of principle*. Supposing £250 is paid by way of deposit in connection with the supply of electricity to the business. This deposit is refundable if and when the business closes down, and therefore is an Asset. If the amount is debited to Heat, Light and Power Account in the Nominal Ledger it will in all probability be written off as an *expense* for the particular period, resulting in an *overstatement of working expenses*, and an *understatement of Assets*.

Secondly, should a part of the Fixtures and Fittings be disposed of to a dealer when the offices are being modernised, and entered as a sale in the Sales Journal, Sales Account will be improperly inflated, *because the goods are not those in which the business is dealing*. Further, the Fixtures and Fittings Account will not record the reduction in value resulting from the disposal. Here also the Trial Balance is of no help in the detection of the errors.

We must not, however, assume that its value as a basis for the preparation of the Final Accounts is seriously lessened. So far as accounts in the Nominal and Private Ledger are concerned, these are not usually numerous, neither are the number of entries appearing in them and great care is taken in practice to record the true facts.

Similarly when the Sales and Purchase Ledger Balances are extracted and totalled, it is usual for the work to be checked before the figures are finally accepted.

Errors which the Trial Balance will show

If there is a 'difference' on the Trial Balance, a search must be made for the probable cause as *any* difference will indicate an error in recording *must* have occurred somewhere in the entry and recording process.

We can compare the names of the accounts appearing in it with those in some previous Trial Balance, and note any omission. We can also scrutinise each item in the light of its description and the definition that:

- a Debit Balance is either an Asset or an Expense, and
- a Credit Balance is either a Liability or a Profit.

Thus, if we regard Sales as a Profit, Sales Returns or Returns Inwards should be considered as an Expense, or Debit Balance. If the returned goods remain in the warehouse unsold we could alternatively look on them as an Asset, but they would still be a Debit Balance.

It will not take long to go through the accounts in the Nominal and Private Ledgers to satisfy ourselves that they are apparently in order, and we should probably do this before re-examining the Sales and Purchase Ledger Accounts. Because they so rarely occur any Credit Balances on the Sales Ledger and Debit Balances on the Purchase Ledger should also be considered as a likely indication of error.

If the error(s) are not discovered by these checks, and assuming the (monthly) totals of the Books of Prime Entry have been checked to the Nominal Ledger, the following steps can be taken:

- Check the additions (or casts) of the Books of Prime Entry.

■ Check the postings in detail from the Books of Prime Entry to the Sales and Purchase Ledgers.

The two latter checks involve a great deal of time and labour, but should result in locating the error, and obtaining agreement in the Trial Balance.

Summary of errors

Trial Balance does not balance

- ■ arithmetical errors in primary records ledger accounts
- ■ posting errors
  - wrong figures
  - amounts omitted
  - wrong side (debit instead of credit and vice versa)
- ■ wrong balance extracted

Trial Balance balances

There may still be

- ■ errors of omission
- ■ compensating errors
  - unrelated, e.g. two or more offsetting errors of similar amounts
  - related, e.g. cash from T Smith credited to LS Smith
- ■ errors of principle.

If the Trial Balance does not balance at the first attempt we may include another account, called a 'Suspense Account' so that the Trial Balance balances and we can proceed. This is only a temporary solution; sooner or later the errors and/or omissions which caused the difference must be identified and corrected. The net effect of correcting them will offset the Suspense Account.

Example 10.1

The following Trial Balance was extracted from the books of F Briers on 31 December xxx1. Do you think that it is correct? If not, rewrite it in its correct form.

	Dr £	Cr £
Capital Account		11 000.00
Stock at 1 January xxx1	3 825.00	
Purchases and Sales	21 275.00	31 590.00
Returns Inwards		80.00
Returns Outwards	70.00	
Discounts Received	80.00	
Discounts Allowed		70.00
Motor Car		4 175.00
Wages and Salaries	10 250.00	
Carriage		70.00
Rent and Rates	3 185.00	
Sundry Debtors	4 760.00	
Sundry Creditors		725.00
Cash in hand	20.00	
Bank Overdraft	4 245.00	
	£47 710.00	£47 710.00

Produce your own correct Trial Balance before looking at the answer below.

Although the total debits equal the total credits, the Trial Balance is very far from being correct. It should instead appear as below:

	Dr £	Cr £
Capital Account		11 000.00
Stock at 1 January xxx1	3 825.00	
Purchases and Sales	21 275.00	
Sales		31 590.00
Returns Inwards	80.00	
Returns Outwards		70.00
Discounts Received		80.00
Discounts Allowed	70.00	
Motor Car	4 175.00	
Wages and Salaries	10 250.00	
Carriage	70.00	
Rent and Rates	3 185.00	
Sundry Debtors	4 760.00	
Sundry Creditors		725.00
Cash in hand	20.00	
Bank Overdraft		4 245.00
	£47 710.00	£47 710.00

The adjustments made, and the reasons for them are:

Returns Inwards. As an expense or Asset (see page 143) this is a Debit Balance.

Returns Outwards, i.e. to *suppliers*. These are sometimes called Purchase Returns, and are a Credit Balance.

Discount Received. As a profit to the business, the amount represents a Credit Balance.

Discounts Allowed. Clearly an expense, and so a Debit.

Motor Cars are an Asset of the business and will be a Debit Balance in the Private Ledger.

Carriage. The cost of carriage is a business expense, and a Debit in the Nominal Ledger.

Bank Overdraft. As a liability due to the bank this must be a Credit Balance in the Cash Book.

Four-column Trial Balance

The purpose of this form of Trial Balance is to assist us further in the preparation of the Profit and Loss Account and Balance Sheet. It demonstrates in a manner which is not apparent in the ordinary form of Trial Balance, the fact that:

■ a *Debit* Balance is either an *Asset* or an *Expense*, and

■ a *Credit* Balance is either a *Liability* or a *Profit*.

The expenses and profits comprise the recurring Revenue aspects of the business, whereas the assets and liabilities reflect longer term Capital aspects.

Let us redraft the Trial Balance of R Ready, shown on page 135, in *four-column* form:

Trial Balance

R READY   28 February xxx1

			Revenue		Capital	
Account	*Ledger*	*Fo*	*Dr*	*Cr*	*Dr*	*Cr*
			£	£	£	£
Cash	Cash Book	2			167.25	
Bank		2			1625.00	
C Clowes	Bought	10				138.00
B Bright						75.00
R Wright	Sales	20			308.30	
M Moses		23			57.50	

			Dr	Cr	Dr	Cr
Purchases	Nominal	30	120.00			
Credit sales		35		302.00		
Cash sales		40		1115.00		
Sales returns		45	10.00			
Discounts allowed		46	3.00			
Discounts received		50		5.00		
VAT		52				193.05
Wages		55	462.00			
Rent		60	120.00			
Furniture and fittings	Private	65			180.00	
Stock, 1 Feb		70	1340.00			
Capital		75				2690.00
Drawings		80			125.00	
			£ 2055.50	£ 1422.00	£ 2463.05	£ 3096.05

Opening Stock, although an Asset, is entered in the *Revenue* column because it represents goods in which the business is dealing. The stock on hand at 28 February xxx1 will be recorded and will be used (see page 154) in:

- the Revenue column (Credit), and
- the Capital column (Debit),

thus enabling us to record:

- the true Profit, and
- the existence of the Asset of Stock at this date.

Summary

	Dr £	Cr £
Revenue	2055.00	1422.00
Capital	2463.05	3096.05
	£4518.05	£4518.05

What we have now done is to show in the *first two columns* of the four-column Trial Balance all those items which are of a Revenue character, and which will be the items to concern us in determining the Profit or Loss.

In the *third and fourth columns* are found the accounts which relate to Assets (except Closing Stock), and Liabilities, and as such comprise the Balance Sheet of the business.

KEY POINTS

On completion of this chapter you should be:

1 aware of the role of the Trial Balance in the records of a business

2 able to prepare a Trial Balance

3 aware of what assurances of correctness it gives

4 aware of errors that may still exist

5 able to prepare a four-column Trial Balance.

Questions

1 Can the arithmetical agreement of the Debit and Credit Columns in a Trial Balance be considered conclusive proof of the accuracy of the book-keeping work?

Illustrate your answer with at least three suitable examples.

2 Write short notes on:

- errors of omission
- errors of commission
- compensating errors

giving two examples of each.

3 On taking out a Trial Balance from a set of books, a book-keeper found that the Dr side exceeded the Cr by £9.

Assuming that this 'difference' was due to a single mistake, mention as many types of error as you can think of, each different in principle, any one of which could have caused it.

4 On preparing a Trial Balance from a set of books the sides are found not to agree, the Dr total being £2530.20, and the Cr £2580.60. You are convinced that nothing has been omitted and that all the figures are arithmetically correct, all postings, additions, etc., having been independently checked.

What is the probable nature of the error made and what will be the correct totals of the Trial Balance?

5 The following errors were discovered in a set of books kept by Double Entry:

- An item of £52 in the Sales Day Book posted to the customer's account as £50.20.

- Bank interest amounting to £60 charged by the bank on an overdraft, entered on the debit side of the Cash Book in the bank column.
- An item of £15 for goods returned by a customer entered in the Returns Outwards Book and omitted to be posted.
- A payment by cheque of £10 to XY, entered in the Cash Book on the credit side in the cash column.

State by what amount the totals of the Trial Balance disagreed.

6 A Trial Balance is extracted to check the arithmetical accuracy of a set of books. If the Trial Balance fails to agree, errors must have been made. However, if the Trial Balance does agree, it does not prove the accuracy of the accounts. There are errors which a Trial Balance does not reveal.

Name and briefly describe *four* types of error which would **not** stop a Trial Balance from balancing. Give one example for each type of error.

7 State what 'difference' would be caused in the books of a business by each of the following errors:

a The omission from the list of debtors' balances, compiled for the purpose of the Trial Balance, of a debt of £12.25, due from P & Co.

b Omission to post from the Cash Book to the Discount Account the sum of £5.35, representing discounts allowed to debtors during July.

c Omission to make any entry in respect of an allowance of £8.50 due to Q & Co in respect of damaged goods.

d Posting an item of wages paid, correctly entered as £231.75 in the Cash Book as £231.25 in the Ledger Account.

e Posting £20 being cash received from the sale of an old office typewriter, to the debit side of 'Office Equipment' Account.

Note: These errors are to be taken as affecting different sets of books having no relation to one another.

8 The following Trial Balance contains certain errors. You are required to discover them and draw up a correct Trial Balance.

	Dr £	Cr £
H Jones, Capital Account		6 000.00
Current Account (Cr)		1 091.00
S Brown, Capital Account		4 000.00
Current Account (Dr)		57.00
Salaries and wages	11 140.00	
Rents and rates	2 520.00	
Sales, less returns		32 556.00
Purchases, less returns	17 245.00	
Stock, opening	5 472.00	

	Dr £	Cr £
Trade debtors	10 314.00	
Trade creditors		3 591.00
Fixtures and fittings	550.00	
Manufacturing expenses	926.00	
Manufacturing expenses (unpaid)	102.00	
Office expenses	341.00	
Carriage inwards	559.00	
Carriage outwards		253.00
Bank overdraft		1 956.00
Interest on overdraft		42.00
Bad Debts written off	112.00	
Bad Debts reserve	250.00	
Cash in hand	15.00	
	£49 546.00	£49 546.00

Note: You could leave this question until you have completed Chapter 18 Partnership.

9 The following is the 'Trial Balance' of Diminishing Returns owned by XY at 31 December xxx1:

	Dr £	Cr £
Capital		2 650.00
Bank	126.00	
Machinery	1 452.00	
Fixtures	78.00	
Stock, 1 January xxx1		340.00
Purchases	12 242.00	
Wages	7 135.00	
Salaries	3 312.00	
Rent	1 100.00	
Sales		24 612.00
Repairs	357.00	
Bad debts	24.00	
Heat and light	748.00	
Debtors	970.00	
Creditors		475.00
	£27 544.00	£28 077.00

Amend the Trial Balance, taking the following into account:

■ The Sales Day book had been undercast £89.

- The bank confirmed the overdraft at the sum shown on 31 December xxx1.
- XY's private drawings of £184 had not been posted to the Ledger.
- A sale of £10 had not been posted to the account of I Jones, a customer.

10 At 31 December xxx1, the accountant of ABC Ltd has failed to balance her books of account. The difference has been carried to the debit of a Suspense Account.

Subsequently, the following errors are discovered:

- The total of the Sales Day Book for June has been posted to Sales Account in the Impersonal Ledger as £2784.25. The Day Book total is £2748.25.
- For the month of November, cash discounts allowed, £37.10, and Discounts received, £19.85, have been posted to the wrong sides of the Ledger Account.
- An allowance to a customer of £1.95 has been posted in the debit of his account in the Sales Ledger.
- A book debt of £14.55, due by L, a customer, has been omitted from the list of Sales Ledger balances.
- Cash drawings of the proprietor, amounting to £20, have not been posted to the Ledger.
- Goods purchased costing £21.10 were posted to the credit of the Supplier's Ledger Account, and also to the credit of 'Sundry Purchases' Account in the Bought Ledger.

After the discovery and correction of the errors mentioned, the books balanced. You are required:

- to show the Suspense Account as it originally appeared
- to make the requisite corrective entries.

11 | WHAT IS PROFIT OR LOSS?

OBJECTIVES

This chapter explains the accounting aspects of profit and loss, in particular its relationship to changes in Assets and Capital of a business. It also discusses the inclusion of closing stock in the Trial Balance.

Question The profit made seems to be represented by an increase in the Assets of the business during the period. Is this always the case?

Answer Yes. The word 'Profit' has no meaning except in the sense of an increase of Net Assets. As the business Assets are directly related to the Capital, you could just as truly say that Profit represents an increase in Capital. Put in another way, if the Capital invested at the commencement is a liability of the business, the liability is greater at the end of the period by the amount of the Profit earned.

Question What, then, is a Loss?

Answer A shrinkage in the Net Assets, or the extent to which they fall short of the Initial Capital for the period. If the latter had at one time comprised £100 worth of stock which owing to a general drop in prices had to be sold for £90 cash, an Asset of £90 would replace one of £100 and a Loss of £10 would have been incurred.

Such a loss would be described as a Revenue Loss, because stock is a part of the Current Assets of the business, or its Trading property. But if Fixed Assets, like Plant and Machinery, are sold at a figure below their book value, a Capital Loss is said to have been sustained.

Question Referring again to the example in Chapter 10, the proprietor had withdrawn £125 from the business for personal use, and yet you put the item in the third, or *Asset* column of the Trial Balance. Should it not have been entered in the first or *Expense* column?

Answer   No, and for this reason. In the majority of businesses the owners will periodically withdraw either cash or goods (sometimes both) for their private use. These withdrawals are probably made to cover their living expenses, and have no relation whatever to the *expenses of the business*. We may regard them as withdrawals *on account of accruing profits*.

Therefore, they properly appear elsewhere than in the Revenue columns of the Trial Balance. To enter them in the third or *Asset* column is the only alternative and is justified if we look upon the initial Capital as a *Liability*. In withdrawing money or goods from the business, the proprietor has really reduced the Capital invested in the first place, assuming no Profits, or insufficient Profits, have been earned to cover the withdrawals.

Question   Should drawings then be set against *Profits* rather than against Capital?

Answer   Often it is found convenient to proceed in this way. The Capital Account, as we have seen, is credited with whatever the proprietor first introduces. Any drawings are then debited to a separate, or *Drawings, Account*. This is sometimes called a *Current Account*. Subsequently, when the figure of profit is determined, it is credited to the Capital Account. At the end of the year the total drawings are transferred from the Drawings Account to the debit of the Capital Account. This is the treatment that several examining institutions expect. An alternative approach would credit the profit for the year to the Drawings or Current Account. The balance would then represent the difference between the amounts withdrawn by the proprietor during the year and the net profit for the year. If the proprietor decided to retain that surplus within the business it will be transferred to the Capital Account (Dr Drawings, Cr Capital). If they wish to use it for private purposes it will be paid to them by a cheque (Dr Drawings, Cr Bank). Withdrawals may be made on account of Capital, and would be debited to Capital Account, but these are exceptional.

Question   Am I right in thinking that the Trial Balance, whether in the ordinary or in the four-column form, does not give all the information needed for preparing the Final Accounts?

Answer   Yes. Even in the simple case of R Ready, in Chapters 9 and 10, certain *adjustments* may have to be made. It is true, however, to say, as we did, that it provides a *basis* for their preparation.

Question   What are these adjustments?

Answer   It will be better for us to consider them after we have become familiar with the ordinary form of *Revenue Account and Balance Sheet*, because they affect both. One of the factors we have to take into account is that of *Stock in Trade*. In determining our profit figure, it is not enough to compare the cost of goods purchased with the proceeds of goods sold. Since a minimum amount of stock has to be held by the business and will usually have been included as part of the cost of purchases, an adjustment is necessary to calculate the cost of goods sold. Thus, at any particular date, for example, the date to which the business makes up its accounts, allowance must be made for the existence of the stock *then in hand*, and its proper value.

In the case of a new business, if we thought in terms of *quantities* only, we might say *purchases* equal *sales* plus *stock in hand at the end* of the period. Therefore, closing stock *must* be included in the second column of the four-column Trial Balance, and as it is a part of the property of the business at the same date, it *also appears* in the third or *Asset* column, i.e. in the former as a credit, and in the latter as a debit, which maintains the 'double entry'.

The need for the explicit inclusion of closing stock into our accounts as an adjustment at the end of the period arises as a conventional Double Entry book-keeping system does not support the management of goods/stock values during the year. Stock purchased during the year is recorded at cost (minus trade discount) in the *Purchases* account and stock sold is recorded at *Sales* price in the Sales account. These two accounts are brought together in the Profit and Loss account as we will see in the next chapter.

Example 11.1

At the beginning of the year the business held stock to the value of £2300. During the year purchases of goods for resale amounted to £35 764, and sales to £57 891. At the end of the year the stock in hand was estimated to have cost £4229.

	£
Opening stock	2 300
add Purchases during the year	35 764
Cost of goods available for sale	38 064

(the whole of this amount will either have been sold during the year or not sold; if not sold it will still be in stock)

	£
Deduct cost of closing stock	4 229
Cost of goods sold	33 835

It is the amount of	£33 835
which will be deducted from the sales figure of	£57 891
to give the gross profit for the year of	£24 056

Clearly any error in estimating the cost (or value if lower than cost) will have a corresponding effect on the profit for the year. The amount of £4229 is an asset of the business at the year end.

KEY POINTS

On completion of this chapter you should:

1 appreciate the accounting nature of profit and loss as they relate to Assets and Capital of a business

2 understand the nature of *closing stock* and how its value is included in the accounts.

12 THE REVENUE ACCOUNT: THE TRADING, PROFIT AND LOSS, AND APPROPRIATION ACCOUNTS

OBJECTIVES

The purpose of this chapter is to introduce you to the Profit or Loss calculation for a business. It describes the calculation for retail businesses and for manufacturing businesses – these being slightly different from each other. It demonstrates that the profit and loss calculation is part of the process of Double Entry recording.

Having prepared a Trial Balance, corrected any errors and made some adjustments, we are now able to proceed to the first section of the Final Accounts.

Our task is to determine the Profit or Loss which has resulted from the carrying on of the ordinary transactions of the business.

One of the major objectives of our Final Accounts is to produce the information in such a way that it is clear and informative, and free from unnecessary detail.

The period for which they are drawn up will vary according to the requirements of the owner of the business. In many cases it is customary to prepare them at yearly intervals, or at the date of the business's financial year end. This may be 31 December, 31 March, or some other date when perhaps there is least pressure of work on the office staff. The reporting of profit to the Government is normally required once a year for all businesses in the UK.

The **Revenue Account** is usually divided into three sections:

- The Trading Account
- The Profit and Loss Account
- The Appropriation Account.

At this stage it is the first two sections which are important. In all three sections, however, we find that the *form* adopted is that of the *ordinary Ledger Account*, as the Revenue Account is treated as an account of the Double Entry system in the Nominal Ledger.

The Trading Account

The purpose of this account is to determine what is called the **gross profit** or **loss**.

In it, making allowance for stocks carried at the beginning and the end of the period, we compare (in a merchanting retail business) the proceeds of sales with the cost of goods sold.

Example 12.1

On 1 January xxx7, A Graham had a stock of goods value £1216. Purchases for the year amounted to £10 340, and sales to £15 000. Transport charges on incoming goods amount to £208. Stock on 31 December xxx7 was valued at £1764. show the Trading Account.

Trading Account
Year ended 31 December xxx7

Dr					Cr
		£			£
Stock, 1 January xxx7		1216.00	Sales		15 000.00
Purchases	£10 340.00		Stock, 31 December xxx7		1 764.00
Carriage inward	208.00				
		10 548.00			
Gross Profit		5 000.00			
		£16 764.00			£16 764.00

It is important we should notice the following points:

■ The account is headed 'Year ended 31 December xxx7', implying that it is a summary of the transactions throughout the year.

■ The cost of purchases is increased by the transport charges paid, and represents *delivered cost* to the business. Apart from this no other kind of expense whatever is included as this is a merchanting or retail business.

■ Gross Profit is seen to be the excess of sales over the purchased cost of the goods sold. It is the first stage in the determination of the final or net profit.

Stock in trade

Sometimes a difficulty may arise as to the measurement of the quantity and value of the Stock at 31 December xxx7, which is shown above at £1764.

We saw on page 154 how necessary it was to take it into account and an essential step in this process is to determine the quantities, usually by means of an actual stocktaking.

In this process the goods on hand will be counted, weighed, measured, etc., listed on stock sheets and priced at purchased cost. They cannot be valued at the higher selling price because they are not yet sold, and may never be sold. It is reasonable to value them at cost price, because in doing so we are merely carrying forward *from one period into another* a part of the Cost of Purchases.

It may be that at the date of stocktaking the market price (or present buying price) is less than the cost price. Provided, however, that there is no selling deficiency, i.e. the cost price, together with any selling expenses yet to be incurred, does not exceed the selling price, no adjustment is required. The general rule for stock valuation is 'cost or market value' whichever is lower.

A point to note is that in the Trading Account the ratio of **gross profit** to **sales** or **turnover** is an important one in all businesses. Expressed as a percentage it amounts in this case to $33\frac{1}{3}\%$ of the Sales (15 000 ÷ 5000) = $\frac{1}{3}$, or $33\frac{1}{3}\%$.

Let us now consider the **closing entries** in the Ledger Accounts concerned.

Private Ledger

STOCK

Dr								Cr
Date	Details	Fo	Amount	Date	Details	Fo	Amount	
			£				£	
xxx7				xxx7				
Jan 1	Balance	b/d	1216.00	Dec 31	Transfer to Trading A/c		1216.00	
Dec 31	Transfer to Trading A/c		1764.00	Dec 31	Balance	c/d	1764.00	
Jan 1	Balance	b/d	1764.00					

- On 1 January xxx7, *stock then in hand* of course appears as a Debit Balance and is transferred on 31 December to the *debit* of the Trading Account.
- At the same time the closing stock figure of £1764 is debited above and posted to the *credit* of Trading Account.
- The debit of £1764 is then brought down on 1 January xxx8.

In making these entries in the Stock Account we are transgressing the rule that no first entry shall be made in any Ledger Account. It may be preferred to use the General Journal as the proper Book of Prime Entry. Its use for this purpose was referred to in Chapter 8. The record in this Journal would then be:

			Dr £	*Cr* £
xxx7				
Dec 31	Trading A/c, xxx7	Dr	1216.00	
	Stock			1216.00
	Being Transfer of Stock at January 1, xxx7			
xxx7				
Dec 31	Stock	Dr	1764.00	
	Trading A/c, xxx7			1764.00
	Being Stock at this date transferred			

It should be noted that the Trading Account is produced by transferring each item from its ledger account to the Trading Account. It is also necessary to journalise the transfers from the other Accounts which will be found in the Nominal Ledger and the closing entries in the accounts will appear as follows:

PURCHASES

Dr							Cr
Date	Details	Fo	Amount	Date	Details	Fo	Amount
xxx7			£	xxx7			£
Dec 31	Total purchases for year*		10 340.00	Dec 31	Transfer to Trading A/c		10 340.00

* The total of the totals for each month.

CARRIAGE INWARDS

Dr							Cr
Date	Details	Fo	Amount	Date	Details	Fo	Amount
xxx7			£	xxx7			£
Dec 31	Total expenses for year		208.00	Dec 31	Transfer to Trading A/c		208.00

As regards *Sales* the transfer will be made from the *debit* of Sales Account to the credit of Trading Account.

SALES

Dr							Cr
Date	Details	Fo	Amount	Date	Details	Fo	Amount
xxx7			£	xxx7			£
Dec 31	Transfer to			Dec 31	Total sales		
	Trading A/c		15 000.00		for year		15 000.00

These entries will, in effect, move the balances for the individual accounts to the Trading Account ready to calculate the profit or loss they represent in total thereby enabling the gross profit to be calculated.

In a *manufacturing* business, on the other hand, the Trading Account will be in somewhat different form. In addition to purchases, remuneration paid to staff employed in the actual production of the goods will be debited.

Purchases here will include in the main *raw materials* and component parts.

As *gross profit* in a *merchanting* business is determined after comparing the proceeds of sales with the cost of goods sold, similarly in a *manufacturing* business the proceeds of sales are compared with the *Direct Cost*, or Prime Cost, of production, which covers *both purchases and manufacturing wages and salaries* and any other identifiable direct expenses.

Our justification for dealing with it in this way may be stated as follows:

a *Merchanting business.* Every sales order booked involves a direct and proportionate increase in Purchases.

b *Manufacturing business.* Every sales order requires not only a direct increase in purchases, but also a direct increase in some of the manufacturing expenses.

In the case of **b**, apart from these direct expenses of production, there are also the general factory expenses to be considered. These include rates on the factory premises, repairs to plant and machinery, power costs for operating the plant, and so on. It would be incorrect for us to include these in the Trading Account unless we are instructed to do so, because their inclusion would convert the Account into a Manufacturing, or Production Account.

In practice this will usually mean that a merchanting business will produce a trading account, and a manufacturing business will produce a manufacturing account and a trading account. The manufacturing account will provide a cost of goods manufactured which will be transferred to the trading account where it will take the place of 'goods purchased'.

The Profit and Loss Account

The Profit and Loss Account follows immediately after the Trading Account, of which it is really a continuation.

If the total Revenue is greater than the total cost charged in the Trading Account the balancing figure will be a Gross Profit. This will be debited in the Trading Account and carried down as a credit in the Profit and Loss Account, and vice versa.

Its purpose is to ascertain the final or *net profit* of the business for the period by including:

- the remaining *expenses*, other than those already dealt with in the Trading Account
- the *incidental sources of income*, such as Cash Discounts received, Bank Interest received, etc.

In form it is similar to the Trading Account, the expenses or debits appearing on the left-hand side, and the incidental sources of income or credits on the right-hand side. That is, it too is produced as part of the Double Entry process, including the need to transfer the items included in it from their Nominal Ledger accounts.

As regards both debits and credits in the Profit and Loss Account, care must be taken that:

- the expenses are those *of the business only (excluding* such items as Proprietor's drawings, or private payments made by the business on their behalf)
- the *whole of the expenses* relating to the period under review are brought in.

We shall see at a later stage the importance of the latter point, but meanwhile let us look at the form and construction of the Profit and Loss Account.

Example 12.2

From the items set out below select those which should appear in the Trading and Profit and Loss Account, prepare those accounts (only) showing the Gross Profit and the Net Profit or Loss.

Capital	22 400.00
Freehold Premises	21 350.00
Stock at 1 January xxx9	650.00
Debtors	360.00
Creditors	1 512.00
Purchases	13 500.00
Sales	25 000.00
Returns Inwards	20.00
Discounts Allowed	52.00
Salaries	7 220.00
Sundry Expenses	2 753.00
Rates	490.00
Fixtures and Fittings	1 062.00
Cash at Bank	450.00

The stock in hand at 31 December xxx9 was £215.

Trading and Profit and Loss Account

Year ended 31 December xxx9

Dr				Cr
	£			£
Stock, 1 January xxx9	650.00	Sales	£25 000.00	
Purchases	13 500.00	*Less* Returns	20.00	
Gross profit c/d	11 045.00		————	24 980.00
		Stock, 31 Dec xxx9		215.00
	————			————
	£25 195.00			£25 195.00
	═════			═════
Salaries	7 220.00	Gross profit b/d		11 045.00
Sundry expenses	2 753.00			
Rates	490.00			
Discounts allowed	52.00			
Net profit	530.00			
	————			————
	£11 045.00			£11 045.00
	═════			═════

The remaining items in the list, with which we have not dealt, are of a Capital nature, and will appear in the Statement of Assets and Liabilities or Balance Sheet of the business.

The information below the 'Gross Profit' line comprises the *Profit and Loss Account*. If required the Trading Account could be presented separately from the Profit and Loss Account. The matching credit entry for the Net profit figure will appear in the capital account recording the net affect on the capital of the business transactions of the period.

An alternative form of presentation which is increasingly being adopted is a vertical one. The same example is presented below in this form. The information presented is identical and is still produced as part of the Double Entry System. The only thing that has changed is the layout of the Account. The vertical form of layout is usually preferred as it improves the understandability of the information – one of the major aims of the Final Accounts.

Trading and Profit and Loss Account

Year ended 31 December xxx9

	£	£
Sales	£25 000.00	
less Returns	20.00	
		24 980.00
deduct		
Cost of goods sold:		
Stock, 1 January	650.00	
Purchases during year	13 500.00	
Available for sale	14 150.00	
Stock, 31 December	215.00	13 935.00
Gross profit		11 045.00
deduct expenses:		
Salaries	7 220.00	
Sundry expenses	2 753.00	
Rates	490.00	
Discounts allowed	52.00	
		10 515.00
Net profit		£ 530.00

The transfer from the Accounts in the Nominal Ledger will be made as follows:

SALARIES

Dr							Cr
Date	Details	Fo	Amount	Date	Details	Fo	Amount
xxx9 Dec 31	Total salaries for year		£ 7220.00	xxx9 Dec 31	Transfer to Profit and Loss A/c		£ 7220.00

TRADE EXPENSES

Dr							Cr
Date	Details	Fo	Amount	Date	Details	Fo	Amount
xxx9 Dec 31	Total for year		£ 2753.00	xxx9 Dec 31	Transfer to Profit and Loss A/c		£ 2753.00

RATES AND TAXES

Dr   Cr

Date	Details	Fo	Amount	Date	Details	Fo	Amount
xxx9			£	xxx9			£
Dec 31	Total for year		490.00	Dec 31	Transfer to Profit and Loss A/c		490.00

DISCOUNTS ALLOWED

Dr   Cr

Date	Details	Fo	Amount	Date	Details	Fo	Amount
xxx9			£	xxx9			£
Dec 31	Total for year		52.00	Dec 31	Transfer to Profit and Loss A/c		52.00

Alternatively, instead of making the transfers direct to the Profit and Loss Account, we could use the *General Journal*, with the result that the following Journal entries will appear as *closing entries*:

			Dr £	Cr £
xxx9				
Dec 31	Sundries			
	Profit and Loss A/c	Dr	10 515.00	
	Sundries			
	Salaries			7220.00
	Sundry expenses			2753.00
	Rates			490.00
	Discounts allowed			52.00
	Being transfer of Expense Account balances to Profit and Loss Account as above.			

If the latter method is adopted the word 'Sundries' with the appropriate Journal reference will describe the credit entries in each of the Ledger Accounts, in place of 'Transfer to Profit and Loss Account'.

Example 12.3

The financial year of Excelsior Pressings, a manufacturer of small household equipment, ends on 31 December. The following balances are in the books of the firm as at 31 December Year 8:

	£
Stocks as at 1 January Year 8:	
Raw materials	28 315
Work in progress (at factory cost)	6 200
Finished goods	33 700

	£
Heating and Lighting	3 450
Wages of indirect manufacturing personnel	45 820
Rent and Rates	16 400
Purchase of raw materials	172 300
Manufacturing wages	194 500
Factory power	4 760
Factory expenses and maintenance	3 700
Salaries	32 400
Sales of finished goods	652 500
Advertising	60 800
Administration expenses	27 500

The following information is also available:

■ Stocks have been valued as at 31 December Year 8 as follows:

	£
Raw materials	30 200
Work in progress (at factory cost)	7 100
Finished goods	37 500

■ In respect of Year 8, the following apportionments are to be made:

	Factory	**General Office**
Heating and Lighting	4/5	1/5
Rent and Rates	3/4	1/4
Salaries	1/3	2/3

■ Depreciation is to be allowed as follows:

Plant and Machinery	£20 000
Office equipment	£4 000

You are required to prepare the Manufacturing, Trading and Profit and Loss Accounts of Excelsior Pressings for the year ended 31 December Year 8.

Note: Try to prepare your own accounts and then compare them with the solution that follows. The slightly new requirement means that you have to consider, using the description of the balance and the additional data, the amounts which will be included in each particular account.

Excelsior Pressings

Manufacturing account for the year ended 31 December Year 8

	£	£
Raw materials used		
Opening stock	28 315	
Purchases	172 300	
Available	200 615	
Closing stock	30 200	
Used during the year		170 415
Manufacturing wages		194 500
Other expenses		
Heating and lighting	2 760	
Indirect personnel	45 820	
Rent and Rates	12 300	
Factory power	4 760	
Sundry and maintenance	3 700	
Salaries	10 800	
Depreciation plant and machinery	20 000	
		100 140
Cost of manufacturing during the year		465 055
add opening work in progress		6 200
deduct closing work in progress		7 100
Cost of goods completed during the year		464 155

Trading account for the year ended 31 December Year 8

	£	£
Sales		652 500
Cost of goods sold		
Opening stock	33 700	
Completed during the year	464 155	
Available for sale	497 855	
Closing stock	37 500	
Used during the year		460 355
Gross profit		192 145

Profit and loss account for the year ended 31 December Year 8

	£	£
Gross profit		192 145
Expenses		
Heating and lighting	690	
Rent and rates	3 100	
Salaries	21 600	
Advertising	60 800	
Administration expenses	27 500	
Depreciation of office equipment	4 000	
		117 690
Net profit, before taxation		74 455

Appropriation, or Net Profit and Loss Account

As its name implies, this third section deals with the ascertained Net Profit or Loss, and its distribution among the proprietors of the business.

Therefore, in a partnership firm the Net Profit figure will here be divided in the ratio in which the partners share profits and losses (see Chapter 18).

In the case of a Limited Company, the appropriation account shows how the Net Profits are divided in dividend to the shareholders according to their respective rights and interests and this appropriation sometimes appears in the Profit and Loss Account (see Chapter 19).

The necessity for such an account rarely, if ever, arises where the position of a sole trade is under consideration, the Net Profit being carried direct to the Capital or Current Account of the proprietor, as already explained.

KEY POINTS

On completion of this chapter you should:

1 understand the purpose of the Trading, Profit and Loss Account.

2 appreciate the difference between the Trading, Profit and Loss Account and the Manufacturing, Trading, Profit and Loss Account.

3 be able to produce either form of account by transferring appropriate items from the Nominal Ledger Accounts.

Questions

1 What do you understand by **a** Capital Expenditure; **b** Revenue Expenditure?

State some items coming under each of these headings in the case of a Company carrying on business as manufacturers of aeroplanes.

2 What is the object in preparing a Trading Account as distinct from a Profit and Loss Account? Explain what information may be obtained from the former and its importance to a trader.

3 PQ carries on business as a merchant, but, although stock is taken regularly at the end of December in each year, proper books of account are not kept. A Cash Book, Petty Cash Book and Personal Ledger are the only books.

Explain briefly how you would proceed if requested to ascertain the result of the trading for the past year.

4 What is the object of calculating gross profit and net profit? Does gross profit measure the prosperity of a business? Explain.

5 On 5 January xxx7, Ambrose sold goods to Applejohn.

The goods had cost Ambrose £100, and the selling price was 50% on cost, payment being due on monthly account less 2% for cash.

On 28 January xxx7, Applejohn returned some of the goods, and Ambrose sent him a credit note for £30.

The amount due was paid by cheque on 28 February xxx7, but three days later the cheque was returned by the bank unpaid. Ultimately full settlement was received from Applejohn.

Show:

    a Applejohn's Account in the books of Ambrose.

    b What profit or loss Ambrose made on the whole transaction.

6 A business has three departments, A, B and C. You are asked to calculate the working profit in each department, by reference to the following:

	£
Opening Stocks, B	1280.00
Opening Stocks, C	640.00
Closing Stocks, B	1320.00
Closing Stocks, C	650.00
Purchases	6000.00
Wages	1800.00
General Expenses	1250.00
Sales, B	6800.00
Sales, C	3200.00

All purchases are made for A department in the first instance. A department (which has no sales) processes the goods and then re-issues them to B and C departments at fixed prices.

The issues to B were valued at £5000 and to C at £2400.

25% of the wages are charged to B, 20% to C, 10% to general expenses and the balance to A.

The general expenses are recharged as follows:

Department A, 7% on output value,

Department B, 10% on sales value,

Department C, 7% on sales value,

any difference being carried to the Profit and Loss Account.

This may seem to be a question that you have not been taught how to answer; but think about it. There are three departments and general expenses. You are told how wages and general expenses are charged to the three departments. The output of A is not sales to customers but transfers to B and C at a given value which become the 'purchases' of B and C departments.

13 | THE BALANCE SHEET

OBJECTIVES

In this chapter you will be introduced to the second of the Final Accounts of a business – the Balance Sheet. This chapter describes the purpose of this statement and explains how it is prepared (drawn up) from the Trial Balance. Its relationship with the Profit and Loss Account is also described.

Together with the Profit and Loss (or Revenue) Account, we have described the Balance Sheet as a part of the Final Accounts of the business. It has been fittingly defined as 'a flashlight photograph of the position of affairs of the business at a particular date'.

More precisely, we can speak of it as a Statement of Assets and Liabilities, including the balance of the Profit and Loss Account made up to the date at which the Balance Sheet is prepared.

The fact that it is a Statement of Assets and Liabilities justified us in confining our attention to the 'Capital' columns of the Trial Balance, the *debit balances* which were seen to represent *Assets*, and the *credit balances, Liabilities*.

The fact that it includes the balance on the Profit and Loss Account implies that this balance, if a Credit, will be shown as a Liability and if a Debit, as an Asset.

In other words, the business having an *initial liability* to its proprietor for the amount of Capital invested, now has a *further liability* in respect of the profit earned.

It is important for us to remember that the Balance Sheet is the complement to the Profit and Loss Account and is an essential part of the Final Accounts for this reason. When the business was started, Capital was invested in it, perhaps in the first place in the form of cash. Almost at once this cash would be spent in the acquisition of various forms of property; of the kind we have defined as Fixed Assets or Current Assets.

The former represented property which the business must possess as part of its equipment; the latter consisted of property in which the business was dealing.

If the Current Assets were used by the proprietor or the manager to produce a Profit it would clearly be necessary to draw up a further Balance Sheet at *the end of each trading period*, showing just what Assets existed in the business at that date. Provided no additions to or withdrawals from Capital had taken place, and each Asset held was reasonably and properly valued in each succeeding Balance Sheet, any increase in the Total Assets would represent a *profit*, and conversely any decrease a *loss*.

In the latter case, as the loss appeared in the Balance Sheet as an 'Asset', it could quite well be deducted from the liability of the business to its proprietor on Capital Account, disclosing at that point a *loss of Capital*, which, of course, is in line with the facts.

Assets = Liabilities

and the assets and liabilities will consist of:

Fixed Assets

+ Current Assets

= Owner's Capital

+ Liability to Other Creditors

or rearranged

OWNER'S CAPITAL = FIXED ASSETS + CURRENT ASSETS – CREDITORS

Earning a profit means that, for a retail business, we have bought something for, say, £100 and sold it for £150. If these were cash transactions they could be represented as changes in current assets. Buying for £100 merely means

$$- £100 \text{ cash}$$
$$+ £100 \text{ stock}$$

i.e. a change within the current assets.

Selling for £150 means   + 150 cash

                                                          – £100 stock

and   – £50 profit

As cash is now £50 more than before, the business has made a profit and until this is paid to the owner of the business it remains a liability of the business to the owner, which is why the sign is 'minus'.

The form of the Balance Sheet

We have seen that the Profit and Loss Account is prepared very much in the form of the ordinary Ledger Account, although before presentation to others it may be redrafted into a vertical format.

In form, it is a summarised Ledger Account to which all the Revenue balances appearing in the Trial Balance are transferred at the end of the financial year of the business. By so doing, an ultimate balance (either of Profit or Loss) is struck.

But we still have to deal with the 'Capital' columns. It is these remaining balances, **and the balance of the Profit and Loss Account**, which are entered in a 'sheet of balances' or **Balance Sheet**.

We could, if we wished, show this Balance Sheet in the form of an ordinary Ledger Account, debiting to it the Assets, and putting the Liabilities on the credit side.

As a result, in reading the Balance Sheet in the ordinary way, from left to right, we begin with the Assets, and then turn to a study of the Liabilities out of which they have been financed.

We can also regard the Balance Sheet as a *classified summary* of the Ledger Balances remaining on the books after the preparation of the Revenue Account and including the balance of this Account.

The Balance Sheet and the Trial Balance contrasted

While both are drawn up at a particular date, the former includes only those balances which are, or have become, *Assets* and *Liabilities*; the latter also includes the various Nominal Ledger balances relating to *expenses* and *gains*.

The Balance Sheet is a properly marshalled statement of the Assets and Liabilities, setting them out in their order of permanence. The Trial

Balance merely lists the whole of the balances in the order in which they happen to appear in the Ledgers.

The purpose of the Balance Sheet is to give information to the proprietor of the business as to its financial position, whereas the Trial Balance is extracted primarily to prove the arithmetical accuracy of the book-keeping work.

Finally, the Balance Sheet always includes the value of the Stock in Hand at the end of the period; the Trial Balance does not necessarily show this Asset.

Let us now take two examples involving some of the points we have been discussing.

Example 13.1

From the following items construct the Balance Sheet of L Redfern as on 31 December xxx1 or 'as at' or 'at'.

	£
Capital as at 1 January xxx1	2000
Motor vans as at 31 December xxx1	2200
Cash at bank as at 31 December xxx1	700
Profits for the year	3000
Land and buildings as at 31 December xxx1	4100
Drawings for the year	1500
Stock of goods, 31 December xxx1	2300
Loan from A Herbert repayable 30 Nov xxx2	4000
Debtors as at 31 December xxx1	2000
Sundry creditors as at 31 December xxx1	3800

In this first case, it may be helpful if we list the items as **Assets** (Debits) or **Liabilities** (Credits),

	Dr £	Cr £
Capital, 1 January xxx1		2 000.00
Motor vans, 31 December xxx1	2 200.00	
Cash at bank, 31 December xxx1	700.00	
Profit for the year		3 000.00
Land and buildings, 31 December xxx1	4 100.00	
Drawings	1 500.00	
Stock of goods, 31 December xxx1	2 300.00	
Loan from A Herbert, repayable xxx2		4 000.00

	Dr	Cr
	£	£
Debtors as at 31 December xxx1	2 000.00	
Sundry creditors as at 31 December xxx1		3 800.00
	£12 800.00	£12 800.00

We may then proceed as follows, remembering:

■ that a balance sheet is always prepared at some definite date

■ that the balances on the various Accounts of which it is made up are **not** transferred to it as is the case with the Revenue Account.

L REDFERN

Balance Sheet

as at 31 December xxx1

Assets	£	£	Liabilities	£	£
Fixed Assets			Capital Account	2 000	
Land and Buildings	4 100		Profit for year	3 000	
Motor Vans	2 200				
				5 000	
Total fixed assets		6 300	Less drawings	1 500	
Current Assets					
Stock of goods	2 300		Capital at 31.12.x1		3 500
Debtors	2 000		Current Liabilities		
Cash at bank	700		A Herbert	4 000	
			Sundry creditors	3 800	
Total current assets		5 000			7 800
TOTAL ASSETS		£11 300	TOTAL LIABILITIES		£11 300

It should be noted that:

■ the Assets are stated in their order of permanence beginning with the least liquid asset of 'Land and Buildings'

■ Cash, Debtors and Stock represent Current Assets, while Motor Vans and Land and Buildings are Fixed Assets

■ although Profit and Drawings have been shown in a Capital Account they might equally well have been recorded in Current Account

■ the loan from A Herbert is shown as a Current liability as it is due to be repaid within twelve months of the Balance Sheet date.

As with the Trading and Profit and Loss Account, the Balance Sheet may be presented in a vertical format, for example:

L REDFERN
Balance Sheet
as at 31 December xxx1

	£	£
Fixed Assets		
Land and buildings	4 100.00	
Motor vans	2 200.00	
Total Fixed Assets		6 300.00
Current Assets		
Stock of goods	2 300.00	
Debtors	2 000.00	
Cash at bank	700.00	
Total Current Assets		5 000.00
Total Assets		**£11 300.00**
Capital account		
As at 1 January xxx1	2 000.00	
Add profit for year	3 000.00	
Deduct drawings	(1 500.00)	
As at 31 December xxx1		3 500.00
Current Liabilities		
Loan from A Herbert	4 000.00	
Sundry creditors	3 800.00	
Total Current Liabilities		7 800.00
Total Liabilities		**£11 300.00**

It will be noticed that in this presentation the assets and liabilities are still in the order of permanence.

Example 13.2

From the following particulars construct the Balance Sheet of T Tomlinson as on 31 March xxx2.

Capital 1 April xxx1 was £5000. The loss for the year to 31 March xxx2 was £1200 and drawings were £220. On 31 March xxx2 the Stock was £2480, and the Bank Overdraft £1320, Debtors £3260, the Loan from F Weston £2200 repayable on 31 March xxx8, the Fixtures and Fittings £1480, Creditors £2900, Cash in Hand £50, Machinery £2730.

If you have studied Example 13.1 carefully, it should not be necessary to list the balances again before constructing the Balance Sheet. Try to produce your own Balance Sheet.

Looking at the information given, we see, however, that a *trading loss* of £1200 has been sustained, and in addition there are drawings of £220. The initial Capital has thus *decreased* by £1420.

As regards the Liabilities, we may note here that the Loan is not repayable until xxx8; an Overdraft is usually considered a Current Liability; the item 'Creditors' referring to the Purchase Ledger Accounts of suppliers for *goods* or *services*.

T TOMLINSON

Balance Sheet

as at 31 March xxx2

Assets	£	£	*Liabilities*	£	£
Fixed Assets			Capital Account:		
Machinery	2 730.00		1 April xxx1	5 000.00	
Fixtures and Fittings	1 480.00		Less Loss year to		
			31 March xxx1	1 200.00	
Total Fixed Assets		4 210.00	Drawings	220.00	
Current Assets					1 420.00
Stock	2 480.00				3 580.00
Debtors	3 260.00		At 31 March xxx1		
Cash in hand	50.00		Longer-term Liability Loan		2 200.00
			Current Liabilities		
Total Current Assets		5 790.00	Bank overdraft	1 320.00	
			Trade Creditors	2 900.00	
			Total Current Liabilities		4 220.00
Total Assets		£10 000.00	Total Liabilities		£10 000.00

Having considered separately the Trading and Profit and Loss Accounts, and the Balance Sheet, we may now, as in a practical case, prepare each of them from an ordinary two-column Trial Balance.

Example 13.3

From the following balances prepare the Trading Account, Profit and Loss Account, and Balance Sheet of J Farmer, a retailer, for half year ended 30 June xxx1:

	£	£
Petty cash	50.00	
Sundry creditors		493.00
Cash at bank	986.00	
Furniture, fixtures and equipment	400.00	
Purchases	8 417.00	
Sales		11 618.00
Stock, 1 January xxx1	1 117.00	
Office expenses	45.00	
Rent and rates	997.00	
Lighting and heating	186.00	
Advertising	75.00	

	£	£
Delivery expenses	66.00	
Capital		2 000.0
Drawings	1 560.00	
Carriage on purchases	212.00	
	£14 111.00	£14 111.00

Stock on 30 June xxx1, £1084. Not registered for VAT.

J FARMER

Trading and Profit and Loss Account

Six Months ended 30 June xxx1

Dr   Cr

	£	£		£	£
Stock, 1 January xxx1		1 117.00	Sales		11 618.00
Purchases	8 417.00		Stock, 30 June xxx1		1 084.00
Carriage on purchases	212.00				
		8 629.00			
Gross profit c/d		2 956.00			
		£12 702.00			£12 702.00
Rent and rates		997.00	Gross profit, b/d		2 956,.00
Lighting and heating		186.00			
Advertising		75.00			
Delivery expenses		66.00			
Office expenses		45.00			
Net profit, carried to					
Capital A/c		1 587.00			
		£ 2 956.00			£2 956.00

J FARMER

Balance Sheet

as at 30 June xxx1

Dr   Cr

Assets	£	£	Liabilities	£	£
Fixed Assets			Capital Account	2000.00	
Furniture, fixtures and			*Add* Net profit for		
equipment		400.00	half year to date	1587.00	
				3587.00	
Current Assets			*Less* Drawings	1560.00	
Stock	1084.00				
Cash at bank	986.00		At 30 June xxx1		2027.00
Petty Cash	50.00		Current liabilities		
Total current assets		2120.00	Sundry Creditors		493.00
Total Assets		£2520.00	Total Liabilities		£2520.00

Note that as the Trading Account and the Profit and Loss Account are only divisions of the Revenue Account, they may conveniently be shown together in one statement.

KEY POINTS

On completion of this chapter you should

1 be clear on the purpose of the Balance Sheet

2 understand how it relates to the Profit and Loss Account

3 be able to draw up a Balance Sheet from a Trial Balance

4 be aware of the use of various formats for presenting the information contained in a Balance Sheet

Questions

1 What effect would the following errors made by a book-keeper have upon **a** the Trial Balance, **b** the annual accounts for a business:

■ An item of £50 for goods sold to CD posted from the Sales Journal to the credit of CD's Ledger Account.

■ An item of £212, representing the purchase of a desk, placed in the general expenses column of the Purchase Journal.

■ A sum of £15, representing interest allowed by the banker, entered in the bank column on the credit side of the Cash Book.

2 List the assets you would expect to find on the Balance Sheet of AB, a motor-car manufacturer, grouping them into the different classes.

Why is the distinction between different types of asset important?

3 From the following particulars draw up the Balance Sheet of B Wilton as on 31 December xxx1. Land and buildings, £51 000; Machinery, £7325; Motor vans, £12 120; Fixtures and fittings, £3070; Stock on hand at 31 December xxx1, £5950; Sundry debtors, £3856; Cash in hand, £29; Sundry creditors, £7820; Bank overdraft, £1200; Loan from A Mather, £40 000; Capital as at 1 January xxx1, £30 230; Loss for the year, £4100. State briefly your opinion of the financial position of B Wilton.

4 AB, an engineer, decides to erect a new machine in his works. He dismantles an old machine and uses material from it to the value of £250 in the erection of the new machine. Additional materials are purchased from outside sources at a cost of £840, and the wages amount to £560.

Explain how the items would be dealt with in his books.

5 The following balances were extracted from the books of D Wright on 31 December xxx1. You are required to prepare a Trading Account, Profit and Loss Account and Balance Sheet as on that date.

	Dr £	Cr £
Cash in hand	17.00	
Bank overdraft		175.00
Stock, 1 January xxx1	6 794.00	
Purchases and sales	14 976.00	26 497.00
Wages	3 719.00	
Insurance	155.00	
Bank charges	110.00	
Furniture and fittings	1 115.00	
Returns inwards and outwards	309.00	237.00
Sundry Drs and Crs	1 753.00	615.00
Land and buildings	20 000.00	
Discount		154.00
Capital		21 270.00
	£48 948.00	£48 948.00

Stock at end £1169.00

6 From the following Trial Balance of J Lowe, prepare Trading and Profit and Loss Accounts for the year ended 31 March xxx2, and a Balance Sheet as on that date.

	£	£
Purchases	21 300.00	
Carriage inwards	350.00	
Sales		36 600.00
Stock, 1 April xxx1	4 000.00	
Trade expenses	850.00	
Fixtures and fittings	2 000.00	
Discounts allowed	900.00	
J Lowe: Capital		6 000.00
Returns inwards	750.00	
Cash in hand	150.00	
Sundry debtors	2 400.00	
Salaries	7 200.00	
J Lowe: Drawings	2 500.00	
Discounts received		400.00
Sundry creditors		4 000.00
Cash at bank	2 700.00	
Rent	500.00	
Rates	1 400.00	
	£47 000.00	£47 000.00

Stock at 31 March xxx2 was £5500

7 The following Trial Balance was extracted from the books of R Parr on 31 December xxx1:

	Dr £	Cr £
Capital		35 000.00
Drawings	1 450.00	
Stock at 1 January xxx1	26 000.00	
Purchases and sales	45 000.00	65 000.00
Returns outwards		600.00
Returns inwards	1 000.00	
Salaries	4 750.00	
Trade expenses	2 050.00	
Bad debts	230.00	
Discount account (balance)		350.00
Sundry debtors	35 750.00	
Sundry creditors including VAT		19 600.00
Insurance	220.00	
Fixtures and fittings	1 850.00	
Motor vans	2 650.00	
Rent and rates	3 550.00	
Bank overdraft		3 950.00
	£124 500.00	£124 500.00

The value of the stock on hand was £17 950.

You are required to prepare Trading and Profit and Loss Accounts for the year ended 31 December xxx1, and a Balance Sheet as on that date.

8 The following balances were extracted at 30 April xxx2, from the books of CD:

- ■ Prepare a Trading and Profit and Loss Account for the year ended on that date, and also a Balance Sheet.

- ■ Do the results of the business for the year justify the drawings of £350 by CD? Explain.

	£
Office salaries	7 628.00
Insurance of plant	61.00
Discounts received	33.00
Sales	27 350.00
Bad debts	69.00
Plant and machinery	7 430.00
Commission	127.00
Investment Interest received	30.00
Stock, 1 May xxx1	1 110.00
Repairs	98.00
Sundries	46.00

	£
Goods returned by customers	100.00
Discounts allowed	115.00
Rent and rates	1 322.00
Purchases	4 290.00
Sundry debtors	3 143.00
Travelling expenses	263.00
Wages and National Insurance	13 004.00
General insurance	34.00
Carriage inwards	87.00
Sundry creditors	1 426.00
CD: Capital, 1 May xxx1	13 250.00
Cash at bank	109.00
Coal, gas and water	2 177.00
Goods returned to suppliers	74.00
Investment in Utopia Ltd	600.00

The stock at 30 April xxx2 was valued at £1275.00.

9 The following is the Trial Balance extracted at 31 December xxx2 from the books of S Printer, who carries on business as a manufacturer of sports equipment:

	Dr	Cr
	£	£
Petty Cash Book	28.00	
Nominal Ledger:		
Carriage outwards	504.00	
Carriage inwards	266.00	
Travelling expenses	2 169.00	
Discount allowed	933.00	
Discount received		218.00
Repairs and incidentals	820.00	
Rent and rates	872.00	
Factory wages	10 655.00	
Heating and lighting	137.00	
Sales, less Returns		30 750.00
Factory National Insurance	318.00	
Packing and dispatch expenses	1 252.00	
Purchases, less Returns	10 546.00	
Salaries and National Insurance	2 735.00	
Private Cash Book		853.00
Private Ledger:		
Stock, 1 January xxx2	3 915.00	
S Printer: Capital at 1 January xxx2		10 000.00
S Printer: Drawings	1 200.00	
Office fixtures and general equipment		
1 January xxx2	1 567.00	
Equipment sold		136.00

	Dr £	Cr £
Equipment purchased	608.00	
Bank interest account	46.00	
Sales Ledgers:		
Accounts receivable	6 002.00	
Purchase Ledger:		
Accounts payable		2 616.00
	£44 573.00	£44 573.00

The stock at 31 December xxx2, was valued at £5200.

You are required to:

■ Prepare a Trading and Profit and Loss Account for the year ended 31 December xxx2, and a Balance Sheet at that date.

■ State the percentages of Gross Profit and of Net Profit to Turnover.

■ Show the Office Fixtures and General Equipment Account as it would appear in the Private Ledger.

10 In the form of a three-column Cash Book, after properly heading each column, enter all the money transactions below and balance the book.

Journalise the opening balances and remaining transactions. (Note: Purchases and Sales Books may be used, if preferred.)

Post the entries to the Ledger. Extract a Trial Balance.

Draw up a Profit and Loss Account and Balance Sheet.

On 1 May xxx2, D Robinson, nurseryman, reopened his books with the following balances in addition to his Capital Account: Cash, £40; Rent outstanding, £80; Bank overdraft, £470; M Merritt (Cr), £232; S Service (Dr), £327; Stock, £1565.

During the month his transactions were:

			£
May	3	Received cheque from S Service and paid into bank	300.00
	5	Sold to S Service:	
		Rose bushes	146.00
		Rose standards	139.00
		Misc plants	127.00
	7	S Service's cheque returned dishonoured	300.00
	10	S Service paid in cash (banked)	275.00
	14	Bought from M Merritt:	
		Fruit trees	356.00
		Shrubs	42.00
	18	Paid M Merritt by cheque to settle account to 1 May	230.00
	21	Returned to M Merritt damaged shrubs	4.00
	25	Cash sales	48.00
	26	Bought for cash sundry plants at auction	17.00

		£
27	Paid rent outstanding by cheque	80.00
29	Drew cheque for self	80.00
31	Wages and expenses for month:	
	Paid by cheque	120.00
	And in cash	52.00
	Bank charges	6.00
	Rent accrued	40.00
	Interest on capital at 6% pa	
	Stock on hand valued at	1701.00

11 The following is the Trial Balance extracted from the books of JB as at 31 December xxx1.

	Dr £	Cr £
Private Ledger:		
Capital, 1 January xxx1		4 137.00
Drawings	1 000.00	
Stock, 1 January xxx1	2 035.00	
Fixtures and fittings, 1 January xxx1	2 119.00	
Creditors		268.00
Debtors	238.00	
Nominal Ledger:		
Purchases	5 911.00	
Sales		30 782.00
Discounts allowed	223.00	
Discounts received		104.00
Packing expenses	192.00	
Office expenses	74.00	
Salaries	7 826.00	
Repairs	58.00	
Lighting and heating	1 087.00	
Rates	1 146.00	
Rent	1 200.00	
Wages (workpeople)	11 644.00	
Sundry expenses	61.00	
Cash book		781.00
Petty cash book	27.00	
Creditors (Personal Ledger)		1 433.00
Debtors (Personal Ledger)	2 664.00	
	£37 505.00	£37 505.00

The stock on hand at 31 December xxx1, was valued by JB in the sum of £3157.

Prepare Trading and Profit and Loss Account, and Balance Sheet.

Read Chapter 15 before attempting questions 12, 13 and 14.

12 The following 'statement of affairs' has been drawn up to give the financial position, as on 31 March xxx1, and 31 March xxx2, respectively, of A Brown who keeps her books on a single entry basis:

Statement of Affairs, 31 March xxx1

	£		£
Capital	6192.00	Fixtures	250.00
Creditors	742.00	Stock	2305.00
		Debtors	4176.00
		Cash	203.00
	£6934.00		£6934.00

Statement of Affairs, 31 March xxx2

	£		£
Capital	5933.00	Fixtures	230.00
Creditors	817.00	Stock	2562.00
		Debtors	3777.00
		Cash	181.00
	£6750.00		£6750.00

Brown has transferred £100 a month regularly from her business banking account to her private banking account by way of drawings, and she has taken £25 worth of stock for her private use. The alteration in the value of the fixtures represents an amount written off by way of depreciation.

Calculate Brown's trading profit for the year.

13 The only books kept by Green are Personal Ledgers. At 1 January his position is as follows:

	£		£
Capital	17.00	Creditors	635.00
Debtors	3109.00	Capital	3023.00
Stock	102.00		
Equipment at cost	430.00		
	£3658.00		£3658.00

At 31 December following, he informs you that the following are the figures concerning his Assets and Liabilities:

	£
Cash	15.00
Bank (overdraft)	230.00
Stock	98.00
Debtors	3036.00
Creditors	502.00

He has had his equipment valued, and thinks that it is now only worth £350. He has taken notes as to his drawings, and informs you that he has spent £1332 for household purposes, etc., £140 for a life assurance premium, and £110 for fire insurance for business assets. In addition, he has taken home goods, of which the cost price was £90 and the sale price £120.

Prepare a Statement showing Green's profit for the year, and his general position at 31 December.

14   **Balance Sheet**

	£		£
Creditors	721.00	Freehold premises	21 560.00
Capital	33 150.00	Machinery and plant	7 420.00
		Stock	2 876.00
		Debtors	1 982.00
		Cash	33.00
	£33 871.00		£33 871.00

The above is a copy of Samuel Wood's Balance Sheet as on 31 December xxx1. The only books kept are a Cash Book and a Ledger. The following is a summary of his receipts and payments for the year ended 31 December xxx2.

Receipts	£	*Payments*	£
Cash on account of		Creditors for goods	
credit sales	4 276.00	purchased	3 954.00
Cash sales	12 863.00	Wages	10 743.00
Capital paid in	4 200.00	General expenses	627.00
		Additions to	
		machinery	4 160.00
		Drawings	536.00
	£21 339.00		£20 020.00

On 31 December xxx2, the amount due to Creditors was £816, and the Debtors and Stock amounted to £2918 and £1854 respectively. You are required to prepare Trading and Profit and Loss Accounts for the year ended 31 December xxx2, and a Balance Sheet as on that date, after making adjustments in respect of the following:

- Depreciation of 10% is to be written off the Machinery and Plant, including additions during the year.
- £150 is to be provided as a Reserve for Doubtful Debts.
- The sum of £38 for goods supplied to the proprietor was included in the Debtors' balance at 31 December xxx2.

14 | ADJUSTMENTS IN THE FINAL ACCOUNTS

OBJECTIVES

Having been introduced to the Profit and Loss Account and the Balance Sheet as two Final Accounts produced by a business, you now need to ensure that these accounts contain all the correct information. This chapter introduces you to a number of so called 'adjustments' which need to be made to ensure that the Final Accounts accurately reflect the reality of the financial activities and position of the business.

Question You said on page 153 that certain adjustments may be necessary in preparing the Final Accounts, and that the Trial Balance does not show what they are. Can we consider them now?

Answer As we have dealt with the simple form of Profit and Loss Account and Balance Sheet, in which no adjustments were called for, we may now look a little more closely at the problem of ascertaining *true Profit and Loss* as it arises in practice.

In the first place, our task is not merely to prepare the Final Accounts from the information given in the books of the business as they may stand. We must examine the Ledger Accounts, particularly the accounts in the Nominal Ledger, with a view to seeing that they are *complete for the period under review.*

Question Is there any likelihood of their being incomplete?

Answer When we speak of the function of the Profit and Loss Account, for example, as the statement of the Profit or Loss over a definite period, it is essential that we include in it *all the expenses incurred as well as the whole of the gross income* of the business.

If any expenses *attributable to the period* were inadvertently omitted, the final figure of Profit would be untrue, and would be *overstated*. Similarly, Profit is *understated* if we neglect to bring in every kind of income, however incidental to the main purpose of the business, which has been *earned* during the period and for which it may properly take credit.

Question   Can you give me examples of such items, and explain why they are termed 'adjustments'?

Answer   Examples of the most commonly occurring adjustments are those for wages, stock and debts.

Wages

Normally wages may be paid on Fridays in respect of the week ended on the preceding Wednesday. The wage sheets or cards for the week have to be checked and certified, the pay roll prepared, deductions made for National Insurance, and so on. Consequently, if the financial year ended on a Thursday, wages for a whole week and one day would be outstanding, no payment would have been made, and there would be no Credit entry in the Cash Book, and no Debit entry in the Wages Account for the amounts involved when the books were closed.

In effect, the *expense* figure for wages would be less than the true amount, and the fact that the workpeople were *creditors* of the business would be ignored. The expense should be included in the Profit and Loss Account and the creditors in the Balance Sheet. Therefore we must make an adjustment raising the wage figure to its true level (an additional Debit), and at the same time record the liability for wages in the Balance Sheet (an additional Credit).

Stock

The adjustment to purchases of goods for resale to reflect the opening and closing stocks has been explained earlier but these are, in effect, adjustments. There may be other stocks, for example stationery, which should be treated as an asset of the business rather than written off as an expense in the year when purchased (if the amounts are significant).

Debts

Another instance arises in connection with the Book Debts, or 'Sundry Debtors', as we have more recently described them.

At the end of the financial year, a certain amount will be due from customers for goods sold to them. The value of these goods appears as 'Sales' in the Trading Account, as we have seen, and is the main source of Profit. Unless we are quite convinced that our customers are willing and able to pay what they owe, a part of the Book Debts may become Bad Debts. Any loss that is likely to arise in this way must be charged against the Profit earned in the period otherwise such estimated loss, if and when it becomes an actual or ascertained loss, is a burden on the Profits of the *subsequent* trading year. Neglecting to reserve an estimated sum for Bad or Doubtful Debts has the effect of *overstating Profits*, and *also overstating Assets* as the debtors appear in the Balance Sheet of the business at more than they will ultimately realise.

The adjustment required in this case is to *debit* a sum to the Profit and Loss Account by way of 'Provision for doubtful debts', along with the debts actually written off as Bad during the period.

The amount of this provision should be calculated by analysing each debt by the date of sale (for a year ending 31 December); any sales made in September but not yet paid would be considered unusual. Careful assessment of all the September and earlier months' sales, in relation to terms of trade and any particular circumstances, would lead to an estimate of those considered doubtful. Many businesses would also make a general provision in respect of October, November and December sales – a general percentage provision reflecting the expectation that some will not be paid but we don't know which ones. (If we did we wouldn't have allowed credit.)

The corresponding Credit balance can be shown on the Liabilities side of the Balance Sheet, or better, as a *deduction* from the total Sundry Debtors on the Assets side, thereby reducing them to their estimated collectible value.

Question   With all these adjustments, then, both the Profit and Loss Account and the Balance Sheet are affected?

Answer   Yes, either as a Debit to Revenue and a Credit on the Balance Sheet, with what is called a **Liability Provision**, or as a Credit to Revenue and a Debit on the Balance Sheet, in the form of an **Asset Provision**.

The following are examples:

Example 14.1

Merryweather & Co pay a rent of £2400 per annum for their business premises. The estimated business rates are £3000 payable half yearly in advance on 31 March and 30 September.

The rent is payable on the usual quarter days, but on 30 September xxx6, the firm sublet a part of the premises to Tenant & Co at £800 per annum, the first half-yearly payment being due on 31 March xxx7.

The Rates and Rent Accounts in Merryweather's books was as follows on 1 January xxx6:

Rates

Dr					Cr
xxx6		£			
Jan 31	Balance b/d, Rates prepaid	750.00			

Rent

			xxx6		£
			Jan 31	Balance b/d, Rent due 25 December	600.00

You are required:

■ To write up the account for the year, bringing down any necessary balances at 31 December xxx6.

■ To state in which section of the Final Accounts for the year xxx6 these balances would appear, giving reasons in brief.

Before we begin, let us take the information given, and consider it. The following points must be borne in mind:

■ The financial year end of the business is 31 December xxx6.

■ In the year ended on that date we shall expect to find in the Profit and Loss Account:

– an expense for rent payable of £2400.

– an expense for rates of £3000.

– a provision for rent receivable from Tenant & Co of £200 (3 months at £800 per annum).

■ And in the Balance Sheet:

- an Asset or Debit Balance of £750 representing *rates paid in advance for the 3 months to 31 March xxx7.*
- a similar Asset of £200, being rent accrued due at 31 December xxx6.

■ The opening balances represent half the rates paid on 30 September xxx5 (one half of £1500) and the rent due (one quarter £2400).

The Rent and Rates Accounts in the Nominal Ledger will then appear as shown below assuming all payments are made on the due dates.

Rates

Dr					Cr
Date		Rates	Date		Rates
xxx6		£	xxx6		£
Jan 1	Balance b/d, Rates prepaid	750.00	Dec 31	Provision for 3 months, Rates paid in advance c/d	750.00
Mar 31	Cash, Rates 6 months to 30 September xxx6	1500.00	31	Transfer to Profit and Loss A/c: Rates	3000.00
Sept 30	Cash, Rates 6 months to 31 March xxx7	1500.00			
		£3750.00			£3750.00
xxx7					
Jan 1	Balance b/d, Rates prepaid	750.00			

Rent

Dr					Cr
Date		Rates	Date		Rates
xxx6		£	xxx6		£
Jan 2	Cash, Rent	600.00	Jan 1	Balance b/d, Rent due December 25	600.00
Mar 25	Cash, Rent	600.00	Dec 31	Provision for 3 months' Rent accrued from Tenant & Co at this date at £800.00 per annum c/d	200.00
June 24	Cash, Rent	600.00			
Sept 29	Cash, Rent	600.00			
Dec 25	Cash, Rent	600.00			
31	Transfer to Profit and Loss A/c: Rent Receivable	200.00	31	Transfer to Profit and Loss A/c: Rent Payable	2400.00
		£3200.00			£3200.00
xxx7	Balance b/d				
Jan 1	Rent accrued due	200.00			

Note: If there were many properties it would be useful to open separate Rent receivable and Rent payable accounts.

We notice that the *two provisions* carried down appear as the opening figures for the year xxx7. Since they are Debit Balances they may rightly be described as Asset Provisions.

One more illustration may be taken of a provision, which is in the reverse direction.

Example 14.2

During xxx5, the first year of business, a merchant wrote off Bad Debts amounting to £100, and at 31 December made a provision for Doubtful Debts, amounting to £50.

During xxx6, a final dividend, £30, was received in respect of one of the debts (£40) written off in xxx5, further debts amounting to £60 were written off, and at 31 December xxx6, the merchant considered it prudent to make a provision against existing debts of 60% for one of £40, and 30% for one of £30.

In addition it was estimated that a final dividend of £0.75 in the £ would be received in xxx7 in respect of a debt standing in the books at £28.

You are required to produce, for the two years, the Bad Debts Account, Provision for Doubtful Debts Account, and (as far as possible) Profit and Loss Account.

In this example, we are instructed to open separately an account for the Provision for Doubtful Debts.

The recovery of £30 during xxx6 serves to reduce the expense of £60 for debts written off during that year, and the balance is transferred at the year end to the Provision Account. The Provision required at 31 December xxx6 is brought down as a Credit Balance on 1 January xxx7, and may as such be termed a Liability Provision.

Alternatively, the Profit and Loss Account for xxx6 could show a debit (charge) for Bad Debts of £30 and a credit of £10, being the difference between the opening provision of £50 and the required closing provision of £40. This would be a more accurate use of the two accounts.

Why do bad debts arise? Because the business has agreed to sell to a customer on a credit basis instead of requiring cash. Nobody *has* to grant credit, but it is often essential if you wish to sell your products and services. The decision should only be made after a review of the information provided by the customer when credit was requested.Usually this will include a bank reference, other suppliers who already give credit and one of the trade or commercial organisations who provide detailed reports. The credit controller can then decide whether to grant credit, and if so what the limit will be. (Similar to the procedure for a credit card from a bank for individuals.) After experience the account will be reviewed and if there is a satisfactory record of payments the credit limit will be increased, and if poor the facility will be withdrawn.

Nominal Ledger

BAD DEBTS

Dr		£			Cr
xxx5			xxx5		
Dec 31	Sundry customers' debts written off	100.00	Dec 31	Transfer to Profit and Loss A/c	100.00
xxx6			xxx6		
Dec 31	Sundry customers' debts written off	60.00	Jan 1	Cash, final dividend of £0.75 in £ on debt of £40.00 written off in xxx5	30.00
			Dec 31	Transfer to Provision For Doubtful Debts A/c	30.00
		£60.00			£60.00

Nominal Ledger

PROVISION FOR DOUBTFUL DEBTS

Dr			£			Cr
xxx5				xxx5		
Dec 31	Provision c/d, being provision at this date		50.00	Dec 31	Transfer to Profit and Loss A/c	50.00
xxx6				xxx6		
Dec 31	Transfer from Bad Debts A/c		30.00	Jan 1	Provision b/d	50.00
31	Provision c/d, being provisions at this date:			Dec 31	Transfer to Profit and Loss A/c	20.0
	X 60% of £40.00	£24.00				
	Y 30% of £30.00	9.00				
	Z 25% of £28.00	7.00				
			40.00			
			£70.00			£70.00
				xxx7		
				Jan 1	Provision b/d	40.00

Profit and Loss Accounts (extract)

Year ended 31 December xxx5

Dr	£		Cr
Bad debts, including Provision	150.00		

Year ended 31 December xxx6

Dr	£		Cr
Bad debts, less Recoveries, and including Provision	20.00		

Example 14.3

This illustrates the preparation of financial statements after the Trial Balance has been adjusted.

The Trial Balance of Bilton Potteries prepared after calculation of the gross profit is shown below.

Bilton Potteries

Trial Balance as at 31 January xxx9

Details	Debit £	Credit £
Capital		7 000
Premises	5 000	
Bank	3 218	
Debtors	434	
Stock (31 January xxx9)	1 000	
Creditors		870
Drawings	3 800	
Insurance	450	
Rent Receivable		225
Rates	500	
Wages	5 200	
Gross Profit for year ended 31 January xxx9		11 507
	£19 602	£19 602

A detailed review by the accountant revealed that the following adjustments were outstanding:

■ Rates amounting to £100 had been paid in advance.

■ Rent receivable of £75 was still outstanding at 31 January xxx9.

■ The insurance total included the payment of £50 for private house contents insurance.

■ Wages owing amounted to £300. An example of an accrual.

You are required to:

■ Open up the appropriate ledger accounts and post the above adjustments. Balance off these ledger accounts.

■ Prepare a profit and loss account for the year ended 31 January xxx9 and a balance sheet as at that date, after the above adjustments have been posted.

Note: As the gross profit has already been calculated the Trial Balance includes this item and the Stock at 31 January xxx9.

There are four accounts to be considered. All follow the same principle but think about them carefully and attempt to produce them before comparing with the solution.

Dr   **Rates**   Cr

xxx9			£	xxx9				£
Jan 31	Balance		500	Jan	31	In advance	c/f	100
					31	P & L a/c		400
			500					500
Feb 1	In adv b/f		100					

Dr   **Rent**   Cr

xxx9			£	xxx9				£
Jan 31	P & L a/c		300	Jan	31	Balance		225
					31	Due	c/f	75
			300					300
Feb 1	Due b/f		75					

Note that these are both debit balances, i.e. assets, but one is a payment in advance made by Bilton and the other is rent due to Bilton.

Dr   **Insurance**   Cr

xxx9			£	xxx9			£
Jan 31	Balance		450	Jan	31	to Drawings	50
					31	P & L a/c	400
			450				450

Dr   **Wages**   Cr

xxx9			£	xxx9			£
Jan 31	Balance		5200	Jan	31	P & L a/c	5500
	31	Owing c/d		300				
			5500				5500
				Feb	1	Due b/d	300

Consignment and Branch accounts

A Consignment account is used when a supplier has agreed to provide a customer with a stock of goods stored under the control of the customer but which remain the property of the supplier until the customer uses them.

Bilton Potteries

Profit and Loss Account for the year ended 31 January xxx9

			£	£
Gross profit brought forward				11 507
Rent receivable	(225 + 75)			300
				11 807
deduct Expenses				
	Wages	(5200 + 300)	5 500	
	Rates	(500 – 100)	400	
	Insurance	(450 – 50)	400	
				6 300
Net profit				5 507

Balance sheet as 31 January xxx9

			£	£	£
Fixed assets	Premises				5 000
Current assets	Stock			1 000	
	Payment in advance			100	
	Debtors	(434 + 75)		509	
	Bank			3 218	
				4 827	
deduct Current liabilities					
	Creditors		870		
	Wages due		300		
				1 170	
	Net current assets				3 657
	Total net assets				8 657
Representing					
Capital				7 000	
Profit for the year				5 507	
				12 507	
deduct drawings	(3 800 + 50)			3 850	
					8 657

Clearly the revenue and profit will not be recognised until the sale takes place. Until then it is usual to record the transfer of the stock from the supplier to the customer in a separate account, 'stock on consignment'.

If transferred at cost, when the customer notifies the supplier that he has used items which cost £1060 these will be evaluated at selling price. A sales invoice will be prepared and a transfer (supported by a Journal entry) from 'Stock on Consignment' to 'Cost of goods sold' will be made.

Sometimes the stock on consignment is valued at selling price. Then there must be a separate account 'Unrealised profit on stock on consignment' which will not become realised until the sale is recognised.

Similar accounting procedures may arise when there is a Branch for which some separate records are kept. The amount of authority given to the

Branch manager will affect the precise form of these records and accounts. Usually these will include stock, expenses and perhaps debtors subject to local control.

Example 14.4

Smart Goods Ltd has a branch at Southness and for control purposes keeps the books of account at head office.

All goods are purchased by head office and invoiced to the branch at cost price plus 50%.

The branch transactions during the year ended 31 December xxx1 were:

	£
Opening stock at invoice price	12 000
Branch debtors at 1 January xxx1	16 600
Goods sent by head office at invoice price	147 000
Credit Sales during the year	85 600
Cash Sales during the year	56 600
Goods returned to head office at invoice price	6 300
Petty cash balance at 31 December xxx1	30
Cash received from debtors and paid direct into head office Bank Account	83 900
Branch expenses paid direct by head office	14 500
Petty cash balance at 1 January xxx1	20

On the first day of each week the head office sent £40 to the branch for petty cash payments.

The result of the physical stocktaking on 31 December xxx1 agreed with the stocks account.

You are required to write up the following accounts for the year ended 31 December xxx1 for the Southness branch:

■ Stock account.

■ Branch adjustment account.

■ Debtors' account.

■ Petty cash account.

■ Profit and Loss account.

The books are kept by head office – the Branch may also keep its own memorandum records but we are not considering those.

In this example it is the 'Branch adjustment account' which reflects the unrealised profit movements following the transfer of stock and its subsequent sale.

The given data includes the assets of the branch at the beginning of the year, stock, debtors, petty cash balance and the unrealised profit on the stock. These four accounts can be opened remembering that the first three are debit balances and the last one, unrealised profit, a credit balance. Stock (Dr) at selling price minus unrealised profit (Cr) equals Stock (Dr) at cost price. The transactions for the year can be recorded in the accounts and the end of the year transfers to the Branch Profit and Loss Account provide a summary of the activities.

Prepare your own accounts before checking with the solution.

Dr		SOUTHNESS BRANCH STOCK ACCOUNT				Cr
xxx1			Fo	xxx1		Fo
Jan 1	Opening stock b/d		12 000	Dec 31	Goods returned	6 300
Dec 31	Goods from HO		147 000	31	Credit sales	85 600
				31	Cash sales	56 600
				31	Closing stock c/d	10 500
			159 000			159 000
	Opening stock b/d		10 500			

Dr		SOUTHNESS BRANCH ADJUSTMENT ACCOUNT				Cr
xxx1				xxx1		
Dec 31	Unrealised profit on goods returned		2 100	Jan 1	Unrealised profit on opening stock b/d	4 000
31	Gross profit realised during year		47 400	Dec 31	Unrealised profit on goods transferred	49 000
31	Unrealised profit in closing stock c/d		3 500			
			53 000			53 000
					Unrealised profit b/d	3 500

Dr		SOUTHNESS BRANCH DEBTORS ACCOUNT				Cr
xxx1			Fo	xxx1		Fo
Jan 1	Balances b/d		16 600	Dec 31	Cash received	83 900
Dec 31	Credit sales		85 600	31	Balances c/d	18 300
			102 200			102 200
	Balances b/d		18 300			

SOUTHNESS PETTY CASH ACCOUNT

xxx1			xxx1		
Jan 1	Balances b/d	20	Dec 31	Sundry expenses	2 070
Dec 31	Cash from HO	2 080	31	Balances c/d	30
		2 100			2 100
	Balances b/d	30			

SOUTHNESS BRANCH DEBTORS ACCOUNT

Profit and Loss Account
year to 31 December xxx1

Expenses by HO		14 500	Gross profit		47 400
Sundry petty cash expenses		2 070			
Profit		30 830			
		47 400			47 400

KEY POINTS

On completion of this chapter you should:

1 be aware of the reason for year end adjustments to the double entry accounts

2 be clear as to how adjustments to expenses (e.g. wages), stock and income (e.g. debtors) are made

3 be aware of how the adjustments are reflected in the Profit and Loss Account and Balance Sheet

4 be able to write up the appropriate records for consignment transactions and branch accounts.

Questions

1 Explain briefly the object of a bad debts reserve. Upon what basis is it usually formed? How does it affect the Profit and Loss Account and the Balance Sheet? Illustrate your answer with a specimen account.

2 During the year ended 31 December xxx9, C P Kilham made the following bad debts: A B, £13.13; X Y, £5.49; and R Z, £12.91.

Submit the entries Kilham should make when closing books as on 31 December xxx9.

3 X sets up in practice as a doctor on 1 January xxx2. During xxx2 the fees received were £33 545, and at the end of the year £237 was owing. During xxx3 the fees received were £33 831, and at the end of the year £364 was owing. The expenses amounted to £11 265 in xxx2 and £11 320 in xxx3, there being no liabilities outstanding at the end of either year.

Ascertain the profit for each of these years.

4 On 1 October xxx5, the Bad Debts Reserve Account of a business stood at £3768. During the ensuing twelve months bad debts amounting to £3389 were written off. On 30 June xxx6, a payment of £80 was received on account of a debt which had been treated as irrecoverable two years previously. The debts outstanding at 30 September xxx6 were examined, and the book-keeper was instructed to make a reserve of £3400 to cover the anticipated loss.

You are required to show the Ledger Account or Accounts as they appear after the closing of the books had been completed.

5 On 1 January xxx6, H Jacks owed J Dixon £220. On 31 March Jacks purchased goods from Dixon valued at £246, of which he returned goods to the value of £16 on 3 April. On 6 April Jacks paid Dixon £120 on account. On 1 July Dixon received notice of the bankruptcy of Jacks, and on 5 October he received first and final dividend of £0.35 in the £ from the Trustee in Bankruptcy. Show the account of H Jacks in the Ledger of J Dixon as it should appear after Dixon had balanced his books at 31 December xxx6.

6 The Rates Account of G Baker is shown in the Ledger as follows:

RATES ACCOUNT

xxx4
31 Dec   To Balance, in advance, b/f £360.
xxx5
31 May   To Cash, half-year to 30 September xxx5, £734.50.
18 Nov   To Cash, half-year to 31 March xxx6, £734.50.

Balance the account by transfer to Profit and Loss Account at 31 December xxx5, bringing forward the appropriate amount in advance. (Remember that rates are due on 31 March and 30 September.)

7 At 31 December xxx1, the Ledger of T Atkins contained the following balances for debts due:

	£
Arthur	436.08
Carol	215.50
Henry	314.09
Peggy	120.50

The estate of Arthur is being administered in Bankruptcy, and it is feared, pending realisation, that not more than £0.50 in the £ will be recoverable. Henry has died and his estate has no assets whatever. For the sake of prudence 5% is to be reserved on the debts of Carol and Peggy.

Show the four accounts, together with Bad Debts Account and Reserve for Doubtful Debts Account. Journal need not be given.

8 In xxx2 a trader, X, wrote off as a bad debt £319.77, the balance of an account due to him by Y.

In xxx3 Y paid the debt in full. Show by means of Journal entries how the recovery of this debt would be dealt with in closing X's book for xxx3, on the assumption that:

- the cash received was posted to the credit of Y's account.
- the cash was posted to a nominal account.

9 The payments made by X Ltd to its travellers on account of commission and salaries during xxx4 amounted to £121 547.18 and during xxx5 to £141 752.67. The amounts accrued and unpaid under this heading were as follows:

	£
31 December xxx3	2036.96
31 December xxx4	3441.18
31 December xxx5	3122.89

Draw up a statement showing the amount to be charged against profits in xxx4 and xxx5 respectively, and show what would have been the effect of accidentally omitting to make the proper reserve at the end of xxx4.

10 The Rent and Rates Account in the Ledger of Riley Bros showed that on 31 December xxx5, the rent for the quarter to Christmas was outstanding, and that the rates for the half-year ending 31 March xxx6, amounting to £876.38, had been paid. During the ensuing year the following payments relating to the rent and rates were made:

			£
Jan	4	Rent for Christmas quarter	590.00
Mar	29	Rent for Ladyday quarter	590.00
June	26	Rates for half-year ending 30 September xxx6	974.73
July	7	Rent for Midsummer quarter	590.00
Sept	30	Rent for Michaelmas quarter	590.00
Dec	28	Rent for Christmas quarter	590.00

The rates for the half-year ending 31 March xxx7, which amounted to £980.88, were paid on 6 January xxx7.

You are required to show the Rent and Rates Account as it would appear after the books for the year ended 31 December xxx6 had been closed. Make any calculations in months.

11 The financial year of Sanctions Ltd ended on 31 December xxx5.

At that date, the following balances appeared, among others, in their Nominal Ledger:

Rates, £3225 (15 months to 31 March xxx6).
Wages, £47 098 (to 27 December xxx5).
Stationery, Advertising, etc., £864.
Bad and Doubtful Debts, written off, £126.

The wages for the week ending 3 January xxx6 were £2562 (7-day week).

Stationery stocks for which an adjustment is required amounted to £117.

The Sundry Debtors totalled £5660, and a reserve is to be made of 5% for doubtful debts, and 2% for discounts.

Show the Ledger Accounts involved after giving effect to the above.

12 XY, who owed £200 to AB for goods supplied on 1 June xxx4, became unable to pay his debts in full and offered a composition of £0.25 in the £ to his creditors and this was accepted. A cheque for the dividend was received by AB on 1 December xxx4.

When XY called his creditors together, AB had on his premises a machine belonging to XY and claimed a right of lien in respect of it. This was admitted and the machine was valued at £80. AB's claim was consequently reduced by this amount.

AB decided that instead of selling the machine he would retain it as part of his plant. When making up his annual accounts on 31 December xxx4, the balance of XY's account was written off as a bad debt.

You are required to show, by means of Journal entries and Ledger Accounts, how the transactions would be recorded in AB's books.

13 In the books of Hazel Holborn at 31 December xxx6, the financial year end, the Ledger Account for 'Heat, Light, Power and Water' shows a Debit Balance of £1253. Investigation discloses the following points:

■ A deposit of £100 (returnable on cessation of supply) was paid on 1 April xxx6, in respect of electric power.

■ The charge for electric power is made quarterly, and the last debit in the account is for the three months to 30 November xxx6. The demand note for the three months to 28 February xxx6, amounted to £135.

■ A half-year's water rate, amounting to £94, was debited to the account in October xxx6, in respect of the period to 31 March xxx7.

Make such adjustments in the Ledger Account as appear to you to be necessary and state how, if at all, they would be shown in Holborn's Balance Sheet at 31 December xxx6.

14 The firm of J Clark & Son trades from both Head Office and a Branch depot. All purchases are made by Head Office and goods sent to the Branch are invoiced at cost. The Branch sells goods on credit and for cash.

The following information relates to the Branch for the financial year ended 31 December Year 8:

	£
Debtors at 1 January Year 8	5 720
Stock at 1 January Year 8	9 000
Stock at 31 December Year 8	8 340
Goods sent from Head Office	40 480
Goods returned to Head Office at cost	420
Cash sales	20 100
Credit sales	36 000
Allowances to credit customers	210
Returns from credit customers	330
Discount allowed to credit customers	1 440
Bad debts	360
Cash received from credit customers	29 520
Rates	1 080
Wages and salaries	3 600
Selling expenses	780

In the Head Office ledger of J Clark & Son, you are required to prepare the following accounts for the year ended 31 December Year 8:

- ■ Goods sent to Branch.
- ■ Branch Stock.
- ■ Branch Debtors.
- ■ Branch Profit and Loss.

15 DEPRECIATION

OBJECTIVES

In this chapter you will be introduced to the concept and practice of depreciation as a 'cost-spreading' activity performed by businesses who purchase and use Fixed Assets. This chapter introduces the two primary depreciation methods commonly used – the straight-line method and the diminishing or reducing balance method.

We have seen in the preceding chapter how very important it is that all matters affecting the determination of true profit shall be properly taken into account whenever an attempt is made to produce a Trading and Profit and Loss Account and a Balance Sheet. Thus, any outstanding income, even though not actually received yet in cash, and any expense incurred but not yet paid must, if relating to the period under review, be provided for either as an *Asset or a Liability Provision*.

In doing so, we are taking steps to ensure *the genuineness of the profit figure* which the Profit and Loss Account discloses, but we should not forget that the Balance Sheet drawn up at the end of the period likewise calls for attention. If the Balance Sheet is concerned with the proprietor's Capital, and the property or Assets by which it is represented, it is just as necessary to consider the correctness of the values put upon these Assets. Generally speaking, it is sufficient for the Assets as a whole to be shown at their 'going concern' values, i.e. at a figure which reflects their worth to the business as an established concern, producing a normal and reasonable profit on the total Capital invested. By way of contrast we can speak of *break-up* values of the property, representing its realisable value if sold in the market. Between the two, there is a very wide gap, particularly noticeable with Fixed Assets, as distinct from Current Assets.

Examples of Current Assets are:

- Stock in Trade, and
- Book Debts or Debtors

and we have seen that they are typical of the property *in which the business is dealing from day to day.* The Stock held by the business must be capable of sale at the prevailing market price; Book Debts must also (usually) be capable of collection from customers at their full value.

We can, therefore, appreciate that for Current Assets, the test of their *realisable value* is all-important, and their *book value* shown in the Books of Account should not be in excess of this value.

In the case of Fixed Assets, however, being property *purchased for retention* and *not* for *resale*, altogether different considerations apply. Examples of this class of property are:

- plant and machinery
- motor vehicles for delivering goods to customers.

Without assets such as these the business cannot begin to function, and they are clearly an essential part of its Capital equipment.

Although these assets may last for a number of years, because they represent property *used* for the purpose of the business, we have to recognise that they will not last forever. Therefore, although they are retained within the business, a limit must be set to their *effective working life*, or the period of time during which they can be economically operated. Beyond this period, no matter how carefully they have been repaired and overhauled, it will usually be found that charges for renewals and replacements of parts are increasing to the point that *these Assets must be replaced.*

The effective working life will naturally vary between one class of Fixed Asset and another; sometimes it may be from 20 to 30 years, while with motor vehicles three to five years is often the maximum period during which useful service can be rendered to the business.

As a result, we can recognise a progressive shrinkage in value of these classes of property, which we term *depreciation*, and it is very important that we take a note of it as a *shrinkage of value caused by the use of the property for the purpose of profit-earning.*

We can extend this idea, and argue that against the profits earned in each trading year should be put as an expense the depreciation estimated to have taken place during that trading year.

In other words, we may say that the loss in value is just as truly a business expense as the wages paid to workpeople, or the charge for rent and rates.

The real working expenses will be understated if the factor of depreciation is ignored year by year, and ultimately, when the machinery is worn out, or obsolete, the proprietor of the business may have to introduce fresh Capital to replace it, or else shut down.

This point of view brings us to the second reason for charging depreciation. Net Profit as determined by the preparation of the Trading and Profit and Loss Account is the yield upon the Capital invested, and may be wholly withdrawn by the proprietor in the form of cash. If depreciation is charged as a business expense, this Profit figure will be accordingly reduced, and also the amount of *cash withdrawable from the business*. Put in yet another way, cash or its equivalent, representing the charge for depreciation, will be retained within the business, and may, over a period of time, accumulate to provide the amount required for eventual replacement. Although making a charge for depreciation reduces profit, the charge by itself does not provide extra cash for the business. The cash that is not distributed becomes part of the total resources of the business and may be used for any purpose. If it is used for some other purpose it will not necessarily be available to buy a replacement.

For these reasons, it is the general practice to depreciate or *write down* the Fixed Assets, usually on a percentage basis. This calculation is usually performed annually when the Final Accounts are to be prepared.

The result is that we have:

- ■ a Debit to Profit and Loss Account, and
- ■ a Credit to the particular Asset Depreciation Account.

The two methods most generally employed are:

- ■ the Straight Line, or Fixed Instalment method
- ■ the Diminishing Balance, or Reducing Instalment method.

They have in common the fact that a percentage of either the cost or book value of the Asset is written off against profits period by period, with or without allowance for any *residual* or *scrap* value.

Straight-line (or fixed instalment) method

The straight-line method relies on writing off yearly a part of the *original or purchase cost*. When the Asset is bought its effective working life is estimated as being a certain number of years, and the difference between cost and estimated residual value is recovered at the same rate per month or year over this period.

Example 15.1

Sanders and Son have a delivery van which cost £13 185 on 1 January xxx5. Depreciation is to be provided using the straight-line method over a period of three years, at the end of which it is expected that it will be bought back by the supplier for £2400. Show the Ledger Account of the Asset and the Asset Depreciation Account in the firm's books for the years xxx5, xxx6 and xxx7.

Calculation of depreciation

	£
original cost	13 185
resale value	2 400
loss in value	= 10 785
over 3 years, i.e.	£3 595 per annum

At 31 December xxx5 the van would appear in the Balance Sheet as below, being the balances on the two accounts:

Assets		
	£	£
Delivery van at cost	13 185.00	
Less Depreciation	3 595.00	
		9 590.00

i.e. its net book value would then be £9590 only, the cost minus the depreciation.

At 31 December xxx5 the depreciation balance relates to the charge for the year. At 31 December xxx6 it will be £7190 and is the total (**or aggregate**) for the two years. At 31 December xxx6, the van will be sold so will not appear in the Balance Sheet for that date. There will be a charge for Depreciation in the Profit and Loss Account for the year ended on that date, 31 December xxx6. Depreciation is usually charged on assets in use at the beginning of a year. Sometimes, particularly for high cost items, straight line depreciation may be charged in relation to months instead of on a yearly basis.

Private Ledger

DELIVERY VAN

Dr							Cr
Date	Details	Fo	Amount	Date	Details	Fo	Amount
xxx5			£	xxx5			£
Jan 1	Cash, Purchase cost		13 185.00	Dec 31	Balance	c/d	13 185.00
			£13 185.00				£13 185.00
xxx6				xxx6			
Jan 1	Balance	b/d	£13 185.00	Dec 31	Balance	c/d	£13 185.00
xxx7				xxx7			
Jan 1	Balance	b/d	£13 185.00	Dec 31	Transfer to disposal of delivery van A/c		13 185.00
			£13 185.00				£13 185.00

PROVISION FOR DEPRECIATION OF DELIVERY VAN

Dr							Cr
Date	Details	Fo	Amount	Date	Details	Fo	Amount
xxx5			£	xxx5			£
Dec 31	Balance	c/d	3 595.00	Dec 31	Transfer to Profit & Loss A/c		3 595.00
xxx6				xxx6			
Dec 31	Balance	c/d	7 190.00	Jan 1	Balance	b/d	3 595.00
				Dec 31	Transfer to Profit & Loss A/c		3 595.00
			£7 190.00				£7 190.00
xxx7				xxx7			
Dec 31	Transfer to disposal of delivery van A/c		10 785.00	Jan 1	Balance	b/d	7 190.00
				Dec 31	Transfer to Profit & Loss A/c		3 595.00
			£10 785.00				£10 785.00

DELIVERY VAN DISPOSAL ACCOUNT

Dr | | | | | | | | Cr

Date	Details	Fo	Amount	Date	Details	Fo	Amount
xxx7			£	xxx7			£
Dec 31	Transfer cost	JI	13 185.00	Dec 31	Transfer Accumulated depreciation	JI	10 785.00
				31	Sale	CBI	2 400.00
			£13 185.00				£13 185.00

When the van has been sold at 31 December xxx7 journal entries will transfer the cost of the van and the balance on the van depreciation accounts to a van disposal account. The Debits and Credits are equal and this means that all the loss in value over the three years has been charged to the Profit and Loss Account.

If the accumulated depreciation plus sales proceeds did not equal cost the difference would be transferred to the Profit and Loss Account. In practice it would be usual to have a small difference. A large difference might suggest that the depreciation rate had not been estimated correctly. If the accumulated depreciation plus sales proceeds are less than the cost then there is an additional charge to the Profit and Loss Account, i.e. Dr Profit and Loss Account, Cr Disposal Account.

Diminishing (or reducing) balance method

In this case, *a fixed percentage is written off the book value* of the Asset as it appears *at the commencement of each year*. This method is sometimes used by smaller firms, usually for assets with a small value. Most firms would keep a detailed register for each particular motor car or lorry and for each significant item of plant and machinery.

Example 15.2

At 1 January xxx6, the balance on the Plant and Tools Account was £4730. During the year a lathe was purchased costing £575, and on 31 March xxx7, three drilling machines which cost £900 when purchased three years ago were sold for £520.

Show the Asset Account, reckoning depreciation at 10% per annum on the diminishing balance method.

Private Ledger

PLANT AND TOOLS

Dr   Cr

Date	Details	Fo	Amount	Date	Details	Fo	Amount
xxx6			£	xxx6			£
Jan 1	Balance	b/d	4730.00	Dec 31	Profit & Loss A/c Depreciation 10% of £4730.00		473.00
June 30	Cash Lathe		575.00	31	Balance	c/d	4832.00
			£5305.00				£5305.00
xxx7				xxx7			
Jan 1	Balance	b/d	4832.00	Dec 31	Cash 3 Drilling Machines sold		520.00
				31	Profit & Loss A/c Loss on sale		136.10
				31	Profit & Loss Depreciation 10% on £4832.00		483.20
				31	Balance	c/d	3692.70
			£4832.00				£4832.00
xxx8							
Jan 1	Balance	b/d	£3692.70				

	N.B.	Cost three years ago	900.00
		1 year 10%	90.00
			810.00
		2nd year 10%	81.00
			729.00
		3rd year 10%	72.90
			656.10
		Selling price	520.00
		Loss:	£136.10

At 31 December xxx6, the following would appear in the Balance Sheet:

Assets

Plant	£	£
At 1.1.xxx6	4730.00	
Add Additions at Cost	575.00	
	5305.00	
Less Depreciation at 10% per annum	473.00	
		4832.00

Although this is the net book value (NBV) it does not show the aggregate cost and depreciation provided which 'best practice' would consider desirable. This is why separate asset and depreciation accounts, as in example 15.1, are preferable.

The reducing balance method is open to the criticism that Fixed Assets so depreciated tend to be dealt with in groups, and that with ordinary rates of depreciation its slowness in writing down the values is not sufficiently recognised. If the life of the asset is short the percentage required may be prohibitively high; e.g. to depreciate a tool having a life of three years only would require a 90% rate.

The Journal is used to avoid making a Prime Entry in the particular Ledger Account:

Example 15.3

xxx6			Dr	Cr
Dec 31			£	£
	Profit and Loss A/c	Dr	473.00	
	Plant and Tools Depreciation A/c			473.00
	Being depreciation at 10% p.a. now written off.			

As the example shows, an account for Depreciation as a business expense may be opened in the Nominal or Private Ledger, *but the Debit Balance on it must ultimately be transferred to Profit and Loss Account.*

Comparison of the two methods

A comparison of the two methods using the data in 15.1 is shown below.

The reducing (or diminishing) balance would require 43.5% (approximately) to be written off each year.

			Straight-line depreciation
Cost		13 185	
Yrx5	Depreciation	5 735	3 595
	Net book value	7 450	
Yrx6	Depreciation	3 241	3 595
	Net book value	4 209	
Yrx7	Depreciation	1 831	
	Net book value	2 378	3 595

This is less than the amount received for the van at 31 December xxx7 so there would be a small surplus on the sale of the motor van.

The depreciation charged using the straight-line method is shown above for comparison. You can see that the straight-line method charges much less in xxx5 but much more in xxx7.

KEY POINTS

On completion of this chapter you should:

1 be aware of the need for depreciation of fixed assets

2 be capable of calculating depreciation charges for the final accounts using the two methods shown – straight-line method and reducing balance method

3 be able to draw up the double entry records for depreciation

4 be clear as to how these accounts affect the calculation of Profit or Loss of a business and its financial position in the form of a Balance Sheet.

Questions

1 How is the shrinkage in the value of fixed assets provided for in accounts kept on the double entry principle?

2 Explain briefly, but as clearly as you can, why it is generally necessary when preparing the accounts of a business to make provision for depreciation of the fixed assets.

If you know of any exceptions to this general rule, mention them and give your reasons

3 On 1 January xxx1, a business purchased a delivery van for £8800. Show how the account would appear in the books of the business for the four following years assuming that depreciation is written off **a** by the fixed instalment method, and **b** by the diminishing balance method, the rate of depreciation being 20% in each case.

State, giving your reasons shortly, which method of depreciation you consider is more appropriate for an asset of this sort.

4 On 1 January xxx2, Dix Ltd purchased machinery costing £1240. For the years xxx2, xxx3 and xxx4 depreciation was written off at the rate of 5% on the diminishing balance. During xxx5, it became apparent that the machinery would not be of service after 31 December xxx6, and for these latter two years the fixed

instalment method was substituted to write off the remaining balance. In December xxx6, the machinery realised £15 on sale. You are required to write up the Machinery Account (including depreciation) from the commencement, determining depreciation to the nearest £.

5 X Ltd purchased a seven-year lease of certain shop premises for £8000. A further sum of £2000 was expended in various alterations, and it was estimated that at the end of the lease the cost of restoring the premises to their original condition (for which the company was liable) would be about £500.

Show the Ledger Account for the first two years, providing for depreciation.

6 From the following particulars, write up the Machinery Account for the year ended 30 November xxx6.

The balance from the previous year was £26 882.

On 31 May xxx6, new machinery was purchased for £1164, and wages amounting to £124 were paid for its erection. The old machinery replaced by the above was sold for £144, which was its written-down value on 30 November xxx5.

Depreciation at the rate of 12½% per annum is to be written off (for this question half a year is significant – only half a year of depreciation should be included for the items purchased and sold).

7 The Balance Sheet of PQ & Co Ltd, drawn up as on 31 March xxx7, showed plant and machinery valued, after writing off depreciation, at £25 500.

Depreciation had been written off regularly, from the dates of purchase of the various items, at the rate of 10% per annum on the diminishing value.

On 1 June xxx7, a vehicle, which had been bought on 1 November xxx2, for £5750, was sold for £1250 and replaced by a new one costing £7700.

Show the Plant and Machinery Account as it would appear in the Company's books for the year ended 31 March xxx8, after writing off the appropriate depreciation for the year. (For this question work in months.)

8 CD purchased factory premises (subject to a lease of 10 years from 30 June xxx0) from the Liquidator of H Ltd on 30 June xxx4, the purchase price being £30 000.

To enable him to complete the purchase, he borrowed £16 500 from Happy Bank Ltd, the loan being repayable in three years by equal annual instalments of principal, reckoning interest at 10% per annum. Provide depreciation on the fixed instalment basis, and show the Property Account and the Loan Account in CD's books for the three years to 30 June xxx7.

9 On 1 January xxx4, a manufacturer acquired a machine at a cost of £1200.

During xxx4 repairs to the machine cost £50 and a new attachment, which cost £250, was added to it.

The repairs during the year xxx5 amounted to £180.

It was decided to depreciate the machine at the rate of 10% per annum on the reducing instalment method.

From the foregoing particulars you are required to write up the Machinery Account for the two years ended 31 December xxx5.

10 The following is the Trial Balance extracted from the books of J Falconer at 31 December xxx6.

	Dr £	Cr £
Salaries	12 414.00	
Discounts received		132.00
Repairs and renewals	318.00	
Sales		68 505.00
Carriage outwards	163.00	
Creditors, including VAT		674.00
Wages	26 116.00	
Sundry expenses	86.00	
Sundry debtors	3 445.00	
Commission	196.00	
Capital, 1 January xxx6		7 200.00
Stock, 1 January xxx6	1 572.00	
Discounts allowed	578.00	
Returns outwards		295.00
Plant and machinery, 1 January xxx6	7 460.00	
Cash in hand	2.00	
Purchases	7 336.00	
Rates	3 575.00	
Warehouse expenses	4 537.00	
Office fixtures, etc., 1 January xxx6	4 200.00	
Cash at bank	1 200.00	
Rent of premises	2 788.00	
Drawings	1 000.00	
Bad debts reserve, 1 January xxx6		200.00
	£77 006.00	£77 006.00

You are required to prepare:

    a Trading and Profit and Loss Account for the year to 31 December xxx6.

    b Balance Sheet at 31 December xxx6, showing per cent net Profit to Capital at 1 January xxx6.

Note: The following adjustments are necessary:

    ■ the stock on hand at 31 December xxx6, was valued at £1769

    ■ three months' rates are prepaid in the sum of £715

■ the rent of premises is £3717 per annum, payable quarterly, and has been paid to 29 September xxx6

■ depreciation is to be charged at 5% on plant and machinery, and 10% on office fixtures, etc.

11 Give the Journal entries necessary to record the following transactions:

Dec 2 Bought fixtures and fittings value £345 on credit from S Maxton and Sons.

15 A cheque value £76.25 received from Perkins Ltd was wrongly posted to Brampton Bros' Account.

19 Exchanged one motor car value £1220 for three typewriters value £200 each and the balance in cash.

31 Plant and machinery is to be depreciated by £2173.

31 O Carfax, a debtor for £55, having become insolvent, pays £0.20 in the £ settlement of the amount owing.

12 A firm acquired a 25 years' lease of its business premises for £18 000 at the beginning of the year. The firm's bankers advanced £12 000 towards the purchase price on the security of the lease.

Repayment of the bank loan is made by monthly instalments, in advance, of £250 which the bank debit to the firm's current account together with interest at the rate of 10% per annum on the balance at the beginning of the year.

You are required to make the entries in the firm's books at the end of the first year to record the above arrangements, including depreciation of the lease according to the method you consider most suitable in the circumstances.

16 | CLUBS, SOCIETIES AND CHARITY BOOK-KEEPING

OBJECTIVE

To introduce two simpler forms of a Trading and Profit and Loss Account often used by clubs, societies and charities where the aim of the organisation is to provide a service rather than make as much profit as possible.

Basic recording

In the smaller 'not-for-profit' organisations the usual basic objective will be to record the receipt and payment of cash and cheques – the role of the Cash and Bank Books. Without the use of a purchases or sale journal the Cash and Bank Books provide most of the required information by the use of analysis columns – just like those we have already used for the analysis of purchases and sales, and illustrated for the Petty Cash Book.

A similar analysis, totalled for the year, provides the total receipts and payments. These can then be used to produce a Receipts and Payments Account or an Income and Expenditure Account.

Receipts and Payments Account

If the organisation is so small that it does not bother with the adjustments for debtors, creditors, accrued expenses or prepayments then the revenue statement is called a **Receipts and Payments Account**. This is nothing more than a summary of the cash and bank book. In the horizontal layout it will show, as the cash book does, the income on the debit (left-hand) side and the balance sheet will not be required.

Like the cash book, the first entry will be the balance of cash in hand and at the bank, followed by all the receipts suitable classified and the total will represent the whole of the resources available to the organisation. Similarly with the payments. All the payments will be shown as expenditure, whether they are revenue items or capital items. The balance – the difference between the opening balance plus receipts minus the payments – equals the closing balance of cash in hand and at the bank.

There is no need for a balance sheet but it may be appropriate to show in a brief note the value of assets used and any liabilities.

Example 16.1

The Hixley Arts Club started meeting on 1 April xxx7. The analysis and summary of the Cash and Bank receipts and Expenditure Book for the year to 31 March xxx8 produced the following amounts:

	£
	£
Members' subscriptions	475
Sales of refreshments	275
Annual outing ticket sales	200
Sundry expenses	160
Rent	230
Purchase of refreshments	235
Annual outing expenses	50
Purchase of equipment	75

Prepare a Receipts and Payments Account for the financial year ended 31 March xxx8.

Using the vertical layout:

THE HIXLEY ARTS CLUB
Receipts and Payments Account
year ended 31 March xxx8

	£	£
Balance at beginning of the year		0
Receipts: Members' subscriptions	475	
Sales of refreshments	275	
Ticket sales for annual outing	200	
Total receipts	950	
Payments: Rent	230	
Sundry expenses	160	
Purchase of refreshments	235	
Annual outing expenses	50	
Purchase of equipment	75	
Total payments	750	
Surplus of receipts over payments		200
Balance at end of year		200
(represented by cash in hand and at bank		

Although this layout provides totals for receipts and expenditure, which may be useful, most readers would prefer to see related items brought together, to show the net result of that activity:

		£	£
Members' subscriptions			475
Refreshments: Sales		275	
Purchases		235	
	Surplus		40
Annual outing: Receipts		200	
Expenses		50	
	Surplus		150
			665
Rent		230	
Sundry expenses		160	
Purchases of equipment		75	
			465
	Surplus for the year		200
Add: Balance at beginning of year			–
Balance at end of year			200

There is no distinction between revenue and capital items as all expenditure has been included in this statement so there is nothing to record in a balance sheet. The only asset is the amount of cash in hand and at the bank which is shown at the end of the statement. Equipment costing £75 has been purchased and in practice a note would be made so that it was not forgotten or lost.

Remember that both these formats reflect only the Receipts and Payments. No adjustments have been made to reflect Debtors, Creditors, unpaid bills, etc. If these items are significant then to show a fairer picture they should be reflected in a slightly more complicated statement – the income and expenditure account.

Income and Expenditure Account

Like the Receipts and Payments Account this is based on an analysis and summary of the cash receipts and payments. Adjustments are made for debtors, creditors and other items, in particular, subscriptions and capital items to ensure that everything relating to the accounting period is included. A balance sheet will also be prepared.

Example 16.2

The balance sheet of the Spartan Fitness Society at 31 December Year 4 showed:

		£
Equipment at valuation		23 100
Subscriptions due for Year 4		265
Prepaid rent		126
Bank		2 976
	£	26 467
Less: Subscriptions in advance for Year 5	195	
Accrued expenses	55	
		250
Total net assets		26 217
Club Fund		26 217

During Year 5:

■ Subscriptions received were:	£
– for Year 4	265
– for Year 5	20 975
– for Year 6	94
■ Rent paid	4 840
■ Staff salaries paid	13 280
■ Equipment purchased	2 940
■ Other expenses paid	1 086

At the end of Year 5:

■ Club equipment is valued at	24 190
■ Subscriptions are owing for Year 5	180
■ Other expenses due	40
■ Rent prepaid	135

You are required to:
■ Prepare an Income and Expenditure Account for the Spartan Fitness Society for the year ended 31 December Year 5.

Note: In a horizontal Income and Expenditure Account, income appears on the Credit (right-hand) side and expenditure on the Debit (left-hand) side.

■ Present the Balance Sheet of the Society as at 31 December Year 5.

There are several new items in this example.

Firstly the subscriptions. Many societies treat this on a cash basis, but not Spartan. No new principles are used but you should think carefully about the entries which should appear in the account.

Subscriptions

Year 5			£	Year 5			£
Jan 1	Due for year 4	b/f	265	Jan 1	In advance for year 5	b/f	195
Dec 31	In advance for year 6	c/f	94	Dec 31	Subs received during year	c/f	21 334
31	I & E a/c		21 350	31	Due for year 5	c/f	180
			21 709				21 709
Year 6				Year 5			
Jan 1	Due for year 5	b/f	180	Jan 1	In advance for year 6	b/f	94

Secondly there is the equipment at valuation. At the beginning of the year this was £23 100 and equipment purchased during the year amounted to £2 940. Adding these together gives a total of £26 040 but the year end valuation was £24 190, a difference of £1850. At this stage it can be recognised as a loss of value, i.e. an expense for the year, usually called depreciation, as was discussed in Chapter 15.

Finally, before the financial statements are produced, the bank balance should be calculated.

			£
Opening balance, from the old balance sheet			2 976
add receipts during the year, subscriptions			21 334
			24 310
deduct payments,	Rent	4 840	
	Staff salaries	13 280	
	Equipment	2 940	
	Other expenses	1 086	
			22 146
Balance at 31 December Year 5			2 164

Note: this reconciliation should be made at regular intervals, say monthly.

Spartan Fitness Society

Income and expenditure account for the year ended 31 December Year 5

Expenditure		£	Income	£
Staff salaries		13 280	Subscriptions for year 5	21 350
Loss in value of equipment		1 850		
Rent paid	(126 + 4840 – 135)	4 831		
Other expenses	(1086 – 55 + 40)	1 071		
Surplus for the year		318		
		21 350		21 350

The question suggested a horizontal format for the revenue statement but many societies use the vertical, and the vertical will be used for the balance sheet.

Balance Sheet at 31 December Year 5

		£	£	£
Fixed assets	Equipment at valuation			24 190
Current assets	Subscriptions owing		180	
	Rent in advance		135	
	Bank balance		2 164	
Total current assets			2 479	
deduct current liabilities				
	Subscriptions in advance	94		
	Other expenses due	40		
Total current liabilities			134	
Net current assets				2 345
Total net assets				26 535
Representing				
Society fund at the beginning of the year			26 217	
Surplus arising during the year			318	
Total Society fund at end of the year				26 535

KEY POINTS

You should now be able to

1 prepare a Receipts and Payments Account

2 prepare an Income and Expenditure Account and the related Balance Sheet.

Note: Two publications by the Charity Commissions which provide useful additional information are *CC54 Accounting for the smaller charity on the receipts and payments basis* and *CC55 Accruals accounting for the smaller charity.*

Questions

1 The Broadway Needlecraft Society was formed on 1 September xxx7. The Treasurer has recorded all receipts and payments in the Cash and Bank Book. At the end of the year, 31 August xxx8, the summary of receipts and payments showed:

	£
Members' subscriptions	1425
Sundry expense	480
Rent	390
Rates	300
Annual dance expenses	150
Sales of dance tickets	600
Equipment	225
Purchases of refreshments	705
Sales of refreshments	825

Additional information from the records showed that there was an unpaid bill for printing for the dance for £25, which is regarded as a 'sundry'. Note also that the amount paid for rates included £30 in respect of the next year.

You are required to:

    a prepare a Receipts and Payments Account for the financial year

    b prepare an Income and Expenditure Account for the financial year

    c calculate the accumulated fund on 31 August xxx8

    d explain why the sundry expenses and rates amounts in the Income and Expenditure Account differs from the amounts shown in the Receipts and Payments Account.

2 The Borough Social Club presents you with the following Receipts and Payments Account for the year ended 31 July xxx7.

You are required to compile an Income and Expenditure Account for that year. The profit or loss on each activity should be clearly shown. A Balance Sheet at 31 August xxx7 should also be prepared.

The following information is to be taken into consideration:

Stocks held at the beginning of the year, Refreshments £60, Stationery £10. Both stocks were nil at the end of the year. Dance prizes to the value of £100 had not been awarded and would be used in the following year.

Receipts and Payments Account for the year ended 31 August xxx7

Receipts	£	Payments	£
Balance at beginning	1000	Draw prizes	250
Subscriptions	3500	Printing of draw tickets	50
Sales of draw tickets	1000	Hire of dance band	250
Sales of dance tickets	2500	Prizes for dances	500
Sales of flowers after		Flower show prizes	150
flower show	50	Purchase of refreshments	700
Flower show entry fees	50	Purchase of new tables	
Sales of refreshments	1750	and chairs	1500
		Purchase of crockery	100
		Printing of dance tickets	60
		Cleaning	1855
		Heating and lighting	700
		Rates	345
		Postage and stationery	100
		Balance at end of year	3290
	£9850		£9850

3 The Bumpy Pitch Cricket and Social Club produced the following Trial Balance on 31 December xxx7.

	Dr £	Cr £
Capital at 1 January xxx7		21 360
Clubhouse	20 000	
Club room equipment	4 200	
Sports equipment	2 700	
Sale of refreshments		2 430
Purchase of refreshments	1 850	
Interest free loan from a member		5 000
Subscriptions received for xxx7		3 700
Subscription outstanding from xxx6	50	
Receipts from club room games		1 820
Maintenance of games and sports equipment	975	
Postages	305	
Sundry expenses	685	
Printing and stationery	715	
Wages (50% refreshments, 50% cleaning)	2 080	
Cash at bank	620	
Cash in hand	130	
	£34 310	£34 310

You are required to prepare:

> **a** an account to show the profit or loss on sale of refreshments
>
> **b** the Income and Expenditure Account for the year ended 31 December xxx7 and a Balance Sheet at that date.

The following information is to be taken into account:

> ■ sports equipment is to be depreciated at 20% per annum and club room equipment at 10% per annum.
>
> ■ Subscriptions due for xxx7 and not yet paid £150. Assume that all unpaid subscriptions will be paid eventually.
>
> ■ There is an unrecorded account for refreshments amounting to £120.
>
> ■ The stock of refreshments on hand at 31 December xxx7 was £160.

4 The following particulars relate to the Riverside Social Club for the year ended 31 December xxx8. From them prepare the club's Income and Expenditure Account and Balance Sheet for presentation to the members.

	£
Capital account (1 January xxx8)	3370
Book value of Games and Dramatic Equipment (1 January xxx8)	1050
Book value of Furniture and Fittings (1 January xxx8)	970
Cash at bank (31 December xxx8)	1180
Petty cash in hand	50
Payments during the year	
Rent of premises	2500
Rates	580
Printing and stationery	170
Postages	100
Sundry expenses	60
Purchase of new Games Equipment	280
Expenses of Dramatic Performances	290
Repairs and cleaning	330
Lighting and heating	200
Receipts during the year	
Subscriptions for xxx8	3920
Sales of tickets for Dramatic Performances	430
Catering officer – profit from refreshments	40

The following matters must also be taken into account:

> ■ subscriptions due but unpaid for xxx8 amount to £180
>
> ■ rates paid in respect of next year, £120
>
> ■ expenses still unpaid for the last Dramatic Performance, £10
>
> ■ electricity account unpaid, £80
>
> ■ the old Games and Dramatic equipment is to be depreciated by 20%, that purchased in the year by 10%, and the Furniture and Fittings by £100.

17 | INFORMATION TECHNOLOGY AND BOOK-KEEPING

OBJECTIVE

This chapter introduces the reader to the use of Information Technology in Book-keeping. It briefly discusses what types of function a computer is designed to perform, describes the role the computer could play in the function of keeping business accounts, and describes how this might change the way in which the Book-keeping function is organised.

Although this Teach Yourself text has referred to the use of information technology in various places it largely assumes you will be doing book-keeping work by hand. For a small business, or for keeping your personal accounts, this may be the case in reality. However, as a business grows, producing accounts by hand can become very difficult to do and a computer can often be used to reduce the workload and improve the usefulness of accounting information.

As the book-keeper it is *very* important that you understand what the computer is doing in order to give it the right information and to enable you to understand what it produces. A certain amount of the routine work, however, such as posting entries and doing arithmetic, can be taken over by the machine. This chapter introduces you to the use of the computer in this way.

Basic functions of the computer

A computer has four basic functions to perform that are repeated in almost all uses of this technology.

■ Handling inputting of data – using the pieces of the computer such as the keyboard and the mouse a computer user can input data into the computer.

- Storing data – once the information has been input into the computer it will need to be stored in some way to prevent the need for it to be input again next time. The computer will use devices that can store information electronically for this purpose, such as computer disks.
- Manipulating data – having got the data into the computer it will be possible to ask it to manipulate the data for you in almost whatever way is appropriate for the job you need to perform.
- Output data – the results of the computer's manipulation of data will need to be shown to the computer user. This may be performed via a computer screen, on paper via a printer, or stored back onto a computer disk to be used as input to future manipulations.

The pieces that go together to make up a computer can be separated into two groups – hardware and software. Hardware refers to the pieces of the computer that you can touch and see, such as the keyboard, the mouse and the computer screen. The software refers to the instructions that are given to the computer to describe what it should do with the data you have given it.

People who write software for computers will often put together sets of instructions to perform standard tasks that can then be reused by other people. These sets of software instructions are referred to as computer packages. Packages can be designed to fulfil very general functions such as spreadsheets and databases, or to perform more specific functions. Packages designed to help with book-keeping functions are examples of this latter kind of package.

Role of information technology in business

Information technology in the form of the computer has been applied to a wide range of business activities. They have been used to perform tasks including word-processing, such as typing and storing client correspondence, for statistical analysis, such as performance data analysis, and to help in planning of future activities. They are also useful in supporting electronic communications and information handling using ways of linking different computers together, such as the Internet.

Computers and book-keeping

Computers are very good at manipulating numbers and can therefore do many of the tasks that make up the book-keeping function. Computer packages are available to help with a number of these functions, or just to take over the role of one of the functions. In either case the computer will need to be integrated with the normal manual book-keeping system that will supply the input data and then use the computer output. The computer will become part of the book-keeping role.

The book-keeping functions most commonly taken over by a computer, either singly or in an integrated form, are:

- managing the Books of Prime Entry
- managing the Sales Ledger
- managing the Purchase Ledger
- managing the General Ledger
- production of a Trial Balance and Final Accounts.

Where the computer package performs all of these tasks the user will be required to enter the data from the source documents into the computer, which will then complete the Books of Prime Entry and post the correct totals to the Ledgers automatically. The user will be able to view what the computer has done at any stage of the operation in the same way as a user is able to view the manual process. They will also be able to correct errors that occur due to changes in circumstances or incorrect information given to the computer at the start of the process.

The computer will store the information added by the user over a period of time and will output the account information on request. At the end of the book-keeping period the computer package will produce a Trial Balance or Final Accounts using the data it has stored during the period.

In some cases it may be desirable not to use a totally integrated package of the nature just described. It is possible to use a computer to perform one of the functions and continue to keep the rest of the accounts manually in the way described in the rest of this text.

Advantages of using a computer in book-keeping

The use of a computer as part of a book-keeping function offers the user a number of benefits over an entirely manual system.

- ■ Accuracy is improved – as a computer is not prone to arithmetic and procedure errors like humans, once the correct data has been entered, correct principles will be applied throughout the computer's operation and all the arithmetic will be performed correctly. This greatly reduces the likelihood of errors occurring in the book-keeping process.

- ■ Storage of data is better – as the computer must store information between its data manipulation stages, the need to keep manual records is reduced. The computer can also reuse data entered for one purpose for other reasons so information only needs to be kept in one place for all the uses to which the business may wish to put it.

- ■ Flexible access to data – the computer offers the user more flexible access to the data by helping them to look at it in different ways, to output it in different forms and formats and to use it as input to other packages.

- ■ Traceable history – the computer will keep an accurate listing of all the actions it has performed so that they can be retraced if it is necessary. This is useful when looking to correct errors or to check the accounts are accurate.

Management of information technology in book-keeping

Although the computer may take over a number of the routine functions of the book-keeping, it will be rare that the knowledgeable book-keeper can be done away with when a computer is introduced. There is still the need for someone who is experienced in the recording function to assess what the computer has generated and to ensure the correctness of the accounts it has produced. There is also still a data preparation role that needs to be performed when taking data from the source documents and preparing it for entry into the computer.

It is also likely that the output from the computer will not appear in an identical format to the old manual system. For example, the format of accounts produced by the computer may appear differently. This is noticeable, for example, when comparing the T form of accounts with the account statement received from the bank. It is important that the book-keeper is aware of the different formats in which this data can appear.

The computer will not replace the role of the book-keeper in its entirety in any business, however, the use of the computer is likely to affect the functions performed by the book-keeper. It will remove much of the routine work they conventionally have performed and replace it with more specialist roles that continue to require good knowledge of the practice of book-keeping.

18 | PARTNERSHIP

OBJECTIVE

This chapter introduces you to the meaning of 'partnership' and how the profit earned is divided between partners. It also illustrates the accounting between partners when the partnership is formed, when a new partner is admitted and when one leaves.

In the previous chapters we have assumed the business to be owned by a sole proprietor, or, alternatively, a **sole trader**. This was the earliest form of proprietorship, and still exists in the typical small business, often of the merchanting and distributive type.

With the growth in the size of the business, the Capital required to provide the necessary equipment and to finance ordinary trading is usually found to be larger than the resources of any one individual. A further handicap must be recognised in the fact that, in the event of the business failing, the proprietor is liable to the last penny for the payment of the business creditors. The liability is said to be **unlimited**. This contrasts to that of the shareholders in a Limited Company, which is restricted to the amounts, if any, unpaid on the shares they have contract to take (see Chapter 19 for further details).

Between these two extremes we have the situation where two, or more, individuals agree to work together, sharing their resources and any profits earned. This situation is referred to as a *partnership*. Just as in the case of the Sole Trader, each partner usually has unlimited liability as regards the whole of the debts of the **partnership firm**.

A partnership is a very suitable form of business proprietorship where:

- a large amount of Capital is not required
- liabilities to suppliers and others are unlikely to be considerable
- the business is of a size in which each partner can take part in the general supervision.

For these reasons, partnerships are often found in the professions and in the smaller merchanting and manufacturing businesses.

UK Partnership Act 1890

In the UK a measure of statutory control over the organisation of a partnership was imposed by this Act. It defines partnership as *the relation which subsists between persons carrying on business in common with a view to profit.*

The Act of 1890 provides certain rules which, in the absence of written or verbal arrangement between the partners, can be applied in defining the duties of the partners to each other, and their responsibility to persons outside the firm with whom they have business dealings.

As it is usually desirable to make special arrangements in each individual case, and to have a permanent record of what is agreed upon, a **Deed**, or **Articles of Partnership**, is often drawn up by which each of the partners consents to be bound. These also provide for such modifications of the Act of 1890 as may be thought necessary.

The Deed may state:

a the period for which the partnership is entered into

b the nature of the business to be carried on

c the amount of Capital to be introduced and in what circumstances it may be withdrawn

d the ratio in which Profits and Losses shall be shared

e how much each partner shall be entitled to draw on account of accruing profits

f whether Interest shall be allowed on Partners' Capitals

g the salaries, if any, to be paid to individual partners.

As regards **a**, if no period is stated, or the partnership is continued without any fresh agreement after the original period has expired, it is said to be a **Partnership at Will**.

Of the above, items **c**, **d**, **e**, **f** and **g** have special bearing on the *accounts*, and must therefore be considered separately.

Capital

The Capital brought into a partnership may take the form of cash, or property in kind, such as machinery, buildings, stock, etc.

In any event, the agreed value must be credited to the Partner's Capital Account, and the proper Asset Account debited. If the Capitals are **fixed** the profit shares and drawings on account of them will be dealt with in separate Current Accounts instead of treating them as part of Capital, as in the case of a sole owner.

Profits and losses

Partners may share Profits and Losses on any agreed basis. In the last resort the Partnership Act provides that they are entitled to share equally. Sometimes Profits and Losses may be divided in the ratio of the Fixed Capitals; in other cases where one partner takes a more active part than another, this may be rewarded with a bigger proportionate share.

Drawings

It is better to agree at the outset upon a limit for each partner's drawings. As the cash so withdrawn depletes the circulating Capital, interest may be charged thereon from the date withdrawn to the end of the firm's financial year. To avoid this calculation the agreement may stipulate that drawings on account of profit throughout the year will be in the profit-sharing proportion. Drawings may be in the form of goods or the use of business services for private purposes as well as cash, in which event the Purchases or expense account will be credited and the partner's Current Account debited.

Interest on capitals

Prior to the division of the Net Profit, the Partnership Deed may provide for charging Interest on the Capital of each partner. If this were not done in a case where, for example, Capital Accounts were unequal, but Profits and Losses were divided equally, the partner having the larger (or largest) Capital would lose.

Such Interest on Capital is in no sense a business expense, and would be debited in the Appropriation or Net Profit and Loss Account when dealing with distributions of profit or sharing out of losses.

Partnership salaries

A management salary may be paid to one or more of the partners if they devote more time to the business than their co-partners, or if they are *active*, as distinct from *sleeping* (or *dormant*), partners. The latter may be regarded as those who have contributed Capital, but take no part in the daily supervision of business affairs.

Salaries paid or payable to the partners will, like interest on Capital, be debited in the Appropriation Account. They are, in effect, and as regards each partner, a part of the determined profit due to the proprietor.

Partners' advances

If a partner, to assist the firm, advances cash as a *loan*, it is probable that it will need to be treated in the books in a manner different from the Capital invested. The amount should therefore be credited to a separate Loan Account.

The Act of 1890 provides that the partner making the *advance* shall be entitled to interest at the rate of 5% per annum from the date of the advance, but a more appropriate rate is usually agreed.

Goodwill

Goodwill is a business Asset, which may be defined as the worth inherent in an established business producing a normal and reasonable profit on the Capital employed in it.

It is *worth* or *value* over and above that represented by the *Tangible* Assets, such as buildings, plant, stock and book debts, and can so be termed an *Intangible* Asset.

If the business were sold, it would clearly be to a purchaser's advantage to pay something for the right to enjoy a continuity of the profits arising, and this is well brought out in the case of a *partnership*.

An incoming partner can be expected to pay the existing partners for the goodwill represented by the share of profit, and an outgoing partner is entitled to have goodwill taken into account in determining the sum due to them from the business. The Deed of Partnership will often indicate how the value of the goodwill is to be determined e.g. by reference to past profits or an estimate of future maintainable profits.

The best way to illustrate the similarities and differences between accounting for a sole trader or for a partnership is by way of examples.

Example 18.1

A joins B in partnership on 1 January xxx5. The Capital is provided as £15 000 by A, who is a dormant partners, and £5000 by B, who works full-time for the business and is wholly dependent on it.

Assuming the gross receipts for xxx5 are £60 000, and the working expenses £19 000, prepare a Profit and Loss Account incorporating these items, and also the distribution of profit, allowing 10% Interest on Capital, and dividing the balance equally.

A AND B

Profit and Loss Account

Year ended 31 December xxx5

Dr				Cr
		£		£
Working expenses		19 000	Gross receipts	60 000
Net profits c/d		41 000		
		£60 000		£60 000
Interest on capital			Net profit b/d	41 000
A 10% on £15 000		1 500		
B 10% on £5 000		500		
		2 000		
Balance				
A 1/2 share	£19 500			
B 1/2 share	£19 500			
		39 000		
		41 000		41 000

We can see the benefit to A of charging interest on Capital. B would perhaps think it appropriate that a salary should be paid, but if the agreement does not include a reference to it, none will be due.

The interest due to each partner and the amount of the profit share can be carried direct to Capital Account, but is more usually credited to a Current Account. The following example illustrates the use of Current Accounts in this way.

Example 18.2

Rogers and Shaw enter into partnership on 1 January xxx7, and agree to divide Profits and Losses equally, after charging Interest on Capital at 10% per annum.

On 31 December xxx7, the following Balances are extracted from their Books:

	Dr £	Cr £
Rogers: Capital		13 000.00
Drawings	1 156.00	
Shaw: Capital		12 000.00
Drawings	1 156.00	
Sales		34 257.00
Discounts received		81.00
Purchases	5 413.00	
Discounts allowed	187.00	
Salaries	11 497.00	
Wages	12 500.00	
Sundry debtors	4 200.00	
Rates	1 075.00	
Printing and stationery	292.00	
Travelling expenses	596.00	
Bad debts	24.00	
Repairs and renewals	133.00	
Cash in hand	11.00	
Bank overdraft		34.00
Subscriptions	8.00	
Bank charges	46.00	
Sundry creditors		662.00
Factory and warehouse premises	19 234.00	
Plant and machinery	2 506.00	
	£60 034.00	£60 034.00

The stock at 31 December xxx7 was valued by the partners at £1125.

You are required:

■ to prepare Trading and Profit and Loss Account for the year
to 31 December xxx7, and a Balance Sheet at that date

■ to show the Partners' Current Accounts.

The following adjustments are necessary:

■ Provide £150 for wages accrued due.

■ Provide 1% on the amount of the Sundry Debtors for Bad
and Doubtful Debts.

■ Provide £500 depreciation in respect of Plant and
Machinery.

In this example we should be careful to note how the provisions for **wages**,
doubtful debts and **depreciation** are dealt with in the Balance Sheet.

ROGERS AND SHAW
Trading and Profit and Loss Account
Year ended 31 December xxx7

	£	£			£
Purchases		5 413.00	Sales		34 257.00
Wages	£12 500.00		Stock, 31 December xxx7		1 125.00
Add Provision	150.00				
		12 650.00			
Gross profit c/d					
(50% to turnover)		17 319.00			
		35 382.00			35 382.00
Salaries		11 497.00	Gross profit b/d		17 319.00
Travelling expenses		596.00	Discount received		81.00
Printing and stationery		292.00			
Discounts allowed		187.00			
Repairs and renewals		133.00			
Rates		1 075.00			
Bad debts	£24.00				
Add Provision	42.00				
		66.00			
Bank charges		46.00			
Subscriptions		8.00			
Depreciation of plant and machinery		500.00			
		14 400.00			
Net profit c/d		3 000.00			
		17 400.00			17 400.00
Interest on capitals:			Net profit b/d		3 000.00
Rogers 10% on £13 000		1 300.00			
Shaw 10% on £12 000		1 200.00			
		2 500.00			
Rogers, 1/2 share	£250.00				
Shaw, 1/2 share	250.00				
		500.00			
		£3 000.00			£3 000.00

Note: In practice, the Provisions are seldom shown separately in the Profit and Loss Account, e.g. Wages would be shown in the one sum of £12 650.00 only.

ROGERS AND SHAW
Balance Sheet
As at 31 December xxx7

	£	£
Fixed Assets		
Factory and warehouse premises		19 234.00
Plant and machinery	2 506.00	
less depreciation	500.00	
		2 006.00
TOTAL FIXED ASSETS		21 240.00

	£	£		
Current Assets				
Stock in trade		1 125.00		
Debtors	4 200.00			
less provision	42.00			
		4 158.00		
Cash in hand		11.00		
			5 294.00	
deduct Current Liabilities				
Sundry creditors		662.00		
Wages accrued		150.00		
Bank overdraft		34.00		
			846.00	
NET CURRENT ASSETS				4 448.00
TOTAL ASSETS minus CURRENT LIABILITIES				£25 688.00

Financed by			
Current Accounts			
Rogers			
Interest on capital		1 300.00	
Profit share		250.00	
		1 550.00	
less drawings		1 156.00	
			394.00
Shaw			
Interest on capital		1 200.00	
Profit share		250.00	
		1 450.00	
less drawings		1 156.00	
			294.00
Capital Accounts			
Rogers		13 000.00	
Shaw		12 000.00	
			25 000.00
			£25 688.00

Private Ledger

ROGERS – CURRENT ACCOUNT

Dr						Cr
xxx7			£	xxx7		£
Dec	31	Drawings	1 156.00	Dec 31	Interest on capital	
	31	Balance c/d	394.00		10% on £13 000	1 300.00
				31	One half Profit, year to date	250.00
			1 550.00			1 550.00
				xxx8		
				Jan 1	Balance b/d	394.00

SHAW – CURRENT ACCOUNT

Dr						Cr
xxx7			£	xxx7		£
Dec	31	Drawings	1 156.00	Dec 31	Interest on capital	
	31	Balance c/d	294.00		10% on £12 000	1 200.00
				31	One half Profit, year to date	250.00
			1 450.00			1 450.00
				xxx8		
				Jan 1	Balance b/d	294.00

When two sole traders amalgamate to form a partnership it is usually necessary to value the assets that each is contributing to the new business. They may agree the values themselves or employ a professional valuer, and goodwill (as described on p. 232) should be taken into account.

Similarly when a new partner is joining the firm, or an old one is leaving, a revaluation of assets will usually be necessary so that the correct amount can be attributed to each partner.

Example 18.3

A and B are partners who share equally in the profits and each has contributed £10 000 capital. The net assets therefore total £20 000. When they decided to accept C as an equal partner it was agreed that Goodwill should be recognised with a value of £12 000. This extra asset will be balanced by crediting the capital accounts of A and B with their share, i.e. equally, £6000 each. If the partnership agrees to retain this Goodwill in the accounts then interest, if payable, would be payable on the increased capitals of A and B, and on the £16 000 capital introduced by C . If it is agreed that Goodwill should not be shown on the Balance Sheet it will be written off in the new profit-sharing ratio. This is done equally and so £4000 will be deducted from each partner's capital.

Summarised balance sheets:

		£	£
■ Originally	Sundry net assets		20 000
	Capital accounts		
	A	10 000	
	B	10 000	20 000

■ After valuing goodwill at £12 000

		£	£
	Sundry net assets		20 000
	Goodwill		12 000
			32 000
	Capital accounts		
	A	16 000	
	B	16 000	32 000

■ C joins, paying £16 000 into the business for an equal share in the profits

			£
	Sundry net assets		20 000
	Goodwill		12 000
	Cash		16 000
			48 000
	Capital accounts		
	A	16 000	
	B	16 000	
	C	16 000	
			48 000

■ Goodwill is written off

			£
	Sundry net assets		20 000
	Cash		16 000
			36 000
	Capital accounts		
	A	12 000	
	B	12 000	
	C	12 000	
			36 000

> **KEY POINTS**
>
> On completion of this chapter you should:
>
> **1** have a brief understanding of the legal position
>
> **2** appreciate the importance of a legal agreement governing the division of profit in a partnership, in particular the rules for salary, interest on capital and loan interest and their application
>
> **3** know the basis of valuation of the business when there is a change in the partners, in particular goodwill and its allocation between the partners
>
> **4** be able to produce the separate capital and current accounts for each of the partners.

Questions

1 Explain why interest may be credited to a partner.

2 Define Goodwill and explain its importance in partnership accounting.

3 Earle and Yeoman are considering establishing a dairy to be run by them in partnership. Earle is to provide nine-tenths of the capital required, but, having no practical knowledge of the work, is not expected to take much active part in its operation. Yeoman is experienced in running a dairy and she will manage the business.

You have been asked by them for your advice on the financial provisions to be included in the Partnership Deed. What would you suggest, and why?

4 In the absence of agreement, to what extent are partners entitled to interest on capital in and loans to the firm?

Illustrate your answer by reference to the following:

	£
A. Capital	10 000.00
B. Capital	5 000.00
A. Loan	3 000.00

Profits of the firm (before charging any interest), £2500.

5 On 1 January xxx6, A and B entered into partnership but without any formal deed of partnership. A provided £10 000 as capital, and B provided £500. On 1 July xxx6, A advanced £2000 on loan to the firm.

Accounts were prepared and disclosed a profit of £6000 for the year to 31 December xxx6, but the partners could not agree as to how this sum should be divided between them. A contended that the partners should receive 5% interest on capital and that A should receive 6% interest on the loan to the firm, and the balance then available should be divided equally. B contended that, as B did most of the work, B should be paid a salary before any division of profit was made.

You are required to show how the profits of the firm should be divided and to state what different division, if any, would be made if A had written a letter to B agreeing that a partnership salary of £1500 should be paid to B.

6 A, a sole trader, prepared accounts as on 31 March xxx4, when the Capital Account showed a balance of £9000. On 1 April B joined A as a partner on the terms that before B's entry a Goodwill Account of £4000 should be raised, that B should bring in £3000 in cash as capital, interest at 5% per annum should be allowed on Capital Accounts and the balance of profit be divided between A and B, in the proportion of 3 to 1.

The profit for the year to 31 March xxx5, before charging interest, was £4050. Show the division of this between A and B. Show also what the division would have been had no provision been made as to goodwill, the other arrangements being as stated above.

7 X and Y are partners, and they admit Z as a partner, profits to be shared as follows: X four-ninths, Y three-ninths, Z two-ninths.

Y is credited with a partnership salary of £4500 per annum, and X and Y guarantee that Z's share of profits shall not be less than £8000 in any year.

The profits for the year ended 31 December xxx9, prior to providing for Y's salary, amounted to £38 214.

Prepare the Appropriation section of the firm's Profit and Loss Account.

8 A, a sole trader owning an established business, took B into partnership on 1 January xxx3, at which date the goodwill of the business was agreed to be worth £6000. A's capital (exclusive of goodwill) was £10 000, and B brought in £3000 as his capital. Interest on Capital Accounts was to be allowed at 5%, and A and B were to divide the remaining profit in the ratio of 2 to 1.

The profit for xxx3 before charging interest, was £35 600.

Calculate the division of this sum between A and B on the alternative assumptions that:

■ goodwill was ignored on B's entering the business
■ goodwill was taken into account at its correct value.

9 Bright and Smart carry on business in partnership, sharing profits in the proportion of three-fifths and two-fifths respectively.

On 1 January xxx6, the Capital Accounts showed the following credit balances: Bright, £8000; Smart, £6000.

The Partnership Agreement provides that the partners shall be allowed interest on capital at 5% per annum and that Bright shall be entitled to a salary of £6000 per annum and Smart to one of £4000 per annum. During the year ended 31 December xxx6, the partners' drawings were: Bright, £3550; Smart, £2425.

The profit for the year, prior to making any of the above adjustments, was £23 500.

You are required to write up the Profit and Loss Appropriation Account and to show how the Capital Accounts of the partners would appear on the Balance Sheet at 31 December xxx6.

10 A and B entered into partnership on 1 January xxx6, sharing profits and losses equally.

A contributed £5000 as capital, comprising £2000 in cash, and fixtures and plant valued at £3000.

B could only introduce £1000 in cash, but it was agreed he should be given credit in the sum of £1500 for his sales connection, and also receive a salary at the rate of £4800 per annum.

On 30 June xxx6, B paid in an additional £500, and at the same date C entered the firm, paying £1600 for a quarter share of the profits and goodwill and bringing in £1000 cash as his capital, all of which it was agreed should be left in the business.

A and B continued to share the profits in the same relative proportions as before, and it was arranged that as from the date of C's entry, B's salary should cease, but 10% per annum interest on capitals should be allowed.

The profits for the year to 31 December xxx6, prior to charging such interest and B's salary, were £16 800. Draw up a Statement showing the division of this amount between the partners, making any necessary apportionments on a time basis, and open Ledger Accounts to record the whole of the above.

11 Joan and John entered into partnership as merchants on 1 January xxx6. Joan brought in cash £500 and stock in trade £1000; John brought in cash £2300 and a lorry £8700. The agreement provided that John was to have a salary from the firm of £2250 per annum and that each partner might draw (on account of salary and profit) £100 per month plus £3000 each on 15 December; otherwise the terms of the Partnership Act, 1890, were to apply.

At the end of xxx6 the following Trial Balance was extracted from the books:

Trial Balance
31 December xxx6

	Dr	Cr
	£	£
Capital Accounts		12 500.00
Debtors	950.00	
Cash	25.00	
Carriage inwards	500.00	
Bank		135.00

Stock	1 000.00	
Rent paid	1 550.00	
Sales		36 000.00
Lorry	8 700.00	
Carriage outwards	130.00	
Discounts received		575.00
Petty cash expenditure	52.00	
Purchases	11 500.00	
Drawings	12 400.00	
Creditors		697.00
Discounts allowed	50.00	
Rates paid	1 200.00	
Salaries (not Partners)	10 850.00	
Fixtures and fittings (cost)	1 000.00	
	£49 907.00	£49 907.00

Notes

- Stock 31 December xxx6, valued at £1800.
- Rent accrued but not paid, £150.
- Rates paid in advance, £140.
- Depreciate the lorry at 10% per half-year on the diminishing balance system, and the Fixtures and Fittings at 5% per half-year on original cost.
- Bank charges not yet entered in books, £50.

Prepare Trading and Profit and Loss Accounts for xxx6 and a Balance Sheet at the end of the year.

12 The following Trial Balance has been extracted as at 31 March xxx7, from the books of C Spargo and W Penna – partners sharing profits and losses in the proportion of 2 to 1 respectively.

	Dr	Cr
	£	£
Stock, 1 April xxx6	3 690.00	
Purchases and sales	36 892.75	89 469.97
Bad Debts written off	291.67	
Plant and machinery (cost £7000)	6 650.00	
Furniture and fittings (cost £1200)	1 164.00	
Returns	371.56	297.54
Discounts	351.71	403.69
Drawings: C Spargo	3 560.00	
W Penna	2 380.00	
Debtors and creditors	5 620.00	4 872.68
Light and heat	1 397.80	
Rent and rates	3 650.63	
Insurances	1 131.50	

	Dr £	Cr £
Salaries	11 215.68	
Wages	26 394.93	
General expenses	445.62	
Bad Debts reserve		200.00
Commissions		363.97
Capital: C Spargo		5 800.00
W Penna		3 800.00
	£105 207.85	£105 207.85

Value of stock on 31 March xxx7, £1793.

You are asked to draw up Trading and Profit and Loss Accounts for the year, using the following data for making necessary adjustments:

- Depreciate plant and machinery 10% on cost.
- Depreciate furniture and fittings 5% on cost.
- Amount of insurance pre-paid, £131.75
- Amount of wages due but unpaid, £511.65.
- The Bad Debts Reserve is to be increased to an amount equal to 5% of debtors' balances.
- Amount of commissions due but not received, £34.94
- Capital Accounts to be credited with interest at 5% per annum.

(No interest to be charged on drawings.)

No Balance Sheet is to be drawn up. Instead, you are to show the following accounts in full for the year ended 31 March xxx7:

- Plant and Machinery Account.
- Insurance Account.
- Bad Debts Reserve Account
- Commission Account.

13 The firm of John Smith & Sons, makers of engineering equipment, consists of John and Magnus Smith. They share profits equally, after each has been credited with interest at 5% on his capital at the beginning of the year.

At 31 January xxx7, the end of the firm's financial year, the following are the balances in the Ledger:

	£	£
Purchases: Raw materials	18 562.00	
Finished goods	860.00	
General office expenses	934.00	
Returns inwards	413.00	

	£	£
Creditors, including an unsecured loan of		
£500, maturing in xxx9		2 617.00
Bad Debts provision		205.00
Stock: Raw materials	3 906.00	
Finished goods	101.00	
Wages (factory)	48 687.00	
Salaries (factory)	11 252.00	
Rent, insurance, etc. (factory)	1 246.00	
Rent, insurance, etc. (factory), prepaid	25.00	
Net rents from workmen's cottages		97.00
Fire expense	750.00	
Carriage outwards	909.00	
Factory equipment and machinery	14 315.00	
Factory equipment and machinery		
depreciation provision		2 000.00
Cash	14.00	
Sales		85 200.00
Interest paid on overdraft, etc.	61.00	
Debtors	4 135.00	
Capital: John Smith		12 420.00
Magnus Smith		3 740.00
Drawings: John Smith	837.00	
Magnus Smith	371.00	
Bank		1 099.00
	£107 378.00	£107 378.00

The stock of raw materials at 31 January xxx7 was valued at £4310. There were then no finished goods on hand.

The 'Fire Expense' Account shows the balance of a heavy loss from fire in xxx2. £150 of this amount is now to be written off.

£22 of bank overdraft interest is accrued and has not been allowed for.

The Equipment Depreciation Provision is to be increased by £315.

Prepare suitable Final Accounts and Balance Sheet.

14 On 1 January xxx3, A and B go into business as advertising consultants, on the footing that each contributes £1000 cash as capital, profits and losses to be shared equally.

The £1000 provided by A is borrowed by him privately from his bankers at 8% p.a. interest.

It is agreed that B, who devotes his whole time to the business, shall receive prior to the ascertainment of profit a management salary of £1250 p.a.

Office accommodation is acquired on 1 February xxx3, at a rent of £300 p.a., payable quarterly, the first payment is to be made on 31 March xxx3.

Furniture and fittings are purchased on the latter date from OF Ltd, for a sum of £72 cash, and B introduces other similar equipment of a value of £36 to be credited to his Capital Account.

Apart from the above items, at 31 December xxx3, there has been received in cash by A and B as consultants' fees the sum of £6150, and at that date fees totalling £340 are outstanding and due to them.

Heating, lighting, etc., amounted to £900 during the period, and A and B incurred travelling and entertaining expenses of £763 in connection with visits to clients, all of which has been paid.

Prepare a Profit and Loss Account of the business of A and B for the year ended 31 December xxx3, and a Balance Sheet at that date.

19 | LIMITED COMPANIES

OBJECTIVE

This chapter contains a brief introduction to Limited Liability companies and the legal requirements for their annual accounts. It also briefly illustrates the basic accounting aspects when changing from a partnership to a company.

The limited company, as an artificial 'person' in UK Law, owes its existence to registration under the provisions of the Companies Acts, and must be considered distinct from changing generations of its owners (referred to as shareholders). The latter, when buying shares, are able to limit their liability to the nominal or 'face' value of the shares taken by them. An applicant for 100 shares of £1 each originally offered for sale by the company at £1 each has, when their offer is accepted by the company, a liability to pay £100 *and no more*, even if the company should in future be unable to meet the claims of its creditors. The creditors have contracted with the company, to which alone they can look for payment.

This limited liability has furnished an immense stimulus to the development of business because:

- *the company*, unlike the Sole Trade, or Partnership firm, can obtain capital funds from a very large number of persons
- *the individual shareholder* can take as many, or as few shares as they desire, and, having paid for them, enjoy protection from any further liability.

Public and private companies

All Companies incorporated under the Companies Acts are bound by its provisions and comprise two main classes: Public Companies and Private Companies.

A **Public Company** is one whose name ends with the words 'public limited company' or 'plc'. It must have a minimum allotted share capital of £50 000.

A **Private Company** is any company which is not a Public Company, and it is prohibited from offering its shares or debentures to the public. Instead, it can only obtain its funding by private arrangements.

The book-keeping and accounting requirements are the same for all companies but the disclosure requirements are greater for Public Companies and reduced for small or medium size Private Companies.

A broad distinction is that a Public Company is one in which the public are substantially interested as providers of capital, whereas in a Private Company management and proprietorship are often identical, the company having been formed chiefly to obtain the benefit of limited liability rather than the provision of new money.

Restrictions on the transfer of shares in a Private Company may mean that a would-be seller must first offer their shares to an existing shareholder, or accept a price determined in accordance with the Articles, etc.

The Memorandum and Articles of Association

Any one or more persons may form an incorporated Company by subscribing their names to a *Memorandum of Association* and otherwise complying with the requirements of the Companies Act.

The Memorandum of Association is, in effect, the Charter of the Company, and must state:

- the name of the company, with 'Limited' as the last word of the name
- the situation of the Registered Office of the company
- the objects of the company
- that the liability of the members is limited
- the amount of the Share Capital with which the company proposes to be registered, and the division thereof into shares of a fixed amount

- a public limited company will also state this fact and its name will include plc.

No subscriber of the Memorandum may take less than one share. This implies the minimum number of shares it is possible to establish a company on is one share.

As regards the Memorandum note:

- The name chosen for the new company must not so closely resemble that of an existing company as to deceive or cause confusion in the mind of the public.

- The applicants for registration must state the objects which it is proposed to carry out. If the substratum of the business disappears, particularly where the company is a Public Company, it is only right that the directors should not be able to turn unhindered to some quite unrelated form of business with the residue of the funds originally subscribed.

  Usually the opportunity is taken to provide for eventualities by adding to the main object a number of others which may be regarded as reasonably incidental to it.

- The Capital stated in the Memorandum of Association is variously styled the Registered, Authorised or Nominal Capital, but may be altered from time to time by the company in a general meeting.

Articles of Association, or a series or regulations prescribed for the company, may be registered with the Memorandum, but failing this, a model set of articles, known as Table A-F (and given in the Companies Regulations), is applicable.

The Articles are like the rules of a club or society, and provide for the general conduct of the company's affairs.

All members of the company are bound by the Articles in force, even if they subsequently acquire their shares by purchase in the market, and were not original subscribers when the business was created and the 'rules' drawn up.

The Articles may be altered or added to by passing a special resolution of members at a general meeting, a three-quarters (75%) majority being required and not less than 21 days' notice of the intention to propose the resolution as a special resolution having been given to all current shareholders.

The Articles will concern the following, *inter alia*:

Shares   Issue, transfer and voting rights
Directors   Appointment, powers and remuneration
Meetings   Procedure, and business thereat
Finance   Preparation and circulation of Accounts, payment of dividends, etc.

Share capital

Shares, as units of proprietorship, may be generally classified as Ordinary and Preference Shares. All shareholders are entitled to receive payouts of the companies' profits if any are earned. These payouts to shareholders are called *dividends*. Preference shares carry a fixed rate of dividend. Before payment of this dividend, income tax at the basic rate will be deducted by the company, and the net rate payable is used to describe the shares. Some preference shares may also have the right to be converted into ordinary shares, at stated times and in a stated ratio. These shares are referred to as *Convertible Preference Shares*. Preference Shareholders have a priority for dividends if there are profits available. Ordinary Shares take what remains, and may earn very large dividends in prosperous years, but earn no dividend at all in poor years. The Shareholders also have the opportunity of capital appreciation through an increase in the market price of their shares. This appreciation is referred to as a *capital gain*.

Other forms of shares include Cumulative Preference Shares where any arrears of the agreed fixed dividend are carried forward to the following period and Redeemable Preference Shares are those which are to be redeemed either out of *profits*, or from the proceeds of a fresh issue of *capital*: otherwise the shareholder of any class may only realise their investment by sale of the shares in the market.

The two latter classes represent variations of the simple Preference Share, and are usually of importance in the case of a Public Company, who will try to appeal to the investor in the broadest possible way.

Voting rights are commonly restricted to the Ordinary Shareholders, though Preference Shareholders often enjoy voting rights during any period when their dividend is unpaid.

It must be observed that with both Public and Private Companies the bonus of limited liability is conferred only on the understanding that the capital fund of the company is maintained intact. This means that capital must not be returned to shareholders as dividend. Dividends should only be paid out of profits periodically determined by preparing accounts, and as recommended by the directors and approved by the members in general meeting.

The Articles may give the directors power to pay *interim* dividends which would be paid to shareholders during the year. Other dividends are usually paid after the end of the business year.

Debentures

In addition to issuing shares, a company may issue debentures, which are acknowledgements of *loans* made to the company. The debenture-holder, unlike the shareholder, is a *creditor*, with all a creditor's remedies.

Debentures issued by companies incorporated under the Companies Acts are usually redeemable at a future date. Meantime, the debenture-holder is entitled to receive interest at a fixed rate per cent whether or not profits exist in a particular year out of which to pay it.

A further feature of debentures is that the holders are almost always *secured* creditors. This means that the company pledges or charges some part of its property (e.g. its factory premises) in favour of such creditors specifically, who may, on default by the company, appoint a Receiver (Receiver for debenture-holders), realise the security to the best advantage and repay themselves out of the proceeds.

It will thus be appreciated that an issue of debentures, because of the minimum risk of loss to the holder, may enable money to be *borrowed* at a rate of interest relatively low in comparison with the rate of dividend paid on Preference and Ordinary *Shares*.

Unsecured Loan Stock

Many companies, particularly well-known public companies, are able to borrow without the necessity of providing any security. There will be negotiated rates of interest and repayment terms but the liability is sufficiently different from that associated with debentures for a separate classification to be justified.

Books of account

Statutory Books

The Companies Acts require every company to keep proper books of account to record its:

- Cash receipts and payments
- Trading purchases and sales
- Assets and liabilities.

Proper books of account are such as are necessary to give a true and fair view of the state of the company's affairs and to explain its transactions. They may be kept in bound books, loose cards, or in computer readable form so long as they provide an accurate, accessible record of the transactions.

The *Statutory Books* of the company similarly required to be kept include:

- The Register of Members
- The Register of Charges (e.g. Debentures)
- The Register of Directors and Secretaries
- Separate Minute Book for meetings of directors, and of shareholders.

The Register of Members is the principal statutory book, in which particulars are to be kept of members, their share-holdings, transfers, etc.

Access to the Register of Charges is clearly a help to an unsecured creditor or other person giving credit to the company, enabling them to see what part of the company's property is already charged.

Accounts and audit

The directors of both Public and Private Companies must once in each year lay before the company in a general meeting a Profit and Loss Account.

A Balance Sheet made up to the same date must also be presented, together with a report of the directors as to their dividend recommendations and the general state of the company's affairs.

The Balance Sheet must contain a summary of the Authorised and Issued Share Capital of the company, and particulars of the general nature of its

Assets and Liabilities. The Companies Acts lay down detailed requirements as to the contents of Balance Sheets and Profit and Loss Accounts. (See *Teach Yourself Company Law*.)

Every company must at each annual general meeting appoint an Auditor, or Auditors, who must in general belong to a body of accountants recognised by the appropriate government department. The Auditors are to report to the members on the accounts examined by them, and have a right of access at all times to the books, accounts and vouchers of the company.

Example 19.1

From the following particulars, prepare a Balance Sheet of Wick Plc at 30 November xxx6, grouping the Assets and Liabilities in the form required by the Companies Acts:

	£
12% Debentures, repayable 2000/05	20 000.00
Cash at bank	4 911.00
Stock-in-trade, 30 November xxx6	34 009.00
Goodwill, at cost	30 800.00
40 000 5.6% Preference shares	40 000.00
80 000 Ordinary shares	80 000.00
Doubtful Debts provision	500.00
Contingent liability on bills discounted	250.00
Sundry debtors	12 350.00
Freeholds, at cost	32 750.00
Creditors	6 692.00
Profit and Loss Account, 1 December xxx5 (Cr)	14 900.00
Plant and machinery, at cost, less depreciation, provided to date (£20 000) 1 December xxx5	54 600.00
Deposit with Local Authority	9 800.00
Additions to plant and machinery, at cost	742.00
Profit for the year, *less* Dividends on Preference shares	7 600.00
Depreciation for the year	10 000.00

The Authorised Capital of the company is 50 000 5.6% Preference Shares of £1, and 100 000 Ordinary Shares of £1.

Remember that the presentation of tangible Fixed Assets should include the cost and aggregate depreciation provided to the date of the Balance Sheet.

There is also the requirement to distinguish between Current Liabilities, those due to be paid within one year from the Balance Sheet date, and those not due to be paid until one year or longer after the Balance Sheet date.

You should obtain a copy of the published accounts of a public company for a more detailed example of modern presentation.

WICK PLC

Balance Sheet

at 30 November xxx6

Fixed Assets	*Cost*	*Depreciation*	*Net Book Value*
	£	£	£
Intangible Asset			
Goodwill	30 800.00	–	30 800.00
Tangible Assets			
Freehold land	32 750.00	–	32 750.00
Plant and machinery	75 342.00	30 000.00	45 342.00
Total Fixed Assets	£138 892.00	£30 000.00	108 892.00
Current Assets			
Stock		34 009.00	
Debtors, less doubtful debts provision (£500.00)		11 850.00	
Local Authority Deposit		9 800.00	
Cash and Bank Balance		4 911.00	
		60 570.00	
deduct Creditors – amounts due within one year		6 962.00	
Net Current Assets			53 608.00
Total assets less current liabilities			162 500.00
deduct Creditors – amounts due after one year. 10% Debentures repayable 2000/05			20 000.00
Net Assets			142 500.00
Represented by Capital and Reserves			

Share Capital	*Authorised*	*Issued and Fully Paid*
	£	£
5.6% Preference Shares of £1.00	50 000.00	40 000.00
Ordinary Shares of £1.00	100 000.00	80 000.00
	150 000.00	120 000.00
Reserves		
Profit and Loss Account		22 500.00
		142 500.00

Note: There is a contingent liability of £250.00 in respect of Bills discounted.

Note: There should also be presented the corresponding amounts at the end of the immediately preceding financial year for all items shown in the Balance Sheet. In practice it is unlikely that the pence columns would be shown.

Example 19.2

The following is the Balance Sheet at 30 June xxx0, of Bleak House & Co:

	£	£		£	£
Fixed Assets			*Capital accounts*		
Goodwill	63 000		B Bleak	74 000	
Plant & machinery	4 000		H House	29 000	
		67 000			103 000
Current Assets			*Current liabilities*		
Stock-in-trade	42 140		Trade creditors	8 440	
Debtors	20 780		Bankers	18 600	
Cash	120				
		63 040			27 040
		130 040			130 040

The partners shared profits and losses three-fifths to B Bleak and two-fifths to H House.

A private limited company, Bleak House Ltd, was formed to acquire the business as from 1 July xxx0, the purchase consideration being £106 000. All the Assets and Liabilities were taken over at book values, except as regards the Goodwill and the Plant and Machinery. Plant and Machinery were valued for the purpose of the Sale and Purchase Agreement at £58 000.

In respect of the amount due to him, B Bleak received 20 000 5.6% Preference Shares of £1 each, valued at £1 each, in the new company, and the balance in cash.

H House received the whole of his share in £1 Ordinary Shares, allotted at par, except for £3200 paid to him in cash.

In addition to the above, 30 000 Preference Shares were issued to the public at par for cash, and 60 000 Ordinary Shares at a premium of £0.10 per share; these issues were subscribed and paid up in full (see page 256).

You are required to record the above in the books of Bleak House Ltd and to give the commencing Balance Sheet of the new company.

This is an example of the sale of a partnership to a company. A value will have been agreed for the Tangible Assets and Liabilities to give an agreed Net Asset amount. This is less than the amount of the purchase consideration so the excess must represent the payment made for goodwill. The example also uses the vertical format for the Balance Sheet.

Solution to Example 19.2
Books of Bleak House Ltd
B BLEAK AND H HOUSE – VENDORS

Dr				Cr		
xxx0		£	£	xxx0		£	£
July 1	Sundry creditors		8 440.00	July 1	Sundry Assets:		
	Bankers		18 600.00		Cash	120.00	
	Balance c/d		94 000.00		Sundry debtors	20 780.00	
					Stock-in-trade	42 140.00	
					Fixed assets	58 000.00	
							121 040.00
			£121 040.00				£121 040.00
July 1	*B Bleak:*			July 1	Balance b/d		94 000.00
	5.6% Preference shares	20 000.00			Goodwill		12 000.00
	Cash	55 800.00					
			75 800.00				
	H House:						
	Ordinary shares	27 000.00					
	Cash	3 200.00					
			30 200.00				
			£106 000.00				£106 000.00

GOODWILL

Dr				Cr
xxx0			xxx0	
July 1	B Bleak and H House	£ 12 000.00		

5.6% PREFERENCE SHARES

Dr			Cr
		xxx0	
		July 1	B Bleak	20 000.00
		1	Application and allotments	30 000.00
				£ 50 000.00

ORDINARY SHARES

Dr			Cr
		xxx0	£
		July 1 H House	27 000.00
		1 Applications and allotments	60 000.00
			£87 000.00

APPLICATIONS AND ALLOTMENTS

Dr		Ordinary £	Preference £			Ordinary £	Preference £
xxx0				xxx0			
July 1	Share capital A/cs	60 000.00	30 000.00	July 1	Cash	66 000.00	30 000.00
1	Share premium A/c	6 000.00	–				
		£66 000.00	£30 000.00			£66 000.00	£30 000.00

SHARE PREMIUM ACCOUNT

Dr		Cr
	xxx0	£
	July 1 Applications and Allotments	£6 000.00

CASH BOOK

Dr	£	£			Cr £
xxx0			xxx0		
July1 B Bleak and H House		120.00	July 1	B Bleak and H House	18 600.00
1 Applications and Allotments			1	B Bleak	55 800.00
Ordinary shares	66 000.00		1	H House	3 200.00
Preference shares	30 000.00		1	Balance c/d	18 520.00
		96 000.00			
		£96 120.00			£96 120.00
Balance b/d		18 520.00			

There would also be accounts for sundry creditors, sundry debtors, stock and fixed assets.

BLEAK HOUSE LTD
Balance Sheet
at 1 July xxx0

	£	£
Fixed Assets		
Intangible asset		
Goodwill	12 000.00	
Tangible assets		
Plant and machinery at cost	58 000.00	
		70 000.00
Current Assets		
Stock	42 140.00	
Debtors	20 780.00	
Cash	18 520.00	
	81 440.00	
Deduct Creditors – amounts due within one year	8 440.00	
Net Current Assets		73 000.00
Total Assets less Liabilities		143 000.00
Representing		

Share Capital and Reserve			
		Issued and	
Share Capital	*Authorised*	*Fully Paid*	
	£	£	
5% Preference shares of £1.00	50 000.00	50 000.00	
Ordinary shares of £1.00	100 000.00	87 000.00	
	£150 000.00		137 000.00
Share premium account			6 000.00
			143 000.00

Note: in future years comparative figures will also be shown.

Note to student

	B Bleak	H House
	£	£
Prior to sale the partners' Capitals are	74 000.00	29 000.00
They share profits and losses as 3 is to 2.		
They *lose* £9000.00 on revaluation of Plant and machinery	5 400.00	3 600.00
	68 600.00	25 400.00
The net worth of their business is thus reduced to £94 000.00		
But the Purchase Price is £106 000.00, a *profit* (in effect, Goodwill) of £12 000, shared in the profit-sharing ratio	7 200.00	4 800.00
	£75 800.00	£30 200.00

Alternatively; the partners were paid £106 000 in respect of capital of £103 000, a net gain of £3000, being a loss of £5000 on plant and gain of £8000 to £12 000 on goodwill. This gain of £3000 will be shared in the original profit-sharing ratio. The issue of shares to the public follows the normal debit to cash book, credit to liability accounts. The share premium, £0.10 per share, is credited to a separate account and the nominal amount, £1.00 per share, to the ordinary and preference share accounts.

KEY POINTS

On completion of this chapter you should be aware:

1 of the nature of limited liability status of companies and how a company is established

2 of the differences between Public and Private Limited Companies

3 of the major types of shares a company can issue

4 of the statutory requirement to keep certain records and books

5 that the principles of presentation for company accounts usually provide the 'best practice' for any accounts, subject to the extra information which must be provided when the public have a legitimate interest

6 that the book-keeping entries to record the change to a limited company are related to the capital structure only. All the earlier chapters are relevant to companies, sole traders and partnerships.

Questions

1 AB & Co Ltd has an authorised Capital of £8000, divided into 8000 Ordinary Shares of £1 each. On 31 December xxx3, 6000 shares had been issued and fully paid, and there were also balances on the books of the Company in respect of the following:

	£
Sales	40 350.00
Purchases	14 128.00
Wages	13 084.00
Stock (1 January xxx3)	746.00
Salaries	6 525.00
Rent	2 135.00
Rates	1 348.00
Insurance	729.00
Repairs	37.00

	£
Debenture interest	75.00
Bank charges	14.00
Travelling expenses	197.00
Sundries	188.00
Goodwill, at cost	3 000.00
Patents, at cost	2 506.00
Plant and machinery, at cost	1 240.00
Experimental account (asset)	1 777.00
Trade debtors	2 316.00
Trade creditors	846.00
Bank overdraft	187.00
5% Debenture	2 000.00
Preliminary expenses	142.00
Profit and Loss Account (liability) at 1 January xxx3	804.00

Stock, as taken on 31 December xxx3, amounted to £911, but includes an item of £65 for catalogues, the invoice for which has not yet been passed through the books.

The charges for Carriage Inwards, amounting to £102, have been debited to Sundries Account.

You are requested to prepare a Trading and Profit and Loss Account for the year ended 31 December xxx3, providing 5% depreciation on Plant and Machinery, and £84 for Bad Debts. It is required to provide 2½% for discounts to be allowed to Debtors, ignoring any provision of a similar kind for Creditors.

2 Tompkins, the accountant of Gloria Tubes Ltd, submits to you the following Revenue Account of the Company for the year ended 28 February xxx5.

Dr				Cr
		£		£
Wages		28 200.00	Balance of Profit, 1 March	
Purchases		12 500.00	xxx4	1 250.00
Salaries		13 468.00	Stock, 28 February xxx5	2 350.00
Commission		2 803.00	Rates, prepaid	21.00
Rates		3 105.00	Sales	61 550.00
Carriage inwards		180.00	Discounts received	125.00
Repairs and maintenance		217.00		
Stock, 1 March xxx4		2 120.00		
Depreciation	£			
Plant, 10%	710.00			
Fixtures, 5%	195.00			
Lorries, 20%	280.00			
		1 185.00		
Directors' fees		105.00		
Packing and carriage		486.00		
Insurance		87.00		
Debenture interest		60.00		
Bank interest		22.00		
Sundry expenses		308.00		
Profit		450.00		
		£65 296.00		£65 296.00

The authorised capital of the Company is £15 000, in shares of £1 each. Of these, 14 951 have been issued as fully paid to the vendor, who is the managing director, and his wife.

A 6% Debenture for £1000 is outstanding in favour of the managing director's wife.

£1452 is owing to suppliers, and £2500 by customers, in respect of which latter 2% is to be provided, at 28 February xxx5, the Company had £1767 in the Bank, while at 1 March xxx4, the book values and original cost of the Fixed Assets were:

	£	£
Plant	7100.00	7500.00
Fixtures	3900.00	4200.00
Lorry	1400.00	2000.00

Prepare in proper form Trading and Profit and Loss Account for the year ended 28 February xxx5, and a Balance Sheet at that date.

3 The authorised capital of the Waterloo Engineering Co Ltd is £80 000 in £1 shares. The Trial Balance was extracted from the Company's books as on 31 March xxx4.

You are required to prepare the Manufacturing Account, Profit and Loss Account and Balance Sheet of the Company after taking into consideration the following matters:

- The item 'Delivery Expenses' include £175 in respect of the subsequent trading period.
- Wages £515 and Directors' Fees £100 are outstanding.
- No provision has been made for the half-year's Debenture Interest due on 31 March xxx4.
- The Machinery and Plant is to be depreciated at the rate of 10% of the original cost of £36 450 and the Lorry is to be written down to £3000 being half of the original cost.
- The Bank Statement shows on 31 March xxx4 a credit of £15 for Interest on Deposit, but this item has not been entered in the Company's books.
- The General Reserve is to be increased by £2000.
- The Stock held on 31 March xxx4 was valued at £8765.
- Ignore income tax.

	Dr £	Cr £
Issued capital (60 000 shares)		60 000.00
Sales		138 980.00
Land and buildings	30 000.00	
Machinery and plant	29 530.00	
Sundry debtors and creditors	30 059.00	8 131.00
Purchases	46 150.00	
Interim dividend	3 000.00	
Delivery expenses	3 910.00	
Stock, 31 March xxx3	5 782.00	
Discounts	1 537.00	729.00
Returns inwards	1 100.00	
Salaries	2 697.00	
Travellers' commission and expenses	3 740.00	
Profit and Loss Account, 31 March xxx3		2 530.00
Lorries	3 987.00	
5% Debentures 2000/04		20 000.00
Rent and rates (factory £1650, office £224)	1 874.00	
Wages	61 846.00	
General expenses	892.00	
Factory power and light	2 839.00	
Debenture interest	500.00	
General reserve		6 000.00
Repairs to machinery	1 421.00	
Directors' fees	300.00	
Bank deposit account	3 500.00	
Bank current account	1 696.00	
	£236 370.00	£236 370.00

20 | THE ANALYSIS AND INTERPRETATION OF ACCOUNTS

OBJECTIVE

This chapter explains the importance of the accounts to the proprietor and manager of a business. It describes how to obtain additional information from the accounts by the calculation and use of ratios.

Much of what you have read so far concerns the recording of business transactions from the earliest stage in the Books of Prime Entry to the preparation of the Final Accounts.

It is important, however, that we never lose sight of the fact that accounts are kept in order that they may assist the proprietor or manager of the business.

If the accounts, or any part of them, have no meaning to us, they can have no meaning to others, and we must try to regard the records made as telling a story of what has happened in a business and telling it in a clear and intelligible manner.

A very simple instance of this is seen in the ordinary Ledger Account. Having taken note of the account's heading we should be able to describe to anyone interested not only the nature of the entries appearing in it, but also the final result of the transactions, both from the personal and the impersonal aspect.

Example 20.1

Here is a customer's account as shown in the Sales Ledger. By looking at this account you should be able to describe what activities have occurred relating to this customer in this period. At the beginning of the year £50 was owing by him, and a month later he returned goods to the value of £10, further goods being supplied to him on 28 February.

On 10 March, he remits a sum of £20, which is stated to be 'on account' – in itself often a sign of weakness. Despite this, goods are again invoiced to him on 3 May, and on 4 June a cheque is received for the balance of what was due as far back as 1 January.

The bank subsequently reports that the cheque has not been met, and Brown is accordingly debited with the amount of the cheque *and* discount.

Between then and 8 August, he either settles with his creditors as a whole, or is made bankrupt. A first and final dividend of £0.25 in the £ is received, and £0.75 in the £ has to be written off as a Bad Debt.

H BROWN

Dr							Cr
Date	Details	Fo	Amount	Date	Details	Fo	Amount
			£				£
xxx1				xxx1			
Jan 1	Balance		50.00	Feb 1	Returns		10.00
Feb 28	Goods		25.00	March 10	Cash on A/c		20.00
May 3	Goods		15.00	June 4	Bank		19.50
June 7	Bank, cheque				Discount		0.50
	returned		19.50	Aug 8	Bank, First		
7	Discount		0.50		and Final		
					Dividend of £0.25		
					in the £		15.00
				31	Bad Debts		45.00
			£110.00				£110.00

Analysis of the Final Accounts

It is, however, in regard to the Trading and Profit and Loss Account and Balance Sheet, representing the logical conclusion of the book-keeping work, that the principal points for analysis arise.

To deal firstly with the Trading Account, the following may have to be considered:

■ How does the sales figure compare with that of the previous year, or other period, and how far have alterations in selling prices contributed to any difference noted?

■ Similarly as regards *purchases* and the cost of materials bought.

■ Are the *closing stocks* much in excess of those held at the beginning of the year, and if so, in a manufacturing business, to what extent do they consist of raw material or the finished product? In the former case, have purchases been made in anticipation of a rise in the price of materials? In the latter case, is the turnover partly seasonal so that a large part of the stock is sold early in the following trading period? What is the average stock carried, and what is its relation to the turnover?

■ Does the business earn a fairly consistent rate of Gross Profit, expressed as a percentage to turnover? *If less than the usual Gross Profit is earned*, is it because selling prices have declined or because the closing stock is valued at the then market price which is below the original cost?

Should the Gross Profit percentage rise, is the cause to be found in more favourable selling prices, or in an improper inflation of closing stock values?

The Profit and Loss Account

This section of the Revenue Account includes, as we have seen, the *indirect* or 'overhead' expenses of the business.

To a large extent these do not vary in proportion to the sales or turnover figure, and therefore it is always necessary to watch carefully the individual items, and the total to which they amount.

Broadly speaking, the Profit and Loss Account is concerned with the reconciliation of **Gross** and **Net Profit**. Stated in another way, Gross Profit may be said to consist of the indirect expenses and Net Profit.

Indirect expenses

To assist scrutiny, some suitable arrangement of these expenses is most desirable. *Subheadings* may be inserted, such as:

1 *Production Expenses*
Factory Rent, Rates, etc.
Repairs to Plant.
Depreciation of Plant, etc.

2 *Selling and Distribution Expenses*
Travellers' Salaries and Commission.
Travelling Expenses
Rent of Show Rooms, etc.

3 *General or Administrative Expenses*
Office Salaries.

Bank Interest.

Depreciation of Office Furniture, etc.

A classification of the Profit and Loss Debits in this way is much more helpful than a mere haphazard listing of the balances on the various Ledger Accounts.

Net profit

This is of importance because it represents:

■ the amount which the proprietor may withdraw in the form of cash, *and still leave his Capital intact*

■ the net yield on the Capital invested, which may conveniently be stated as *a percentage return on that Capital.*

The net earnings of the business can only be determined after including all expenses, and all forms of income, as we saw in Chapter 14, and clearly the proprietor will expect to receive something in excess of the rate of interest obtainable from the investment of an equivalent amount of capital in, say, gilt-edged securities. How much more will largely depend on the degree of risk to which his business Capital is exposed in each particular case.

The Balance Sheet

A point to be borne in mind is that the Revenue Account and the Balance Sheet must be read together. Each serves to explain and interpret the other. As an example, if a profit is disclosed at the end of the period, it must be reflected in an increase of the Net Assets. If a loss has been sustained, these Assets will be less at the end of the period than they were at the beginning. Further, when depreciation is charged in the Profit and Loss Account, not only will the profit figure be reduced, but the book value of the Fixed Asset in question will similarly be reduced in the Balance Sheet.

The Balance Sheet is concerned with showing the position of the business *at a particular date*. That position may substantially alter on the day after its preparation, or it may be materially different on the day before it was prepared. The most informative Balance Sheet is that which gives the typical or average state of affairs but this may not always be the one produced and published by a business operating in the commercial world.

When analysing a Balance Sheet we may well begin with the Liabilities:

Who is interested in the business as a provider of Capital? Apart from the liability to the proprietor *on* Capital Account, there may be amounts due to trade creditors, and to bankers. The latter liabilities rank ahead of the former, and the proprietor will usually have to wait until all these claims are met before he can recover any part of his original investment.

The proportion of the Proprietor's Capital to other liabilities should also be noted. If relatively large sums are due to suppliers and others, the position must be further investigated by reference to the total Assets available, and their division between *Fixed*, and *Current Assets*.

Just as liabilities may be divided as between Fixed or Deferred Liabilities – those in favour of the proprietors, and Current Liabilities – or the claims of creditors, so it is from the Current or Floating Assets that the creditors primarily look for payment.

We have already considered the distinction between Fixed and Current Assets and the following example introduces other points.

Example 20.2

The Balance Sheet of T, a haulage contractor, at 28 February xxx6, is set out below.

		£			£
Fixed Assets			**T Capital**		
Leasehold warehouse,			Balance forward	£7 350.00	
offices, sheds, etc., at			*Add* Profit for		
cost, 1 March xxx0		3 511.00	year	1 750.00	
Motor vehicles,				9 100.00	
at cost			*Less* Drawings	1 600.00	
less Depreciation,				———	7 500.00
at cost					
1 March xxx5	£5 700.00				
Less Depreciation	2 037.00				
	———	3 663.00			
Total fixed assets		7 174.00			
Current Assets			**Current Liabilities**		
Stocks of fuel, oil, waste,			Trade creditors	2 118.00	
etc., as estimated by T	495.00		Accrued expenses	432.00	
Book debts, gross	2 606.00		Western Bank Ltd	269.00	
Insurance prepaid	15.00			———	
Cash in hand	29.00				2 819.00
		3 145.00			
		£10 319.00			£10 319.00

You are required:

- to comment carefully upon the position disclosed
- to draw up a statement showing the amount of the Net Current Assets.

1 Analysis and comment

The **Profit** for the year is rather more than 20% on the Capital. Before accepting this as good news, we should look at the **Assets** of the business and the basis of their valuation.

The first item, Leasehold Warehouse, Office, etc., is stated at cost six years ago. No provision for depreciation has been made by reference to the term of the lease.

By contrast, Motor Vehicles have been depreciated, but we do not know the rate. A proper figure for depreciation would probably be from 15 to 20% of the original cost, i.e. on the straight-line method (see page 206).

The Stocks are shown 'as estimated'. Estimates may be of two kinds, good and bad, and information should be sought as to whether the quantities or values, or both, have been estimated, and whether the values are in line with cost or market price, whichever was the lower at the date of the Balance Sheet.

As the Book Debts are described 'gross', their full face value has clearly been taken, and there is no provision for Doubtful Debts. The amount of this provision should be estimated as described on page 191. It would be a charge in the Profit and Loss Account, and would reduce the value of Book debts.

It would seem that the profit for the year may be over-stated because of possible over-valuations of the Assets mentioned.

Lastly, there is a pressing need for the collection of the Book Debts to provide money out of which to pay the trade creditors and accrued expenses. The extent of this urgency will in part depend on the limit set to the Overdraft facilities.

2 Statement of Net Current Assets

This may be drawn up as follows:

Net Current Assets (or net working capital)		£
Stocks of Fuel, oil, etc., as estimated		495.00
Book debts (gross)		2606.00
Insurance prepaid		15.00
Cash in hand		29.00
		£3145.00

Deduct:

	£	
Trade creditors	2118.00	
Accrued expenses	432.00	
Western Bank Ltd	269.00	
		2819.00
Total net current assets		326.00

The insurance prepaid is an asset at the date of the balance sheet. If the business was discontinued it could be recovered from the insurance company and if the business carries on then the following period will received the benefit of it.

It will usually be useful to calculate other ratios or percentages in addition to the Profit Margin. Current Assets as a multiple of Current Liabilities (i.e. 3145/2819 = 1.12 times), which implies that virtually all the stocks and debtors would need to be turned into cash to enable the creditors (short term) to be paid. This is a lower value for the ratio than would be ideal in most businesses and might cause concern to the creditors.

Similarly, Permanent capital as a multiple of Fixed Assets 7500/7174 = 1.05 times which means that the permanent capital is nearly all used to finance the Fixed Assets, with virtually the whole of the Current Assets being financed by the short term creditors.

Ratio analysis

The extent of analysis that can be performed on a business's accounts is virtually unlimited. There are many ratios which can be calculated to quantify the relationships between items in the Trading, Profit and Loss Accounts and the Balance Sheet.

Gross profit margin and return on capital employed have been mentioned earlier see pages 33, 158, 267. They are related by the net asset turnover (the same as the capital turnover as net assets equal capital employed).

GP margin = Gross Profit/Sales

Return (Gross) on capital = Gross Profit/Capital employed

Asset turnover = Sales/Capital employed (same as net assets)

Example 20.3

P James produces the following Trading, Profit and Loss Account and Balance Sheet:

Trading, Profit and Loss Account
for the year ended 31 December Year 2

	£		£
Opening Stock	10 000	Sales (all credit)	177 000
Purchases (all credit)	120 000		
	130 000		
Less closing stock	12 000		
Cost of Sales	118 000		
Gross Profit c/d	59 000		
	177 000		177 000
Wages	35 000	Gross Profit b/d	59 000
Administrative Expenses	1 800		
Light and Heat	400		
Telephone	250		
Rates	1 200		
Repairs and Renewals	800		
Motor Vehicle Expenses	1 100		
Depreciation M/Vehicles	3 000		
Fixtures/Fittings	1 450		
Net Profit	14 000		
	£ 59 000		£ 59 000

Balance Sheet
as at 31 December Year 2

		£			£
Fixed Assets			**Capital**		
Freehold Premises		49 900	as at 1.1 Year 2		86 000
Motor Vehicles 15 000–6 000		9 000	Add Profit for year		14 000
Fixtures/Fittings 7 250–2 900		4 350			100 000
		63 250	Less Drawings		9 250
					90 750
Current Assets	£		**Current Liabilities**		
Stocks	12 000		Creditors		10 000
Debtors	22 125				
Bank	3 375	37 500			
		£100 750			£100 750

The basic ratios can be calculated:

Gross Profit margin   59/177 = 0.3333 or 33.33%
Net Profit margin   14/177 = 0.0791 or 7.91%

Gross return on capital employed. Which capital figure should be used? That at the beginning of the year, the end, or an average? Technically an average would be appropriate but usually the opening amount is used as the capital account is not normally adjusted until the year end. In this example this would be £86 000.

$$59/86 = 0.6860, \text{ or } 68.60\%$$
or for **Net return**   14/86 = 0.1628, or 16.28%

The **net asset turnover**, which indicates how often the capital employed in the business is 'turned over' or sold, during the year is

$$177/86 = 0.0206, \text{ or } 2.06 \text{ times}$$

Using the gross figures we can now see that the gross margin to sales of 33.33% was earned 2.06 times during the year to give a return on capital employed of 2.06 × 33.33 which equals 68.6% approx. Similarly with the net basis, 2.06 × 7.91% = 16.3%, approx.

Profit margin	times	Asset turnover	equals	Return
$\dfrac{\text{Profit}}{\text{Sales}}$	×	$\dfrac{\text{Sales}}{\text{Capital}}$	=	$\dfrac{\text{Profit}}{\text{Capital}}$

This relationship explains how some businesses, for example, food retailing, may only earn a small profit margin to sales but have a very rapid turnover, and so earn this small margin several times a year go give a good annual return on Capital employed. A manufacturer with a much longer cycle from credit customers requires a much higher profit margin to obtain the same return on Capital employed.

Other ratios that may be calculated include:

Stock turnover
Cost of sales / average stock which is (10 + 12)/2 = 11
118   / 11 = 10.7 times, or nearly once a month.

This may be good, as it means that the stock is turning over very quickly, so it is unlikely that there will be any obsolete stock, or it could mean that there is often not enough choice for prospective customers to choose from so that sales are being lost.

Fixed asset turnover
Sales / Fixed assets
177   / 632.5 = 2.8 times, a much lower rate than for the stock.

Have we excess capacity? Could we sublet or sell surplus premises?

Current ratio, sometimes called **working capital ratio**
Current assets / Current liabilities
37.5 / 10 = 3.75 times or 3.75:1

The 'normal' value is 2:1 so this value may be high. A high value suggests that you will be able to pay the creditors on time and that will encourage them to give you good service.

Liquid ratio, similar to the current ratio but excludes stock.
Debtors and cash / Current liabilities
25.5 / 10 = 2.5 times or 2.5:1

Two other useful ratios from the many that are available relate to the amount of credit allowed to debtors and received from creditors.

Debtors at 31.12. Year 2 £22 125.
Sales during the year £177 000, per month 177 000/12 = 14 750

Average credit allowed is 22 125/14 750 = 1.5 months. Most businesses would be very pleased with this ratio if, as is the case with James, all sales are made on a credit basis.

Before calculating the comparable figure for creditors we should consider what purchases are supplied by the creditors. Is it merely the goods for resale, £120 000 in the year, or should some of the expenses be included. If only the purchases (and this is the only item that the data tells us is purchased on credit) then

monthly purchases on credit are 120 000/12 = 10 000, and

Average credit received is

Creditors at 31.12. Year 2 / Average monthly purchases on credit
10 000/10 000 = 1 month, which seems reasonable.

All these ratios use figures from the accounts. Those from the Trading and Profit and Loss Account are those for the whole year, and there may have been seasonal factors or expansion during the year. The Balance Sheet values are those on one specific date and may not necessarily be representative of those throughout the year.

What is 'normal', or more importantly, what should the value be in order to calculate truly representative ratios from final accounts? Several figures will reflect particular policies adopted by the management, or be different in different industries, and the basic comparison should be with the value that was expected. If there is a significant difference then a more detailed analysis must be made of the components making up the ratio.

What is a good ratio, what is bad? Again it mostly depends on what was expected. A high liquidity ratio means that your creditors can be paid promptly but would it be better to have more stock to sell? A manufacturer with spare capacity can accept an order for quick delivery, but what if no customer places that order?

It is important to bear in mind that no two businesses are the same. Although ratios from one business can be compared with another, they should not be taken out of the context of the other ratios and information available about the business if you are to avoid misunderstanding what the accounts are telling you.

KEY POINTS

On completion of this chapter:

1 you should now be able to calculate and interpret significant ratios from the final accounts of a small business, in particular: profit margins, sales turnover and asset turnover and the relationship between them

2 you should now appreciate that ratios must be interpreted in the context of each business and in relation to other ratios.

Questions

1 A trader's Capital appears on the 'liabilities' side of the Balance Sheet. In what sense is it true that the Capital is a liability of the business?

What would you infer if the trader's Balance Sheet (assumed correctly drawn up) showed the Capital on the 'Assets' side?

2 Give an example of one of each of the following:

■ Fixed Asset
■ Current Asset.

Explain the difference (if any) in the purposes for which such Assets are held by a trader or manufacturer.

3 Suppose that you have been newly appointed to an administrative position in a wholesale merchanting business. What data would you call for, and what tests would you apply to this, in order to find out if the general financial position of the business is sound and healthy?

4 The following is an account taken from the Sales Ledger of Herbert Charleston. Explain clearly what information this account gives you.

LILIAN BRYAN

Dr		£				Cr £
xxx4			xxx4			
Jan 1	Balance	102.00	Feb 3	Returns		21.00
March 3	Goods	336.00	April 4	Cheque		401.00
				Balance carried forward		16.00
		£438.00				£438.00
April 4	Balance forward	16.00	Sept 22	Cheque		164.00
June 23	Goods	141.00				
Aug 3	Interest Charged	7.00				
		£164.00				£164.00
Sept 26	Cheque Dishonoured	164.00	Nov 15	Bad Debts A/c	164.00	
		£164.00				£164.00

5 Briefly explain the meaning of the items shown in the following Ledger Account

E SIMPSON – CAPITAL ACCOUNT

Dr		£				Cr £
xxx2			xxx2			
June 30	Cash drawings	2 200.00	Jan 1	Balance		3 636.00
Sept 30	Purchases, motor car for self	9 060.00	June 30	Cash		500.00
Nov 30	Balance	4 116.00	Sept 30	Freehold property		11 225.00
			Nov 30	A Graham		15.00
		£15 376.00				£15 376.00

Note: On 20 november, A Graham, a creditor, for goods supplied had agreed to accept a cash payment of £0.50 in the £ in full discharge of his account of £30.

6 Each year a firm calculates the following percentages:

- Gross profit per cent on sales
- Net profit on gross profit
- Net profit per cent on capital.

What information do you think is obtained from these calculations?

7 From the following figures which were extracted from the books of a manufacturer you are asked to prepare an account or statement in a form which will give the proprietor the maximum information as to his trading results, including the percentages of the various items to turnover, and to state what conclusions can be drawn from the figures:

	Year end 30 September	
	xxx4	*xxx5*
	£	£
Purchases of material	45 823.00	56 494.00
Wages: Productive	25 064.00	36 768.00
Non-productive	10 620.00	10 984.00

	£	£
Returns inwards	472.00	1 903.00
Discount received	180.00	36.00
Salaries	11 560.00	15 584.00
Selling expenses	1 720.00	2 784.00
Discount allowed	420.00	492.00
Works expenses	3 176.00	3 456.00
Office expenses	6 370.00	8 420.00
Stock at commencement of year	2 189.00	2 876.00
Sales	120 472.00	165 903.00

The stock of material at 30 September xxx5 was valued at £1882.

8 Criticise, under the appropriate headings, any five of the items of the Balance Sheet of BM Downfield. In your opinion, is the financial position satisfactory? Give reasons for your answers.

Balance Sheet of BM Downfield
for xxx5–xxx6

Liabilities		Assets		
	£			£
Sundry creditors	12 500.00	Cash		1 300.00
Bank	3 200.00	Bills receivable		2 680.00
Capital	1 040.00	Sundry debtors		3 200.00
		Stock		6 860.00
		Plant	£2 000.00	
		and cost of repairs	200.00	
				2 200.00
		Fittings, cost price in xxx0		500.00
	£16 740.00			£16 740.00

9 The following accounts showing the result of a year's trading, with comparative figures for the preceding year, have been submitted to the proprietor of a manufacturing business, who has forwarded them to you for criticism. Rearrange the accounts in the form you consider will give the maximum information (showing also the percentages of the various expenses to turnover), and state any conclusions which can be drawn from the figures.

Trading and Profit and Loss Accounts

	Year ended 31 Dec xxx0	xxx1		*Year ended 31 Dec* xxx0	xxx1
	£	£		£	£
Stock	2 105.00	2 001.00	Sales	50 000.00	48 000.00
Purchases	5 576.00	5 524.00	Stock	2 001.00	1 495.00
Wages (productive)	15 500.00	15 400.00			
Works expenses	960.00	909.00			
Gross profit c/d	27 860.00	25 661.00			
	£52 001.00	£49 495.00		£52 001.00	£49 495.00
Rent and rates	3 700.00	3 720.00	Balance b/d	27 860.00	25 661.00
Wages (non-productive)	7 800.00	7 990.00			
Salaries	11 808.00	11 818.00			
Travellers' commission and expenses	920.00	900.00			
Office expenses	272.00	270.00			
Bad debts	200.00	414.00			
Net profit	3 160.00	549.00			
	£27 860.00	£25 661.00		£27 860.00	£25 661.00

ANSWERS TO QUESTIONS

For reasons of space, the answers provided here are limited to double-entry and numerical answers only. Answers to other questions can be found in the text and in the sample solutions to examination papers (see next section).

Questions on Chapter 2

1 a Cash total £378.70, Cheques total £623.33, Total paid in £1002
   b see p. 9

2 a Cash columns total £7038.16, Discount allowed £25, Bank cash book balance £4658.16
   b Lodgement not in bank £375, unpresented cheques £1065

3 a £10,45; £5,4; £1,16: 50p,2; 20p,4; 5p,2; 1p,1
   b Total £487.91

4 (Note that the opening stock is valued at £12 per unit and all purchases are at £12 per unit; therefore ALL value amounts will be units multiplied by £12.)
   a see pp. 19–20
   b Balance 10 units and £120
   c Adjustment –2 units, –£24

Questions on Chapter 3

8 Total invoice value £48 + VAT 8.40 = £56.40

9 Total purchases £4719, goods £925

10 Total credit note value £323.75 goods plus VAT £56.66 = £380.41

11 a A £1200 B £300
   b A 20% B 25%
   c A 25% B 33⅓%

12 Purchases Total   £14 541.25
              Goods   £13 791.25
              Sundries   £750.00
   Purchase Returns Total £1008, all goods
   Sales   Total   £7598.00
              Goods   £7580.00
              Sundries   £18.00
   Sales Returns Total £10, all sundries

Questions on Chapter 4

3   a   Debit
    b   Debit
    c   Credit
    d   Credit, normally, as Sales larger than Purchases
    e   Credit

4   Debit balance of £829.00

5   a

	Goods	VAT
Purchases	£545.00	£54.50
Purchase returns	38.50	3.85
Sales	370.00	37.00
Sales returns	56.00	5.60

    b   Due from Customs and Excise £19.25

6   Sales £780Cr   VAT £117Cr   Customers £897Dr

7   a   Purchases £950   Creditors £950   Sales £830   Debtors £830
    b   950   1045   830   913
        VAT £12DR

8   £7623

Questions on Chapter 5

2   a   Credit landlord   **b**   Credit cash
        Debit rent   Debit rent
        Credit cash
        Debit landlord

3   Balance is £40.75 Dr being £48.50 minus £7.75 but all transactions should appear on the statement.

4   Dr Balances   Cash £63.50   Remember the Cash Book is also the
                 Bank £94.85   ledger account but ledger accounts
    Discount Dr £1.00 Cr £2.35   will be needed for Abbott, stamps, etc.

5   Dr Balances Cash £35.00 Bank £612.00
    Discount Dr £6.75 Cr £2.00

6   Cheque payment £354.90

7   Cash Dr Balance £8.75

    Bank Cr Balance £11.75

8   a   Dr side   Personal
                 Impersonal
                 Private
        Cr side   Impersonal
                 Personal
                 Personal
                 Impersonal

9 Dr Balance £124.60
Cr Balance Bank £267.15
Discount Dr £1.25 Cr £2.50

10 a Plant A/c Debit
  b Robinson's personal A/c Credit
     Cash £170.00 and Discount allowed £2.60
  c Fire Loss A/c Credit
  d Motor Van A/c Credit
  e Fitter's personal A/c Debit
     Cash £250.00 and Discount received £10.75

Questions on Chapter 6

4 Extra expense £8.36 to give overdraft of £66.05

6 Cashbook £160 o/d

7 a Favourable Balance £65.82
   b Unfavourable Balance £233.96

8 Favourable Balance £80.39

Questions on Chapter 7

2 Nov 1 Cash from bank £195
Total expenditure for month £330
Dec 1 Cash from bank £330

3 Bank Balance £1646.38. Petty Cash Balance £100
Total PC expenditure £66.72, Analysis £22.40, 12.65, 20.72, 10.95
Discount allowed £17.00, Discount received £15.00

Questions on Chapter 9

1 Balances in TB:

Capital Cr	£6 350.00
Cash Dr	£347.00
Bank Cr	£2 332.00
TB Totals	£20 155.00

2 Balances in TB:

Capital Cr	£10 000.00
Cash Dr	£50.00
Bank Dr	£3 165.95
TB Totals	£11 159.00

3 Balances in TB:

Capital Cr	£6 050.00
Cash Dr	£50.00
Bank Dr	£3 464.50

Discount Cr   £2.50
Discount Dr   £17.50
TB Totals   £7 974.40

4 Balances in TB:
Capital Cr   £4 510.80
Cash Dr   £250.00
Bank Dr   £117.95
Discount Cr   £19.50
Discount Dr   £1.75
TB Totals   £5 666.90

5 Balances in TB:
Capital Cr   £2 500.00
Cash Dr   £162.10
Bank Dr   £255.05
Discount Dr   £5.75
TB Totals   £6 131.30
(including opening and closing stock)

6 Balances in TB:
Capital Cr   £10 650.00
Cash Dr   £100.00
Bank Dr   £4 556.70
Discount Dr   £9.20
Discount Cr   £98.50
TB Totals   £13 474.00

7 Balances in TB:
Capital Cr   £2 000.00
Cash Dr   £23.50
Bank Dr   £5 853.50
Discount Dr   £2.45
Discount Cr   £6.25
TB Totals   £7 543.75

Questions on Chapter 10

4 £2 555.40

5 Short Credit £103.20

7 **a** Short Dr £12.25
   b Short Dr £5.35
   c None
   d Short Dr £0.50
   e Short Cr £40.00

8 TB Totals £49 546.00

9 TB Totals £27 952.00

10 Original Balance short Dr £122.25

Questions on Chapter 12

5 b £40.00 profit

6 Net Profit. Dept   A £72.00

                  B £710.00

                  C £226.00

Dr P/L A/c £8.00 Balance of general expenses

Questions on Chapter 13

1 a Short Debit £100.00: None: Short Debit £30.00

  b Debtors understated £100.00; Fixtures understated £212.00: Profit understated £242.00: Bank balance understated £30.00

3 Balance Sheet Totals £83 350.00

5 Capital £23 264.00
Net Profit £1994.00
Balance Sheet Totals £24 054.00

6 Gross Profit £15 700.00. Net Profit £5250.00
Balance Sheet Totals £12 750.00

7 Gross Profit £11 550.00. Net Profit £1100.00
Balance Sheet Totals £58 200.00

8 Gross Profit £10 108. Net Loss £1769
Balance Sheet Totals £12 557

9 Gross Profit £10 250.00 (33⅓%)
Net Profit £1000.00 (3¼%)
Balance Sheet Totals £13 269.00

10 TB Totals £2717.00
Gross Profit £13.00. Net Loss £100.00
Balance Sheet Totals £2184.00

11 Gross Profit £14 349.00. Net Profit £2586.00
Balance Sheet Totals £8205.00

12 £986.00 less £20.00 depreciation: £966.00

13 Profit £1306.00. Balance Sheet Totals £3499.00

14 Gross Profit £2261.00. Net Profit £326.00
Balance Sheet Totals £37 918.00

Questions on Chapter 14

3 Profits xxx2 £22 517.00. xxx3 £22 638.00

4 P/L Debit £2941.00

5 P/L Debit £214.50

6 P/L Debit £1461.75

7 Bad Debts £314.09. Reserve £234.83

9 P/L Dr   xxx4 £122 951.40
      xxx5 £141 434.38
Omission overstates xxx4 Profits and understates
Liabilities £3441.18

10 P/L Dr Rent £2360.00. Rates £1903.36

11 P/L Dr Rates £2580.00. Wages £48 562.00
Stationery, etc. £747.00
Bad Debts and Reserve £409.00
Discounts £107.54

12 P/L Dr £90.00

13 P/L Dr £1151.00. Payments in advance etc. £147.00
Accrued expenses £45.00

14 Profit £7580

Questions on Chapter 15

3 a Depreciation £1760 each year
      NBV after year 4 £1760
  b Depreciation £1760, 1408, 1126, 901
      NBV after year 4 £3605

4 P/L Dr   xxx2 £62.00
      xxx3 £59.00
      xxx4 £56.00
      xxx5 £532.00
      xxx6 £516.00 (net)

5 P/L Dr £1500.00 p.a. BS net £8500, £7000

6 Depreciation £3432.00 (calculting depreciation for a half-year where appropriate). On new £81, on sold £9, on Balance £3342
Profit on sale £9.00

7 Depreciation (nearest £) £2890.00
Loss on sale £2305.00

8 Depreciation £5000.00 p.a.
Interest   xxx5 £1650.00
                xxx6 £1100.00
                xxx7 £550.00

9 Depreciation (opening Balances):   xxx4 £120.00
                                                            xxx5 £133.00

10 Gross Profit £35 545.00. Net Profit £10 013.00
139% on Capital
Balance Sheet Totals £17 816.00

11 Dr fixtures and fittings. Cr S Maxton and Sons
Dr Brampton Bros. Cr Perkings Ltd
Dr Cash £520.
     Typewriters £600. Cr Motor car £1120
Dr Profit and Loss. Cr Plant and machinery
Dr Cash £11.   Cr O Carfax £11
     Bad Debt £44.   O Carfax £44

12 Dr Lease £18 000. Cr Cash £18 000
Dr Cash £12 000. Cr Loan A/c £12 000
Dr Loan £250. Cr Cash (4 times) £250
Dr Interest payable £1175. Cr Cash £1175
Dr Profit and Loss Account £720. Cr Lease Depreciation £720

Questions on Chapter 16

1 a   £600, **b** £605, **c** £605

2 Draw £700, Dance £1790, Flower show £50, Refreshments £990. Surplus
£3820 after writing off crockery £100 and capitalising £1500. Club capital
£4890

3 a £420, **b** £570 after depreciation of £(540 + 420).
Club capital £21 930

4 Surplus £32, after depreciation of £338
Club capital £3402

Questions on Chapter 18

4 Interest on Loan £150.00
Profit Shares £1175.00

5 a   Interest on Loan £50.00
       Profit Shares £2975.00
b   Salary £1500.00
       Interest on Loan £50.00
       Profit Shares £2225.00

6 a Profit A. £2437.50. B. £812.50. Interest A £650 B £150
b Profit A. £2587.50. B. £862.50. Interest A £450 B £150

7 X. £14 694.00. Y. £11 020.00. Z. £4500.00 + 8000.00 = 12 500.00

8 a A. £23 800.00. B. £11 800.00
b A. £23 900.00. B. £11 700.00

9 Profit Shares, after deducting drawings
Bright £11 530.00. Smart £6995.00

10 A. Profit £5951.25. Interest £290.00
B. Profit £5951.25. Interest £190.00. Salary £2400.00
C. Profit £1967.50. Interest £50.00

11 Gross Profit £24 800.00. Net Profit £9730.00
Balance Sheet Totals £10 862.00

12 Gross Profit £23 699.62
Net Profit (before Interest) £5308.36
Balances carried forward:
Plant A/c £5950.00 Dr. Insurance A/c £131.75 Dr
Bad Debts Reserve £281.00 Cr
Commission A/c £34.94 Dr

13 Manufacturing A/c £80 071.00
Gross Profit £4265.00
Net Profit (before Interest) £2189.00
Balance Sheet Totals £20 879.00

14 Profit £3627.00
Balance Sheet Totals £5663.00

Questions on Chapter 19

1 Gross Profit £13 136.00. Net Profit £1788.20
Balance Sheet Totals £11 690.20

2 Gross Profit £20 900.00. Net Loss £850.00
Balance Sheet Totals £17 803.00

3 Gross Profit
(Manufacturing A/c) £22 787.00
Net Profit £8319.00
Balance Sheet Totals £103 095.00

EXAMINATION PAPERS AND SAMPLE SOLUTIONS

THE ROYAL SOCIETY OF ARTS
EXAMINATIONS BOARD
BOOK-KEEPING (107)
Stage I

(TIME ALLOWED – TWO HOURS)

You have TEN minutes to read through this question paper before the start of the examination.

Questions 1–4 are compulsory. You are advised to complete these questions BEFORE attempting Question 5.

You should attempt Question 5 if you wish to be considered for the award of a Credit.

Calculators may be used; however, a proportion of marks will be awarded for method and you should therefore ensure that workings are shown clearly throughout the examination.

Marks will be lost for untidy work.

Answers should be written in ink pen or ballpoint pen.

Question 1

a John Jennings is the owner of a small engineering firm. During October 1997 the following transactions took place:

3 Oct   New office equipment was purchased from Mega Systems, consisting of 2 computers at £1950 each, 2 printers at £395 each and a photocopier at £2470 all less 12½ per cent trade discount. Twenty-five per cent was paid by cheque, the remainder on credit.

10 Oct   I Hardrup who owes the firm £603.50 has been declared bankrupt. A cheque for 20p in the pound of the amount owed has been received in full and final settlement of the debt. The remainder is to be written off as a bad debt.

15 Oct   A delivery van has been sold for book value of £1950 to R Groves on credit. A cheque for one-third has been received, the balance is to be paid on 15 December 1997.

You are required to show journal entries, with narrations to record the above transactions.

b His accounts were reviewed on 31 October and the following errors were discovered:

i A cash payment of £143 to M Dyson had been entered in the cash book and also posted to the ledger as £341.

ii Goods bought on credit from T Clark costing £390 had been entered in J Clarkson's account.

You are required to show journal entries, with narrations, to record items **i** and **ii**.

c John Jennings' financial year ends on 31 October. From the balances given below prepare the closing journal entries to transfer the figures to the final accounts.

General expenses £2074
Carriage inwards £652
Discount allowed £890.

(26 marks)

Question 2

Helen Gibson runs a small business selling a wide range of garden furniture. On 1 October 1997 her sales ledger contained the following debtors:

	£
C Burrell	956.28
J Coates	639.74
M Kennedy	808.36

During the month of October the following transactions took place:

Sales on credit

October		Goods £	VAT £	Total £
3	J Coates	519.32	51.93	571.25
8	M Kennedy	384.94	38.49	423.43
14	C Burrell	625.18	62.52	687.70

Returns Inward

October		Goods £	VAT £	Total £
20	C Burrell	52.73	5.27	58.00
23	M Kennedy	48.60	4.86	53.46

Payments received by cheque

		Discount allowed £	Cheque value £
October			
17	J Coates	16.99	322.75
24	M Kennedy	40.42	767.94
29	C Burrell	11.95	466.05

You are required to:

a Open ledger accounts for all debtors and enter the balances as at 1 October 1997.

b Enter the transactions which have taken place during the month of October to the appropriate ledger accounts and balance the accounts at the end of the month.

c Show the entries which would appear in the sales, returns inward and VAT accounts in the general ledger.

d Prepare a sales ledger control account for the month of October 1997 and reconcile the balance with the total debtors balances in the sales ledger.

(26 marks)

Question 3

D King works in the assembly unit of a local factory, his clock number is 17. The firm operates a piece work system, piece rates are paid at a rate of £17.25 for every 25 items produced. During week 28, ending 31 October 1997, D King assembled 450 items.

Deductions are to be calculated as follows:

Company pension scheme	6% of gross pay
National Insurance	8% of gross pay
PAYE	£60.23
Social club	£2.50

The company's national insurance contribution to be paid on behalf D King is £18.75.

You are required to complete the following pay slip.

(12 marks)

Insert here:

| Centre Number: |
| Candidate's Name |

Clock No				Week No			Week ending			
					Deductions					
Name	Numbers produced	Rate	Gross Pay	Tax	National Insurance	Pensions	Others	Total	Net Pay	Employers' National Insurance Contribution

Question 4

Excel Products are one of your suppliers. Their account in your ledger is as follows:

1997		£	1997		£
14 Oct	Purchases returns	95	1 Oct	Balance b/d	1350
29	Bank	1330	6	Purchases	1850
29	Discount	20	20	Purchases	1050
30	Purchases returns	75			
31	Balance c/d	2730			
		4250			4250
			1 Nov	Balance b/d	2730

On 2 November the following statement of account is received from Excel Products.

			Debit	Credit	Balance
1997			£	£	£
Oct	1	Balance			2775
	3	Bank		1400	1375
	3	Discount		25	1350
	6	Sales	1850		3200

1997		£	£	£
Oct 14	Returns inwards		95	3105
20	Sales	1050		4155
28	Sales	1550		5705

You are required to:

a Prepare a reconciliation statement, starting with the balance in your books of **£2730** to explain the difference between the balance in your ledger and the closing balance on the statement of account.

b Briefly explain why a supplier may disallow a cash discount.

(12 marks)

Question 5

On 1 November 1996 the Lawnswood Tennis Club had the following assets and liabilities: Club Premises £45 500, Equipment £12 750, Bar stock £980, Bank balance £5220, Cash £326, Creditor for bar supplies £450.

The following receipts and payments were made during the year ended 31 October 1997.

		£
Subscriptions:	98 full-time members, each paying	250
	45 part-time members, each paying	125
Travelling expenses to away matches		1 454
Payments to suppliers for bar purchases		8 428
Lighting and heating		2 962
Payment of league entry fees		545
Rent received from private functions		1 485
General expenses		3 835
Rates		3 180
Insurance premium		2 472
Bar staff wages		5 950
Purchase of new equipment		5 790
Stationery and postage		508
Bar takings		16 592

On 31 October 1997 the following information was available:

i Rent of £395 was owing to the club for private functions.

ii Insurance prepaid was £1854.

iii There was a stock of stationery valued at £96 and a stock of drinks value at £1080. There were no bar creditors.

You are required to:

a Prepare a bar trading account for the year ended 31 October 1997.

b Prepare a receipts and payments account for the year ended 31 October 1997.

c   Prepare an income and expenditure account for the year ended 31 October 1997.

Note: A balance sheet is NOT required. Clearly show how you have dealt with the adjustments. Full and part-time members are listed and accounted for separately.

(24 marks)

Possible solutions

1 a   John Jennings   **General Journal**

		Dr £	Cr £
1997			
Oct 3	Office equipment		
	2 computers @ 1950	3900	
	2 printers @ 395	790	
	1 photocopier	2470	
		7160	
	Less 12½% trade discount	895	
			6265.00	
	Bank 25%		1566.25
	Mega Systems 75% Creditor		4698.75
		£6265.00	£6265.00

Being purchase of office equipment from Mega Systems of which 25% was paid in cash and 75% on credit

Oct 10	Bank	120.70	
	I Hardrup Debtor £603.50 @ 20p in the pound		120.70

Being receipt of cheque for 20p in the pound received in full settlement of debt of £603.50 owing from I Hardrup

	Bad Debts	482.80	
	I Hardrup Debtor		482.80

Being transfer of remaining debt due from I Hardrup now written off as a Bad Debt following his bankruptcy

Oct 15	Bank one-third of £1950	650.00	
	R Groves two thirds of £1950	1300.00	
	Delivery Van Disposal		1950.00

Being sale of Delivery van to R Groves, who paid one-third by cheque with the balance to be paid on 15 December 1997

b

1997		£	£
Oct 3	M Dyson (Creditor)	198.00	
	Bank (Cash Book)		198.00

Being correction of error in Cash book when a payment of £143 had been entered as £341, £198 too much

			Dr £	Cr £
1997				
Oct 31	J Clarkson		390.00	
	T Clark			390.00
	Being correction of error in posting when goods bought from			
	T Clark had been posted to the account of J Clarkson			

c

		Dr £	Cr £
Oct 31	Sundries		
	Sundries		
	Trading Account	652.00	
	Carriage inwards		652.00
	Profit and Loss Account	2074.00	
	General expenses		2074.00
	Profit and Loss Account	890.00	
	Discount Allowed		890.00
	Being the transfer of these expense accounts to the final		
	accounts at the end of the year		

2   a and b

Having read the question you should add up all the columns of figures, and check the cross-casts.

HELEN GIBSON
Sales Ledger
C BURRELL

Dr			£				Cr £
1997				1997			
Oct	1	Balance b/d	956.28	Oct	20	Returns	58.00
	14	Sales			29	Bank	466.05
		plus VAT	687.70			Discount	11.95
					31	Balance c/d	1107.98
			£1643.98				£1643.98
Nov	1	Balance b/d	1107.98				

J COATES

Dr			£				Cr £
1997				1997			
Oct	1	Balance b/d	639.74	Oct	20	Bank	322.75
	3	Sales				Discount	16.99
		plus VAT	571.25		31	Balance c/d	871.25
			£1210.99				£1210.99
Nov	1	Balance b/d	871.25				

M KENNEDY

Dr			£	Cr			£
1997				1997			
Oct	1	Balance b/d	808.36	Oct	23	Returns	53.46
	3	Sales			24	Bank	767.94
		plus VAT	423.43			Discount	40.42
					31	Balance c/d	369.97
			£1231.79				£1231.79
Nov	1	Balance b/d	369.97				

A reference column would be included if references had been given.

c

General (or Nominal) Ledger

SALES

Dr	£	Cr			£
		1997			
		Oct	31	Total for the month	1529.44

RETURNS INWARDS (OR SALES RETURNS)

Dr			£	Cr	£
1997					
Oct	31	Total for the month	101.33		

VAT

Dr			£	Cr			£
1997				1997			
Oct	31	Total for the month	10.13	Oct	31	Total for the month	152.94
		Balance c/d	142.81				
			£152.94				£152.94
				Nov	1	Balance b/d	142.81

d

SALES LEDGER CONTROL ACCOUNT

Dr			£	Cr			£
1997				1997			
Oct	1	Balance b/d	2404.38	Oct	31	Bank	1556.74
	31	Sales				Discount	69.36
		plus VAT	1682.38			Returns	111.46
					31	Balance c/d	2349.20
			£4086.76				£4086.76
Nov	1	Balance b/d	2349.20				

Debtor balances at 31 October 1997

	£
C Burrell	1107.98
J Coates	871.25
M Kennedy	369.97
Total per Control Account	£2349.20

3 Calculate the necessary figures and then complete the pay slip.

		£
For 25 items the gross pay is £17.25 or 69p each		
for 450 items the gross pay will be 450 X 69p =		310.50
deductions Company pension 6%	18.63	
National Insurance 8%	24.84	
PAYE given	60.23	
Social Club given	2.50	
total deductions		106.20
Net pay		£204.30

Remember the Employers' National Insurance, given, £18.75
Now enter ALL the data into the pay slip

Insert here:

Centre Number:	23
Candidate's Name	A. N. OTHER

Clock No 17				Week No 28				Week ending 31 October 1997		
					Deductions					
Name	Numbers produced	Rate	Gross Pay	Tax	National Insurance	Pensions	Others (Social Club)	Total	Net Pay	Employers' National Insurance Contribution
D. KING	450	£ 17.25/25 or 69p. ea.	£ 310.50	£ 60.23	£ 24.84	£ 18.63	£ 2.50	£ 106.20	£ 204.30	£ 18.75

4 a

		£
Balance in Purchase Ledger 31 October 1997		2730
add	Purchase in transit from Excel (29 Oct)	1550
	Purchase returns (30 Oct) not yet credited	
	by Excel	75
	Payment made (29 Oct) not yet credited by Excel	1330
	and related discount	20
Balance on Excel's statement dated 28 October		£5705

b Cash discounts are allowed because a payment has been received in accordance with the previously agreed terms of payment. If these terms have not been met then the discount may be disallowed. A common reason would be that the payment was late, or had not been calculated correctly. Often the later receipt by the supplier is said to be due to delay in the post or the banking system.

4 a   **Lawnswood Tennis Club**

Bar Trading Account for the year ended 31 October 1997

	£	£	£
Sales (Bar takings)			16 592
Opening stock		980	
Payments to suppliers	8 428		
Creditor at 1 Nov 1997	450		
purchase for year		7 978	
		8 958	
deduct closing stock		1 080	
Cost of goods sold during the year			7 878
Gross profit			8 714
Wages of bar staff			5 950
Net profit from bar during the year			£2 764

b It would be possible to use the profit from the Bar Trading Account, which incorporates adjustments for stock and creditors in the Receipts and Payment account, but it is not usual. When trading activities are significant an Income and Expenditure account is usually presented.

Lawnswood Tennis Club
Receipts and Payments Account for the year ended 31 October 1997

			£	£
Receipts	Subscriptions	full-time	24 500	
		part-time	5 625	
				30 125
	Rent from private functions			1 485
	Bar takings			16 592
	Total Receipts			48 202
Payments	Bar purchases		8 428	
	Bar staff wages		5 950	
	League entry fees		545	
	Travelling expenses		1 454	
	Lighting and heating		2 962	
	General expenses		3 835	
	Rates		3 180	
	Insurance premium		2 472	
	Stationery and postage		508	
	New equipment		5 790	
				35 124
Surplus for year				13 078
Cash and bank balance				
	at 1 November 1996 (326 + 5220)			5 546
	at 31 October 1997			£18 624

c

Lawnswood Tennis Club
Income and Expenditure Account for the year ended 31 October 1997

			£	£
Income	Subscriptions	full-time	24 500	
		part-time	5 625	
	Net profit from bar		2 764	
	Rent from private functions (note 1)		1 880	
				34 769
Expenditure				
	Payment of League fees		545	
	Travelling expenses		1 454	
	Lighting and Heating		2 962	
	General expenses		3 835	
	Rates		3 180	
	Insurance premium (note 2)		618	
	Stationery and postage (note 3)		412	
				13 006
Surplus of income over expenditure				£21 763

Notes: 1 Rent received £1485 plus rent owing £395   =   £1880
2 Insurance paid £2472 minus prepaid £1854   =   £618
3 Stationery purchased £508 minus stock £96   =   £412

Learning note. The Balance Sheet was **not** required. However, if you have time in an examination, or as a practical exercise now, it is worth while to produce the outline of one as check on the accuracy of your work.

		1.11.96	31.10.97
		£	£
Accumulated fund	Premises	45 500	45 500
	Equipment	12 750	18 540
	Bar stock	980	1 080
	Bank	5 220	18 624
	Cash	326	
	Creditor	−450	0
	Stationery stock	0	96
	Insurance prepaid	0	1 854
	Debtors	0	395
		64 326	£86 089
	add surplus of year	21 763	
		£86 089	

THE ROYAL SOCIETY OF ARTS
EXAMINATIONS BOARD
BOOK-KEEPING (104)
Stage I

(TIME ALLOWED – TWO HOURS)

You have TEN *minutes to read through this question paper before the start of the examination.*

Marks will be lost for untidy work.

Answers should be written in ink pen or ballpoint pen.

Calculators may be used.

You should answer only *those elements for which you require certification.*

Element 1

You are an employee of James W Lamb Limited which sells musical instruments, music books and sheet music. You have been asked to perform the following tasks:

a Record all the documents, on pages 298–307 inclusive, into the correct books of original entry (as printed in the answer book).

b Enter the correct date and name into the correct columns within these books.

Use the following analysis columns in the purchases and purchases returns day books: Instrument Purchases; Books and Music; Sundry Expenses; VAT; Total.

Use the following analysis columns in the sales and sales returns day books: Net; VAT; Total.

c Enter the figures into the correct columns within these books.

d Total the day books.

e Cross cast the day books.

Element 2

James W Lamb Limited operates an imprest system for petty cash with a float of £250.00. The imprest was restored on 2 May 1995 so there was an opening balance of £250.00. You are required to enter the opening balance into the petty cash book and to perform the following tasks:

a Enter the petty cash vouchers, on pages 308–309 inclusive, into the petty cash book (as printed in the answer book). Use the following analysis columns: VAT; Postage/Carriage; Cleaning; Staff Refreshments; Sundry; Purchase Ledger.

b Total all the columns of the petty cash book. (You are not required to balance the petty cash book.)

c Enter the amount and sign the petty cash reimbursement request in the answer book with the amount required to restore the imprest after these payments have been made.

Element 3

You have been given a cash book with an opening balance overdrawn at the bank of £407.40 as at 2 May 1995. You are required to enter the opening balance into the cash book and to perform the following tasks:

a Enter the receipts on pages 310–313 into the cash book in your answer book. All cash is banked immediately on receipt.

b Enter the payments on page 314 into the cash book, in your answer book.

c Update the cash book from the bank statement on page 315, for standing order payments; bank charges and credit transfers.

d Balance the cash book and bring down the balance to the following month.

e Complete the preprinted bank reconciliation statement in your answer book.

To be used when answering Element 1

INVOICE
H & B Publishing plc, Wentworth Road, New Malden

James W Lamb Ltd   Invoice No: 57/9529/105B
15 Sutherland Terrace   Date: 2.5.95
London WC1 2PS   VAT Reg No: 559 733459

Qty	Description	Unit Price £	Total Net £	VAT Rate %	VAT Amount £	Total £
5	10 Classical pieces for violin & piano by Spencer Harvey	6.00	30.00	0.00	0.00	30.00
2	Learn as you play Clarinet J P Clifford	4.76	9.52	0.00	0.00	9.52
			39.52	0.00	0.00	39.52

TERMS: Net Monthly Account

INVOICE
BULLET MUSICAL INSTRUMENTS PLC
New End Industrial Estate, Birmingham, B14 1TS
0121 942 7493

James W Lamb Ltd   Invoice No: 549127
15 Sutherland Terrace   Date: 3 May 1995
London WC1 2PS   VAT Reg No: 549 2323 14

Qty	Description	Unit Price £	Total Net £	VAT Rate %	VAT Amount £	Total £
1	Bullet B12 Clarinet	215.00	215.00	17.5%	37.62	252.62
			215.00		37.62	252.62

TERMS:

To be used when answering Element 1

SP Office Supplies	**INVOICE**			Invoice No **14797**	

Unit 3 Crayfield Industrial Estate
Crayfield Kent DA2 3DA

James W Lamb Ltd
15 Sutherland Terrace
London WC1 2PS

Date: 4.5.95
VAT Reg No: 922 923500

Your order: 5962   Despatch Date: 4.5.95

Qty	Description	Unit Price £	Total Net £	VAT Rate %	VAT Amount £	Total £
6	Laser Printer Toner Cartridge Code Number: TONER6	13.00	78.00	17.5%	13.65	91.65
			78.00		13.65	91.65

TERMS: 30 Days Net

INVOICE

ACE COMPUTER MAINTENANCE

To

James W Lamb Ltd
15 Sutherland Terrace
London WC1 2PS

Invoice No 5924/27
Date 4 May 1995
VAT Reg No: 238 645842

Description	Total Net £	VAT Rate %	VAT Amount £	Total £
Call out visit to repair in-house computer	49.50	17.5%	8.66	58.16
Total	49.50	–	8.66	58.16

Units 10 & 11, Enterprise Park, London, W2 0BP

To be used when answering Element 1

INVOICE
Shimco UK Ltd
Shimco House, 17 Cornhill, Nottingham

James W Lamb Ltd   Invoice No   5297
15 Sutherland Terrace   Date: 5 May 1995
London WC1 2PS   VAT Reg No: 121 3434 55

Qty	Description	Unit Price £	Total Net £	VAT Rate %	VAT Amount £	Total £
2	Shimco 501 Violins	140.00	280.00	17.5	49.00	329.00
			280.00		49.00	329.00

TERMS: By Return

INVOICE   Invoice No

Laker Envelopes Ltd   **01254**
Laker House
HOLBURN WC1

James W Lamb Ltd   Date: 5.5.95
15 Sutherland Terrace   VAT Reg No: 066 5725 96
London WC1 2PS

Your order: Telephoned   Despatch Date: 5.5.95

Qty	Description	Unit Price £	Total Net £	VAT Rate %	VAT Amount £	Total £
200	A4 Envelopes LL 154	13.00 per 100	26.00	17.5%	4.55	30.55
400	A5 Window Envelopes LL 156	10.00 per 100	40.00	17.5%	7.00	47.00
			66.00		11.55	77.55

TERMS: 30 Days Net

To be used when answering Element 1

Invoice No: 2321
VAT No: 479 9876 31
Date 5 May 1995

COUNTALOT & CO
Chartered Accountants
15 Uxbridge Road
Shepherds Bush
London W12 6XJ

In Account with James W Lamb Limited

	£
Auditing your books and records for the year ended 31 December 1994	1500.00
Submitting a copy of the accounts together with supporting Income Tax computations to the Inspector of Taxes	250.00

Total excluding VAT	1750.00
VAT (17.5%)	306.25
TOTAL	2056.25

INVOICE
BULLET MUSICAL INSTRUMENTS PLC
New End Industrial Estate, Birmingham, B14 1TS
0121 942 7493

James W Lamb Ltd
15 Sutherland Terrace
London WC1 2PS

Invoice No: 549139
Date: 5 May 1995
VAT Reg No: 549 2323 14

Qty	Description	Unit Price £	Total Net £	VAT Rate %	VAT Amount £	Total £
2	E11 Grenadilla Clarinets	370.00	740.00	17.5%	129.50	869.50
1	Bullet Top F# Alto Sax.	456.00	465.00	17.5%	81.37	546.37
			1205.00		210.87	1415.87

TERMS:

To be used when answering Element 1

CREDIT NOTE	No: 7

SHOSAKU VIOLAS (UK) LTD

Date/Tax Point: 3 May 1995

James W Lamb Ltd
15 Sutherland Terrace
London WC1 2PS

VAT No: 542 3078 19

Quantity	Description	Catalogue number	Unit Price £	Total Amount £
1	15½" Viola	HA 200	132.00	132.00
		Total excluding VAT		132.00
		VAT (17.5%)		23.10
		Total credit		155.10

Reason for credit: Wrong model supplied to be replaced by HA300

CREDIT NOTE	No: 629

CENTRAL GASBOARD

Date/Tax Point: 4 May 1994

James W Lamb Ltd
15 Sutherland Terrace
London WC1 2PS

Description	Total Amount £
Credit in respect of Invoice 5742	35.00
Total excluding VAT	35.00
VAT (17.5%)	6.12
Total credit	41.12

Reason for credit: Duplication of charges for repairs

To be used when answering Element 1

CREDIT NOTE
Bullet Musical Instruments plc
New End Industrial Estate
Birmingham, B14 1TS
Tel 0121 942 7493

James W Lamb Ltd   Credit Note No: 316
15 Sutherland Terrace   Date: 9 May 1995
London WC1 2PS   VAT Reg No: 549 2323 14

Qty	Description	Unit Price £	Total Net £	VAT Rate %	VAT Amount £	Total £
1	Bullet B12 Clarinet	215.00	215.00	17.5	37.62	252.62
	Clarinet returned damaged		215.00		37.62	252.62

Ref: Invoice no 549127

CREDIT NOTE   No: 17
LAKER ENVELOPES LTD
LAKER HOUSE, HOLBURN, WC1

Date/Tax Point: 12 May 1995

James W Lamb Ltd
15 Sutherland Terrace
London WC1 2PS

Quantity	Description	Catalogue number	Unit Price £	Total Amount £
400	A5 Window envelopes	LL156	50p per 100	2.00
		Total excluding VAT		2.00
		VAT (17.5%)		0.35
		Total credit		2.35

Reason for credit: Wrong price charged invoice 01254

To be used when answering Element 1

INVOICE
JAMES W LAMB LIMITED, 15 SUNDERLAND TERRACE, LONDON, WC1 2PS
Tel 0171 692 5497

To

Miss L Collins   Invoice No: 1392
59 Chepstow Road   Date: 2 May 1995
Sutton   VAT Reg No: 526 8892 62

Description	Total Net £	VAT Rate %	VAT Amount £	Total £
Yamaha 26 Phenol Resin Bb Clarinet Outfit RR4	312.00	17.5	54.60	366.60
Learn as you play Clarinet by J P Clifford	5.95	0.0	0.00	5.95
Total	317.95		54.60	372.55

Terms: Strictly 30 days net

INVOICE
JAMES W LAMB LIMITED, 15 SUNDERLAND TERRACE, LONDON, WC1 2PS
Tel 0171 692 5497

To

Mrs J Pledger   Invoice No: 1393
72 High Street   Date: 2 May 1995
Wimbledon SW19   VAT Reg No: 526 8892 62

Description	Total Net £	VAT Rate %	VAT Amount £	Total £
"10 Classical pieces for violin and piano" by Spencer Harvey	7.50	0.00	0.00	7.50
Total	7.50	0.00	0.00	7.50

Terms: Strictly 30 days net

To be used when answering Element 1

INVOICE

JAMES W LAMB LIMITED, 15 SUNDERLAND TERRACE, LONDON, WC1 2PS

Tel 0171 692 5497

To

Goodwind Music Ltd	Invoice No: 1394
373 Broad Street	Date: 3 May 1995
Hereford	VAT Reg No: 526 8892 62
Herts	

Description	Total Net £	VAT Rate %	VAT Amount £	Total £
H & B 400 (Czech) 1/2 double Lacquer finish French horn	1075.00			
Shimco 501 (Korean) Violin	210.00			
	1285.00			
20% discount	(257.00)			
Total	1028.00	17.5	179.90	1207.90

Terms: Strictly 30 days net

INVOICE

JAMES W LAMB LIMITED, 15 SUNDERLAND TERRACE, LONDON, WC1 2PS

Tel 0171 692 5497

To

Rosewood Academy of Music	Invoice No: 1395
Rosewood Road	Date: 3 May 1995
Chelmsford	VAT Reg No: 526 8892 62
Essex	

Description	Total Net £	VAT Rate %	VAT Amount £	Total £
2 Daug (Korean) Silver plated flutes at £195.00 each	390.00			
10% discount on flutes	(39.00)			
	351.00	17.5	61.42	412.42
10 copies of "First steps for the flute" by Rose Garney at £4.50 each	45.00	0.0	0.00	45.00
Total	396.00		61.42	457.42

Terms: Strictly 30 days net

To be used when answering Element 1

INVOICE
JAMES W LAMB LIMITED, 15 SUNDERLAND TERRACE, LONDON, WC1 2PS
Tel 0171 692 5497

To

Mr H J Henkel
17 Tulip Grove
Ruislip
Middlesex

Invoice No: 1396
Date: 4 May 1995
VAT Reg No: 526 8892 62

Description	Total Net £	VAT Rate %	VAT Amount £	Total £
Sheffler 5013 short reach Bassoon	1850.00	17.5	323.75	2173.75
Total	1850.00	17.5	323.75	2173.75

Terms: Strictly 30 days net

INVOICE
JAMES W LAMB LIMITED, 15 SUNDERLAND TERRACE, LONDON, WC1 2PS
Tel 0171 692 5497

To

Sarah Linklater
278 Westmorland Road
Barnet
Herts

Invoice No: 1397
Date: 5 May 1995
VAT Reg No: 526 8892 62

Description	Total Net £	VAT Rate %	VAT Amount £	Total £
Bullet top F# lacquer finish Alto Saxe	620.00	17.5	108.50	728.50
Total	620.00		108.50	728.50

Terms: Strictly 30 days net

To be used when answering Element 1

CREDIT NOTE

JAMES W LAMB LIMITED, 15 SUNDERLAND TERRACE, LONDON, WC1 2PS
Tel 0171 692 5497

To

Mrs V Redbridge   Credit Note No: 12
16 Southport Road   Date: 5 May 1995
Dover   VAT Reg No: 526 8892 62

Description	Total Net £	VAT Rate %	VAT Amount £	Total £
Bullet 862E Silver head flute	365.00	17.5	63.87	428.87
Total	365.00		63.87	428.87

Credit in respect of invoice 1350 – Goods returned damaged on arrival

---

CREDIT NOTE

JAMES W LAMB LIMITED, 15 SUNDERLAND TERRACE, LONDON, WC1 2PS
Tel 0171 692 5497

To

Regis Music Ltd   Credit Note No: 13
Seaview Parade   Date: 5 May 1995
Bognor   VAT Reg No: 526 8892 62

Description	Total Net £	VAT Rate %	VAT Amount £	Total £
"10 Classical pieces for violin and piano" by Spencer Harvey	7.50	0.00	0.00	7.50
Total	7.50		0.00	7.50

Credit in respect of invoice 1390. Goods returned ordered in error

To be used when answering Element 2.

| PETTY CASH VOUCHER | Folio 001 |
| Date 2nd May 19 95 |

For what required	AMOUNT	
---	£	P
Stamps	45	00
Trade Magazine	1	50
	46	50

Signature / Marshall
Passed by G. Cooper.

| PETTY CASH VOUCHER | Folio 002 |
| Date 2nd May 1995 |

For what required	AMOUNT	
---	£	P
1 Roll Sello Tape		99
Post-it-notes	1	40
Paper clips	1	00
(includes 50p VAT)	3	39

Signature Joan Daily
Passed by G. Cooper.

| PETTY CASH VOUCHER | Folio 003 |
| Date 3rd May 1995 |

For what required	AMOUNT	
---	£	P
New Mop head	1	60
VAT		28
Teabags		88
	2	76

Signature Sarah Button
Passed by G. Cooper.

| PETTY CASH VOUCHER | Folio 004 |
| Date 4th May 19 95 |

For what required	AMOUNT	
---	£	P
Sarah Button	15	00
Cleaner - wages		
	15	00

Signature Sarah Button
Passed by G. Cooper.

| PETTY CASH VOUCHER | Folio 005 |
| Date 4th May 1995 |

For what required	AMOUNT	
---	£	P
F. Wright	25	00
Window Cleaner		
	25	00

Signature F Wright
Passed by G. Cooper

| PETTY CASH VOUCHER | Folio 006 |
| Date 5th May 19 95 |

For what required	AMOUNT	
---	£	P
Milkman	2	97
	2	97

Signature Peter Monk
Passed by G. Cooper.

To be used when answering Element 2.

PETTY CASH VOUCHER	Folio 007		
	Date 10ᵗʰ May 1995		

For what required	AMOUNT	
	£	P
S & m News Purchase ledger account PL 516	19	57
	19	57

Signature   S. Small
Passed by   G. Cooper.

PETTY CASH VOUCHER	Folio 008		
	Date 12ᵗʰ May 1995		

For what required	AMOUNT	
	£	P
Joan Daily Reimbursement of Petrol Cost for Training course VAT	15	00
	2	62
	17	62

Signature   Joan Daily
Passed by   G. Cooper.

PETTY CASH VOUCHER	Folio 009		
	Date 17ᵗʰ May 1995		

For what required	AMOUNT	
	£	P
Stamps 10 × £1·00	10	00
	10	00

Signature   I. Marshall
Passed by   G. Cooper.

PETTY CASH VOUCHER	Folio 010		
	Date 19ᵗʰ May 1995		

For what required	AMOUNT	
	£	P
Milkman	2	97
	2	97

Signature   Peter Monk
Passed by   G. Cooper.

PETTY CASH VOUCHER	Folio 011		
	Date 23ʳᵈ May 1995		

For what required	AMOUNT	
	£	P
Batteries for wall clock (Inc VAT 29p)	1	98
	1	98

Signature   Joan Daily
Passed by   G. Cooper.

PETTY CASH VOUCHER	Folio 012		
	Date 24ᵗʰ May 1995		

For what required	AMOUNT	
	£	P
Sarah Butter Cleaness wages	15	00
	15	00

Signature   Sarah Button
Passed by   G. Cooper.

To be used when answering Element 3.

Copies of Cheques Received

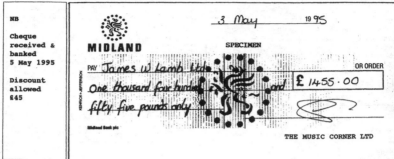

NB

Cheque
received &
banked
5 May 1995

Discount
allowed
£45

3 May 19 95

MIDLAND   SPECIMEN

PAY James W Lamb Ltd   OR ORDER

One thousand four hundred and   £ 1455.00

fifty five pounds only

Midland Bank plc

THE MUSIC CORNER LTD

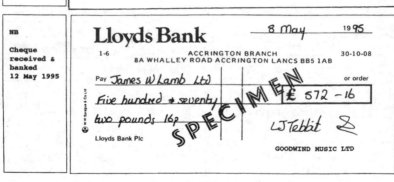

NB

Cheque
received &
banked
12 May 1995

Lloyds Bank   8 May   19 95

1-6   ACCRINGTON BRANCH   30-10-08
          8A WHALLEY ROAD ACCRINGTON LANCS BB5 1AB

Pay James W Lamb Ltd   or order

Five hundred & seventy   £ 572 - 16

two pounds 16p

Lloyds Bank Plc   SPECIMEN

LJTebbit

GOODWIND MUSIC LTD

To be used when answering Element 3.

Copies of Cheques Received

NB
 	
Cheque
received &
banked
17 May 1995
	Girobank
	Bootle Merseyside GIR 0AA ⌐ ⌐ SPECIMEN 72-00-00
	
	Pay _James W lamb ltd_ ∟ ⌐ or order _14th May_ 1995
	Amount _Three hundred & seventy two_ **£372-55**
	pounds 55p only
	                           Signature
	MISS L COLLINS
	59 Chepstow Road
	Sutton _L Collins_
	           Please do not write in the space below

NB
 	
Cheque
received &
banked
19 May 1995
 	
Relates to
Cash Sale
	❖ BARCLAYS _15 May_ 19 _95_
	GOLDERS GREEN BRANCH, 20-34-06
	883/885 FINCHLEY ROAD, LONDON NW11 8RU BARCLAYS BANK PLC
	                            or order
	Pay _James W Lamb_
	Two thousand four hundred & **£2470.00**
	seventy pounds only
	Cheque No. Branch No. Account No. _Rosalica_
	                      MS T P ROSALIA

To be used when answering Element 3.

Copies of Cheques Received

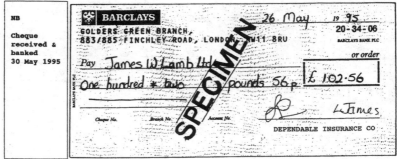

NB

Cheque
received &
banked
30 May 1995

BARCLAYS

GOLDERS GREEN BRANCH,
883/885 FINCHLEY ROAD, LONDON NW11 8RU

26 May 19 95

20-34-06

BARCLAYS BANK PLC

Pay   James W Lamb Ltd   or order

One hundred * two   pounds 56 p   £ 102·56

Cheque No.   Branch No.   Account No.

L James

DEPENDABLE INSURANCE CO

SPECIMEN

NB

Cheque
received &
banked
31 May 1995

Relates to
Cash Sale

Lloyds Bank   29 May   19 95

1-6   ACCRINGTON BRANCH   30-10-08
           8A WHALLEY ROAD ACCRINGTON LANCS BB5 1AB

Pay   James W Lamb Ltd   or order

Five hundred *seventeen   £ 517·50

pounds 50p

Lloyds Bank Plc

P Harper

PAUL HARPER

SPECIMEN

To be used when answering Element 3.

Copies of cash receipts

..6. May................1995   No...316......

Received
   from.....Mrs T Kirkby.......................

The sum of...Thirty..seven..pounds.50.
                    Cash Sale..........

Cheque		
Cash	37	50
Discount		
	37	50

..........G. Cooper..........

WITH   THANKS

..17. May................1995   No...317......

Received
   from......Miss L.M. Sharp.........

The sum of..Ninety...three.pounds.27p
....

Cheque		
Cash	93	27
Discount		
	93	27

..........G. Cooper..........

WITH   THANKS

To be used when answering Element 3.

Copies of cheque counterfoils

3 May 1995	3 May 1995
TO	TO
British Telecom	H & B Publishing plc
Old Balance	Old Balance
Deposits	Deposits
Total	Total
This Cheque £ 697·25	This Cheque £ 215·00
New Balance	New Balance
003106	003107

4 May 1995	12 May 1995
TO	TO
Bullet Musical	Yamaha Instrument
Instruments plc	(UK) plc
Old Balance	Old Balance
	Discount
Deposits	Deposits taken £24·80
Total	Total
This Cheque £1497·20	This Cheque £595·20
New Balance	New Balance
003108	003109

19 May 1995	28 May 1995
TO	TO HM Customs
Shimco UK Ltd	& Excise
Old Discount	Old Balance
Balance taken £23·50	
Deposits	Deposits
Total	Total
This Cheque £727·50	This Cheque £2460·23
New Balance	New Balance
003110	003111

To be used when answering Element 3.

Statement of Account

BANK STATEMENT

Barclays Bank plc
Holborn Branch

James W Lamb Limited
account No 32927797
Sheet No 52   Date 2.6.95

Date 1995	Description	Debit	Credit	Balance
2 May	Balance Forward			407.40 DR
3 May	Westminster City Council s.o.	242.00		649.40 DR
8 May	Cheque		1455.00	
	003106	697.25		108.35
9 May	003108	1497.20		
	Deposit		37.50	1351.35 DR
11 May	University of Guildford Credit Transfer		1597.23	245.88
17 May	Cheque		572.16	
	003109	595.20		
	003107	215.00		7.84
19 May	Deposit		93.27	101.11
22 May	Cheque		372.55	473.66
23 May	Cheque		2470.00	
	003110	727.50		2216.16
26 May	Overdraft Interest 20 Feb – 19 May	14.62		
	Current Account Charge 20 Feb – 19 May	107.98		2093.56

Sample solutions

1 Note: In the examination you would have some printed answer sheets.

James W Lamb   Purchases Day Book

Date	Supplier	Instrument Purchases £	Books & Music £	Sundry Expenses £	VAT £	Total £	
1995							
May 2	H&B Publishing plc		39.52		0.00	39.52	
3	Bullet Musical Instruments PLC	215.00			37.62	252.62	
4	SP Office Supplies			78.00	13.65	91.65	
4	Ace Computer Maintenance			49.50	8.66	58.16	
5	Shimco UK Ltd	280.00			49.00	329.00	
5	Laker Envelopes Ltd			66.00	11.55	77.55	
5	Countalot & Co			1750.00	306.25	2056.25	
5	Bullet Musical Instruments PLC	1205.00			210.87	1415.87	
	Totals	1700.00	39.52	1943.50	637.60	4320.62	Check 4320.62

James W Lamb   Purchases Returns Day Book

Date	Supplier	Instrument Purchases £	Books & Music £	Sundry Expenses £	VAT £	Total £	
1995							
May 3	Shosaku Violas (UK) Ltd	132.00			23.10	155.10	
4	Central Gasboard			35.00	6.12	41.12	
9	Bullet Musical Instruments plc	215.00			37.62	252.62	
12	Laker Envelopes Ltd			2.00	0.35	2.35	
	Totals	347.00	0.00	37.00	67.19	451.19	Check 451.19

James W Lamb   Sales Day Book

Note that you are asked to use three analysis columns only. In practice separate columns for instruments and music might be appropriate.

Date	Customer	Invoice number	Net £	VAT £	Total £	
1995						
May 2	Miss L Collins	1392	317.95	54.60	372.55	
2	Mrs J Pledger	1393	7.50	0.00	7.50	
3	Goodwind Music Ltd	1394	1028.00	179.90	1207.90	
3	Rosewood Academy of Music	1395	396.00	61.42	457.42	
4	Mr H J Henkel	1396	1850.00	323.75	2173.75	
5	Sarah Linklater	1397	620.00	108.50	728.50	
	Totals		4219.45	728.17	4947.62	Check 4947.62

James W Lamb   Sales Returns Day Book

Note that you are asked to use three analysis columns only. In practice separate columns for instruments and music might be appropriate.

Date	Customer	Credit Note number	Net £	VAT £	Total £	
1995						
May 5	Mrs V Redbridge	12	365.00	63.87	428.87	
5	Regis Music Ltd	13	7.50	0.00	7.50	
	Totals		372.50	63.87	436.37	Check 436.37

2 a   James W Lamb   Petty Cash Book

Receipts Date 1995	Receipts amount £	Description	Payments Voucher number	Total £	VAT £	Postage/ carriage £	Cleaning £	Staff refreshments £	Sundry £	Purchase Ledger £
May 2	250.00	Opening balance								
2		Stamps, magazine	1	46.50	0.00	45.00			1.50	
2		Stationery	2	3.39	0.50				2.89	
3		Mop head, teabags	3	2.76	0.28		1.60	0.88		
4		Wages, S Button	4	15.00	0.00		15.00			
4		Window cleaner	5	25.00	0.00		25.00			
5		Milkman	6	2.97	0.00			2.97		
10		S&M News PL 516	7	19.57	0.00					19.57
12		Training course ex	8	17.62	2.62				15.00	
17		Stamps	9	10.00	0.00	10.00				
19		Milkman	10	2.97	0.00			2.97		
23		Clock batteries	11	1.98	0.29				1.69	
24		Wages, S Button	12	15.00			15.00			
b	250.00			162.76	3.69	55.00	56.60	6.82	21.08	19.57

Check 162.76

c Petty Cash Reimbursement Request.   Date   24 May 1997

Expenditure from 2 May 1995 to 24 May 1995   £162.76

signed .... Petty cashier

approved by .... Authorised signatory

Date   25 May 1995

3   James W Lamb   Cash Book

Received Date 1995	Detail	Discount Received	Bank £	Paid Date 1995	Detail	Discount Allowed	Bank £
May 5	The Music Corner L	45.00	1455.00	May 2	Opening overdraft		407.40
6	Mrs T Kirby, Cash sale		37.50	3	British Telecom		697.25
12	Goodwind Music Ltd		572.16	3	H & B Publishing		215.00
17	Miss L M Sharp		93.27	4	Bullet Musical In		1497.20
17	Miss L Collins		372.55	12	Yamaha Instr. (UK)	24.80	595.20
19	Ms T P Rosalia, Cash sale		2470.00	19	Shimco UK Ltd	23.50	727.50
30	Dependable Insurance Co		102.56	28	HM Customs and F		2460.23
31	Paul Harper, Cash sale		517.50	3	Westminster CC S.O.		242.00
11	Uni of Guildford CT		1597.23	26	Interest 20.2–19.5		14.62
				26	Charges 20.2–19.5		107.98
				31	Balance, carried down		253.39
		45.00	7217.77			48.30	7217.77

d

| June 1 | Balance, brought down | | 253.39 | | | | |

e

Bank reconciliation statement at 31 May 1995

	£	£
Balance as shown by bank statement		2093.56
add items paid in but not on statement		
Dependable Insurance	102.56	
Paul Harper	517.50	
		620.06
		2713.62
deduct cheques not yet presented to bank		
HM Customs and Excise		2460.23
Balance as in cash book		£253.39

THE ROYAL SOCIETY OF ARTS
EXAMINATIONS BOARD
BOOK-KEEPING (204)
Stage II
(TIME ALLOWED – TWO HOURS)

You have TEN *minutes to read through this question paper before the start of the examination.*

You are encouraged to show your working for each question as marks will be awarded for method.

Marks will be lost for untidy work.

Answers should be written in ink pen or ballpoint pen.

Calculators may be used.

You should answer only *those elements for which you require certification.*

Element 1

You are an employee of Vigilant Alarms Ltd and you have to perform the following tasks:

a Write up the appropriate personal accounts in the ledgers provided in your answer book from the day books on pages 321 and 322 and the cash book on page 323. (Date order is not important.)

All opening balances are as at 3 April 1995.

You should use the following accounts:

Purchase Ledger
Adel Plastics	– opening balance	£470.30 Cr
Electronic Systems	– opening balance	£329.12 Cr
Spark Components	– opening balance	£586.75 Cr

Sales Ledger
Auto Services	– opening balance	£696.48 Dr
Gibsons Garages	– opening balance	£485.25 Dr
Qwikfit Security	– opening balance	£373.96 Dr

b Correct the running balance after each entry.

c Write up the accounts in the nominal ledger provided in your answer book from the day books on pages 321 and 322 and the cash book on page 323. (Date order is not important.)

All the opening balances are as at 3 April 1995.

You should use the following accounts:

Capital	– opening balance	£14 700.00 Cr
Equipment	– opening balance	£14 500.00 Dr
Rent	– opening balance	£1 000.00 Dr
VAT	– opening balance	£269.80 Cr
Purchases	– opening balance	£8 520.00 Dr
Purchase Returns	– opening balance	£194.00 Cr
Sales	– opening balance	£12 670.00 Cr
Sales Returns	– opening balance	£76.30 Dr
Discount Received	– opening balance	£147.43 Cr
Discount Allowed	– opening balance	£62.37 Dr

d Reconcile the supplier's statement of account on page 324 with the personal account in the purchases ledger as at 30 April 1995 by completing the supplier's reconciliation statement in the answer book.

e Complete the purchase ledger control account in your answer book as at 30 April 1995.

f Complete the sales ledger control account in your answer book as at 30 April 1995.

g Balance the control accounts as at 30 April 1995.

h Write up a creditors' list as at 30 April 1995 using the form in your answer book.

i Write up a debtors' list as at 30 April 1995 using the form provided in your answer book.

Element 2

You are an employee of Broadway Fencentre, a small firm which does not use day books, and you have to perform the following tasks:

a Draft a trial balance using the form in the answer book as at 30 April 1995 from the set of accounts on pages 325–329.

b These accounts contain two obvious errors. A further two errors are noted on the memorandum on page 330. Find the errors in the accounts and correct all four making appropriate entries in the journal using the form provided in the answer book.

c Produce a revised trial balance using the form in the answer book.

To be used when answering Element 1.

VIGILANT ALARMS LTD
PURCHASES DAY BOOK

Date 1995		DETAIL	GOODS £ p	VAT £ p	INVOICE TOTAL £ p
Apr	3	Adel Plastics	118.25	20.69	138.94
	5	Electronic Systems	81.28	14.22	95.50
	10	Adel Plastics	125.00	21.88	146.88
	12	Spark Components	575.96	100.79	676.75
	24	Electronic Systems	142.18	24.88	167.06
	26	Adel Plastics	298.12	52.17	350.29
			1340.79	234.63	1575.42

VIGILANT ALARMS LTD
PURCHASES RETURNS DAY BOOK

Date 1995		DETAIL	GOODS £ p	VAT £ p	INVOICE TOTAL £ p
Apr	10	Electronic Systems	29.45	5.15	34.60
	14	Adel Plastics	24.00	4.20	28.20
	27	Electronic Systems	54.30	9.50	63.80
			107.75	18.85	126.60

To be used when answering Element 1.

VIGILANT ALARMS LTD
SALES DAY BOOK

Date 1995		DETAIL	GOODS £ p	VAT £ p	INVOICE TOTAL £ p
Apr	4	Gibsons Garages	277.02	48.48	325.50
	12	Auto Services	78.47	13.73	92.20
	17	Gibsons Garages	109.45	19.15	128.60
	19	Qwikfit Security	318.98	55.82	374.80
	24	Auto Services	220.68	38.62	259.30
	27	Qwikfit Security	328.00	57.40	385.40
			1332.60	233.20	1565.80

VIGILANT ALARMS LTD
SALES RETURNS DAY BOOK

Date 1995		DETAIL	GOODS £ p	VAT £ p	INVOICE TOTAL £ p
Apr	21	Gibsons Garages	24.17	4.23	28.40
	28	Qwikfit Security	53.45	9.35	62.80
			77.62	13.58	91.20

To be used when answering Element 1.

VIGILANT ALARMS LTD
CASH BOOK

Date 1995	DETAILS	DISCOUNT ALLOWED £	CASH £	BANK £	DATE 1995	DETAILS	DISCOUNT RECEIVED £	CASH £	BANK £
Apr 3	Balances b/d		470.20	3182.84	Apr 3	Rent			250.00
4	Sales		94.15		3	Adel Plastics	23.52		446.78
4	VAT		16.48		5	Bank	c	500.00	
5	Cash	c		500.00	14	Spark Components	29.34		557.41
7	Gibsons Garages	12.13		473.12	19	Purchases		124.80	
12	Sales		272.00		19	VAT		21.84	
12	VAT		30.10		21	Electronic Systems			329.12
19	Auto Services			696.48	28	Adel Plastics	6.95		131.99
24	Qwikfit Security	16.28		373.96	30	Balances c/d		236.29	3320.32
28	Gibsons Garages			309.22					
		28.41	882.93	5535.62			59.81	882.93	5535.62
May 1	Balances b/d		236.29	3820.32					

To be used when answering Element 1.

ADEL PLASTICS
34 Towers Lane
Leeds
West Yorkshire
LS16 8ER

Tel No 0532 16194   VAT No 987 101 62

Our Ref: Date 30 April 1995

STATEMENT OF ACCOUNT

of: Vigilant Alarms Ltd
Control Works, Long Causeway, Leeds

Date 1995		DETAIL	DEBIT £	CREDIT £	BALANCE £
Apr	1	Balance			470.30
	3	Sales	138.94		609.24
	7	Receipt		446.78	162.46
		Discount		23.52	138.94
	10	Sales	146.88		285.82
	21	Sales returns		28.20	257.62

Terms of trading: net 30 days

To be used when answering Element 2.

BROADWAY FENCENTRE
NOMINAL LEDGER

Date 1995		DETAIL	DEBIT £	CREDIT £	BALANCE £
		Bank			
Apr	3	Capital	10 500.00		10 500.00 (Dr)
	3	Cash		400.00	10 100.00 (Dr)
	5	Delivery Van		3 500.00	6 600.00 (Dr)
	12	C Lapwell	295.00		6 895.00 (Dr)
	14	Machinery		1 250.00	5 645.00 (Dr)
	17	Timberland		470.00	5 175.00 (Dr)
	19	Rent		280.00	4 895.00 (Dr)
	26	Manorcraft	429.00		5 324.00 (Dr)
	26	Drawings		250.00	5 074.00 (Dr)
	27	Cash	750.00		5 824.00 (Dr)
	28	Wages		1 090.00	4 734.00 (Dr)
		Capital			
Apr	3	Bank		10 500.00	10 500.00 (Cr)
		Cash			
Apr	3	Bank	400.00		400.00 (Dr)
	5	General expenses		55.00	345.00 (Dr)
	8	Sales	570.00		915.00 (Dr)
	12	Drawings		200.00	715.00 (Dr)
	17	Purchases		145.00	570.00 (Dr)
	26	Sales	490.00		1 060.00 (Dr)
	27	Bank		750.00	310.00 (Dr)
	28	Golden Acres	143.00		453.00 (Dr)
	29	General expenses		69.00	384.00 (Dr)

To be used when answering Element 2.

BROADWAY FENCENTRE
NOMINAL LEDGER *(continued)*

Date 1995		DETAIL	DEBIT £	CREDIT £	BALANCE £
		Delivery Van			
Apr	5	Bank	3 500.00		3 500.00 (Dr)
		Machinery			
Apr	14	Bank	1 250.00		1 250.00 (Dr)
		General Expenses			
Apr	5	Cash	55.00		55.00 (Dr)
	29	Cash	69.00		124.00 (Dr)
		Rent			
Apr	19	Bank	280.00		280.00 (Dr)
		Drawings			
Apr	26	Bank	250.00		250.00 (Dr)
		Purchases			
Apr	3	Timberland	470.00		470.00 (Dr)
	5	C Woodside	360.00		830.00 (Dr)
	11	T Woodstock	165.00		995.00 (Dr)
	17	Cash	145.00		1 140.00 (Dr)
	18	T Woodstock	258.00		1 398.00 (Dr)
	24	C Woodside	242.00		1 640.00 (Dr)
	28	C Woodside	298.00		1 938.00 (Dr)

To be used when answering Element 2.

BROADWAY FENCENTRE
NOMINAL LEDGER *(continued)*

Date 1995		DETAIL	DEBIT £	CREDIT £	BALANCE £
		Purchase Returns			
Apr	17	C Woodside		50.00	50.00 (Cr)
	26	T Woodstock		45.00	95.00 (Cr)
		Sales			
Apr	3	C Lapwell		295.00	295.00 (Cr)
	5	Manorcraft		290.00	585.00 (Cr)
	7	Ranchstyle		284.00	869.00 (Cr)
	8	Cash		570.00	1 439.00 (Cr)
	10	Golden Acres		185.00	1 624.00 (Cr)
	14	C Lapwell		324.00	1 948.00 (Cr)
	17	Ranchstyle		179.00	2 127.00 (Cr)
	18	Manorcraft		175.00	2 302.00 (Cr)
	26	Cash		490.00	2 792.00 (Cr)
		Sales Returns			
Apr	14	Golden Acres	42.00		42.00 (Dr)
	21	Manorcraft	36.00		78.00 (Dr)
		Wages			
Apr	28	Bank	1 090.00		1 090.00 (Dr)

To be used when answering Element 2.

BROADWAY FENCENTRE
PURCHASE LEDGER

Date 1995		DETAIL	DEBIT £	CREDIT £	BALANCE £
		Timberland			
Apr	3	Purchases		470.00	470.00 (Cr)
	17	Bank	470.00		NIL
		C Woodside			
Apr	5	Purchases		360.00	360.00 (Cr)
	17	Purchase returns	50.00		310.00 (Cr)
	24	Purchases		242.00	552.00 (Cr)
	28	Purchases		298.00	850.00 (Cr)
		T Woodstock			
Apr	11	Purchases		165.00	165.00 (Cr)
	18	Purchases		258.00	423.00 (Cr)
	26	Purchases returns	45.00		378.00 (Cr)

To be used when answering Element 2.

BROADWAY FENCENTRE
SALES LEDGER

Date 1995		DETAIL	DEBIT £	CREDIT £	BALANCE £
		Golden Acres			
Apr	10	Sales	185.00		185.00 (Dr)
	14	Sales returns		42.00	143.00 (Dr)
	28	Cash		143.00	NIL
		C Lapwell			
Apr	3	Sales	295.00		295.00 (Dr)
	12	Bank		295.00	NIL
	14	Sales	324.00		324.00 (Dr)
		Manorcraft			
Apr	5	Sales	290.00		290.00 (Dr)
	18	Sales	175.00		465.00 (Dr)
	21	Sales returns		63.00	402.00 (Dr)
	26	Bank		429.00	27.00 (Cr)
		Ranchstyle			
Apr	7	Sales	284.00		284.00 (Dr)
	17	Sales	179.00		463.00 (Dr)

To be used when answering Element 2.

BROADWAY FENCENTRE

Memorandum

<u>To:</u>   Book-keeper   <u>Copy to:</u> Accountant

<u>From:</u> Chief Clerk   <u>Date:</u>   5 May1995

<u>Subject: Further errors discovered in the Ledgers</u>

Two further errors have been discovered in the Ledgers. These errors are detailed below:

<u>Error 1</u>

Purchases on credit from T Woodstock had been incorrectly posted to the account of C Woodside. These purchases amounted to £242.

<u>Error 2</u>

Sales on credit to Ranchstyle amounting to £185 had not been entered in the sales account or in an account for Ranchstyle in the sales ledger.

Sample solutions

1 Vigilant Alarms Ltd

a & b Personal Accounts in the Purchase Ledger

Adel Plastics

Date	Details	Debit £	Credit £	Balance £
1995				
April 3	Opening balance			470.30 cr
3	Goods & vat		138.94	609.24 cr
10	Goods & vat		146.88	756.12 cr
14	Goods & vat return	28.20		727.92 cr
26	Goods & vat		350.29	1078.21 cr
3	Cheque	446.78		631.43 cr
3	Discount	23.52		607.91 cr
28	Cheque	131.99		475.92 cr
28	Discount	6.95		468.97 cr

Electronic Systems

Date	Details	Debit £	Credit £	Balance £
1995				
April 3	Opening balance			329.12 cr
5	Goods & vat		95.50	424.62 cr
10	Goods & vat return	34.60		390.02 cr
24	Goods & vat		167.06	557.08 cr
27	Goods & vat return	63.80		493.28 cr
24	Cheque	329.12		164.16 cr

Spark Components

Date	Details	Debit £	Credit £	Balance £
1995				
April 3	Opening balance			586.75 cr
12	Goods & vat		676.75	1263.50 cr
14	Cheque	557.41		706.09 cr
14	Discount	29.34		676.75 cr

Personal Accounts in the Sales Ledger

Auto Services

Date	Details	Debit £	Credit £	Balance £
1995				
April 3	Opening balance			696.48 dr
12	Goods & vat	92.20		788.68 dr
24	Goods & vat	259.30		1047.98 dr
19	Cheque		696.48	351.50 dr

Gibsons Garages

Date 1995	Details	Debit £	Credit £	Balance £
April 3	Opening balance			485.25 dr
4	Goods & vat	325.50		810.75 dr
17	Goods & vat	128.60		939.35 dr
7	Cheque		473.12	466.23 dr
7	Discount		12.13	454.10 dr
21	Goods & vat return		28.40	425.70 dr
28	Cheque		309.22	116.48 dr
28	Discount		16.28	100.20 dr

Qwikfit Security

Date 1995	Details	Debit £	Credit £	Balance £
April 3	Opening balance			373.96 dr
19	Goods & vat	374.80		748.76 dr
27	Goods & vat	385.40		1134.16 dr
24	Cheque		373.96	760.20 dr
28	Goods & vat return		62.80	697.40 dr

c Nominal Ledger

Date 1995	Details	Debit £	Credit £	Balance £	Date 1995	Details	Debit £	Credit £	Balance £
		Capital					**VAT**		
April 3	Opening balance			14 700.00 cr	April 3	Opening balance			269.80 cr
					4	VAT on cash sales		16.48	286.28 cr
		Equipment			19	VAT on cash purchase	21.84		264.44 cr
April 3	Opening balance			14 500.00 dr	12	VAT on cash sales		30.10	294.54 cr
		Rent			30	VAT on credit purchase	234.63		59.91 cr
April 3	Opening balance			1 000.00 dr	30	VAT on credit purchase return		18.85	78.76 cr
3	Cheque	250.00		1 250.00 dr	30	VAT on credit sales		233.20	311.96 cr
					30	VAT on credit sales return	13.58		298.38 cr
		Purchases					**Purchases Returns**		
April 3	Opening balance			8 520.00 dr	April 3	Opening balance			194.00 cr
19	Cash purchases	124.80	0	8 644.80 dr	30	Credit purchase ret		107.75	301.75 cr
30	Credit Purchases	1 340.79		9 985.59 dr					
		Sales returns					**Sales**		
April 3	Opening balance			76.30 dr	April 3	Opening balance			12 670.00 cr
30	Credit sales return	77.62	0	153.92 dr	4	Cash sales		94.15	12 764.15 cr
					19	Cash sales		272.00	13 036.15 cr
					30	Credit sales		1 332.60	14 368.75 cr
		Discount Allowed					**Discount Received**		
April 3	Opening balance			62.37 dr	April 3	Opening balance			147.43 cr
30	Allowed in month	28.41	0	90.78 dr	30	Received in month		59.81	207.24 cr

d Reconciliation of supplier's statement with ledger account

Adel Plastics at 30 April 1995	£	£
Balance on supplier's statement		257.62 cr
add Goods received, and VAT		350.29 cr
		607.91 cr
deduct Cheque in transit	131.99	
Discount allowed on it	6.95	
		138.94 dr
Balance in our purchase ledger		£468.97 cr

e   Purchase Ledger control account

Date 1995	Details	Debit £	Credit £	Balance £
April 3	Opening balance			1 386.17 cr
30	purchase returns	126.60		1 259.57 cr
30	credit purchases		1 575.42	2 834.99 cr
30	cheques	1 465.30		1 369.69 cr
30	discount received	59.81		1 309.88 cr

f   Sales Ledger control account

Date 1995	Details	Debit £	Credit £	Balance £
April 3	Opening balance			1 555.69 dr
30	sales returns		91.20	1 464.49 dr
30	sales	1 565.80		3 030.29 dr
30	cheques		1 852.78	1 177.51 dr
30	discount allowed		28.41	1 149.10 dr

g The format 'Debit Credit Balance' automatically provides a 'balance' which is confirmed by the lists in **h** and **i**.

h Creditors' list as at 30 April 1995

	£
Adel Plastics	468.97 cr
Electronic Systems	164.16 cr
Spark Components	676.75 cr
	£1309.88

agrees with control account

i Debtors' list as at 30 April 1995

	£
Auto Services	351.50 dr
Gibsons Garage	100.20 dr
Qwikfit Security	697.40 dr
	£1149.10

agrees with control account

2 a Broadway Fencentre Trial balance at 30 April 1995

	originally		(c) revised	
Bank	4734		4734	
Capital		10 500		10 500
Cash	384		384	
Delivery Van	3 500		3 500	
Machinery	1 250		1 250	
General Expenses	124		124	
Rent	280		280	
Drawings	250		450	
Purchases	1 938		1 938	
Purchase Returns		95		95
Sales		2 792		2 977
Sales Returns	78		78	
Wages	1 090		1 090	
Purchase ledger				
C Woodside		850		608
T Woodstock		378		620
Sales ledger				
Golden Acres	0		0	
C Lapwell	324		324	
Manorcraft		27	0	
Ranchstyle	463		648	
	14 415	14 642	14 800	14 800
				balances

b Journal entries

Date				dr	cr
1995					
April 30	dr	Manorcraft		27	
		Sales returns of 36 posted as 63 (21 April, 1995)			
30	dr	Drawings		200	
		Cash withdrawal not posted (12 April, 1995)			

Note there is no credit entry for either of these debits

30	dr	C Woodside		242	
		T Woodstock			242
		incorrectly posted to the credit of C Woodside			
		(memo from Chief Clerk 5 May, 1995)			
30	dr	Ranchstyle		185	
		Sales			185
		item no recorded in Sales day book and therefore not			
		included in sales or the sale ledger (memo from Chief Clerk			
		5 May, 1995)			

INDEX

TEACH YOURSELF

Book-keeping and Accounting
for your Small Business

Mike Truman

This clear and practical book provides guidance on how to keep the books and prepare the accounts for your small business. Forget about debits and credits, journal entries, ledgers and day books – if you can read a bank statement this book will teach you how to prepare accounts for tax purposes and for the bank manager, how to make forecasts of your cashflow, and how to prepare a budget for your business.

With completely up-to-date information, the book follows the layout of the new Inland Revenue self-assessment tax return for preparing accounts. Step-by-step coverage of book-keeping and accounting makes this an accessible and invaluable guide for small business needs.

Mike Truman is a Chartered Accountant and a Fellow of the Chartered Institute of Taxation, as well as being a professional writer in accountancy and taxation.

[ty] **TEACH YOURSELF**

Basic Accounting
J Randall Stott
Revised by Mike Truman

This complete, step-by-step course in elementary accounting, now fully updated, gives clear and concise explanations of accounting principles and practice. New material covers PAYE, Cashflow Statements, Accounting for Share Capital, Accounting Standards and Non-Financial Reporting.

No prior knowledge of book-keeping or accounting is assumed. Clear explanations, diagrams and worked examples enable the student to master the basic principles in easy stages then apply them to example problems.

The book covers the examination requirements of all first-level courses.

Mike Truman is a Chartered Accountant and a Fellow of the Chartered Institute of Taxation. He is a professional writer on accountancy and taxation.

TEACH YOURSELF

Business Studies

Peter Fearns

This best-selling introduction to Business Studies, now in its 5th Edition, looks at business activity in its economic, social, political and legal environments.

The book shows how the separate disciplines of economics, administration, marketing, accounting and law are all interrelated in the real world of business. First it examines the nature of the business environment and the aims of business organisations, the different types of market and the role of marketing. It then describes how business operations are managed and how efficiency and quality are achieved. The book stresses the importance of people in organisations and examines the impact of change. Examples of the main types of financial records and analytical techniques are also included.

Peter Fearns' established text has been fully revised in line with examination requirements. A summary is given at the end of each chapter and a graded series of questions is included at the end of each section to provide an outstanding book for all first level students of business studies.

A selection of bestselling and related titles from Hodder & Stoughton *Educational*

Title	Author	ISBN	Price (UK)
Book-keeping and Accounting for your Small Business	**Mike Truman**	0 340 69721 0	£6.99 ☐
Basic Accounting	**J Randall Stott**	0 340 69776 8	£7.99 ☐
Business Studies, 5th edition	**Peter Fearns**	0 340 70178 1	£8.99 ☐

All Hodder & Stoughton *Educational* books are available at your local bookshop, or can be ordered direct from the publisher. Just tick the titles you would like and complete the details below. Prices and availability are subject to change without prior notice.

Buy four books from the selection above and get free postage and packaging. Just send a cheque or postal order made payable to *Bookpoint Limited* to the value of the total cover price of four books. This should be sent to: Hodder & Stoughton *Educational*, 39 Milton Park, Abingdon, Oxon OX14 4TD, UK. EMail address: orders@bookpoint.co.uk. Alternatively, if you wish to buy fewer than four books, the following postage and packaging costs apply:

UK & BFPO £4.30 for one book; £6.30 for two books; £8.30 for three books Overseas and Eire: £4.80 for one book; £7.10 for two or three books (surface mail)

If you would like to pay by credit card, our centre team would be delighted to take your order by telephone. Our direct line (44) 01235 400414 (lines open 9.00 am–6.00 pm, Monday to Saturday, with a 24 hour answering service). Alternatively you can send a fax to (44) 01235 400454.

Title _____ First name _____ Surname _____

Address _____

_____

_____

Postcode _____ Daytime telephone no. _____

If you would prefer to pay by credit card, please complete:

Please debit my Master Card / Access / Diner's Card / American Express (delete as applicable)

Card number ☐☐☐☐ ☐☐☐☐ ☐☐☐☐ ☐☐☐☐

Expiry date _____ Signature _____

If you would not like to receive further information on our products, please tick the box ☐.